India's Strategy in the Sout]

C000242593

The tensions in the South China Sea pose considerable challenges to the rules-based liberal international maritime order. The situation demonstrates the interplay between maritime nationalism and geostrategic rivalry; fuelling militarisation and endangering freedom of navigation, over-flight and exploitation of natural resources. China's dedicated "terra-claims", land reclamation and island-building spree – enhanced with military sur-veillance, communications and logistics infrastructure-building in the form of port facilities, military installations and airstrips – have escalated these tensions. China declares that these territories are an integral part of its "core interests", taking an uncompromising stance on the question of sovereignty and its determination to protect the domain militarily. India, although not a South China Sea littoral state, sees both the general principle of the rules-based order and the specific issue of navigation between the Indian and Pacific Oceans as core to its own national interest.

Chakraborti and Chakraborty assess the rationale and implications of India's strate-gies and responses *vis-à-vis* the South China Sea dispute, and their impact on its overall "Act East" initiative in Southeast Asia policy. They also analyse the implications of India's stance on the Association of Southeast Asian Nations (ASEAN), five member-states of which (Brunei, Indonesia, Malaysia, the Philippines and Vietnam) are involved in territorial disputes with China in the South China Sea. The analysis focuses on the administrative tenures of both the United Progressive Alliance from 2004 until 2014 and the National Democratic Alliance from 2014 onwards.

Tridib Chakraborti is Professor and Dean of the School of Social Sciences at ADAMAS University, Kolkata, India. He served as Professor and Head of the Department of International Relations at Jadavpur University, Kolkata before taking his present position. He has been the Indian Council for Cultural Rela-tions (ICCR) Chair and the Indian Studies and Visiting Professor at Dublin City University, Ireland. He is an expert on South, Southeast Asian and Indo-Pacific affairs and specialises in South and Southeast Asian politics, foreign relations, strategic issues, Indian Diaspora and ethnic issues in Southeast Asia.

Mohor Chakraborty is Assistant Professor in Political Science at South Calcutta Girls' College (affiliated to the University of Calcutta), Kolkata, India. Prior to this assignment, she held the position of Senior Research Fellow in the Department of International Rela-tions at Jadavpur University, Kolkata. Her research interest is in Indian foreign policy and Area Studies, focusing on South Asia, Southeast Asia and the Indo-Pacific regions.

International Relations in Southeast Asia

India's Strategy in The South China Sea
Tridib Chakraborti and Mohor Chakraborty;
Foreword by Sudhir T. Devare

For more information about this series, please visit: www.routledge.com/
ESL-Applied-Linguistics-Professional-Series/book-series/LEAESLALP

India's Strategy in the South China Sea

Tridib Chakraborti and
Mohor Chakraborty

Foreword by
Sudhir T. Devare

Routledge
Taylor & Francis Group

LONDON AND NEW YORK

First published 2020 by Routledge

2 Park Square, Milton Park, Abingdon, Oxon OX14 4RN

605 Third Avenue, New York, NY 10017

Routledge is an imprint of the Taylor & Francis Group, an informa business

First issued in paperback 2022

British Library Cataloguing in Publication Data
A catalogue record for this book is available from the British Library

Library of Congress Cataloging-in-Publication Data
Names: Chakraborti, Tridib, 1956- author. | Chakraborty, Mohor, author.
Title: India's strategy in the South China sea / Tridib Chakraborti, Mohor Chakraborty.
Description: First. | New York : Routledge, 2020. |
Series: International relations in Southeast Asia |
Includes bibliographical references and index.
Identifiers: LCCN 2019047493 (print) | LCCN 2019047494 (ebook) |
ISBN 9780367136772 (hardback) | ISBN 9780429027994 (ebook)
Subjects: LCSH: South China Sea--International status. |
South China Sea--Strategic aspects-. | India--Foreign relations--Southeast Asia. |
Southeast Asia--Foreign relations--India. | Maritime boundaries--China.
Classification: LCC KZA1692 .C43 2020 (print) |
LCC KZA1692 (ebook) | DDC 327.54059--dc23
LC record available at https://lccn.loc.gov/2019047493
LC ebook record available at https://lccn.loc.gov/2019047494

ISBN: 978-0-367-13677-2 (hbk)
ISBN: 978-1-03-233714-2 (pbk)
DOI: 10.4324/9780429027994

Typeset in Galliard
by Taylor & Francis Books

Dedicated to my parents, my brothers, Sri Prabir Chakraborty and Dr. Anirban Chakraborty; my sisters, the late Pragati Chakraborty and Smt. Srabani Chakraborty; and my wife, Dr. Paramita Bhattacharjee.

Dr. Tridib Chakraborti

Dedicated to the memory of my grandparents, Sri Krishna Chandra Chakraborty, Smt. Suhashini Chakraborty, Sri Pashupati Nath Banerjee and Smt. Anita Banerjee, and my father-in-law, Sri Priyatosh Roy Chowdhury.

Dr. Mohor Chakraborty

Contents

Acknowledgements

In writing this book, we have received valuable counsel and motivation from a host of people and institutions, and we take this opportunity to express our whole-hearted gratitude to all of them.

We are especially indebted to Ambassador Sudhir T. Devare, Former Secretary, Ministry of External Affairs, Government of India, for consenting to write the Foreword of this book, which has added immense value to our work.

We are also grateful to the Staff and Officials of the major libraries in New Delhi and Kolkata for their valuable support and academic assistance. We would like to extend our gratitude to the staff and library staff of the ISEAS-Yusof Ishak Institute, Singapore for their help, guidance and support. We would also like to express our thanks for the editorial assistance and support provided by the Routledge team (Social Sciences), and their encouragement at every step of this endeavour has been a rewarding experience.

This acknowledgement would remain incomplete without extending our heart-felt thanks to our family members for their encouragement and support. Finally, we would like to thank the Almighty for arming us with the spirit, health, tenacity and intellectual capability to successfully bring this book to fruition.

Professor (Dr.) Tridib Chakraborti and Dr. Mohor Chakraborty

Foreword

From ancient times the seas east of India have beckoned the seafarers, sages, princes and traders from India. The existence of India's extensive footprint in Southeast and East Asia even today is a testimony to the longstanding connection that India has had with this region. In the post-World War period if the country's interest in the East appeared to have declined it was largely due to the geopolitical equations which developed as a result of the alliance arrangements of the rival great powers in the Asia-Pacific with which India had chosen not to be associated.

Since the end of the Cold War the situation in this region has undergone a remarkable transformation. While the US naval presence in the western Pacific and its alliance structures with countries like Japan, South Korea, Thailand and Australia remain in force the rise of China and the rapid modernisation and expansion of its armed forces has introduced a significantly new factor in the dynamics of the region. For the past decade or so, China, which for long had chosen not to concentrate on or to highlight its disputes with Japan on the Senkaku islands in the East Sea or with the five states – Vietnam, the Philippines, Malaysia, Brunei and Taiwan on the South China Sea (SCS) islands and the sea itself, has been addressing the SCS as one of the three national "core interests". With its ongoing Maritime Silk Road project (as a part of the ambitious Belt and Road Initiative) the Chinese are expected to give even closer attention to it. For over a decade now the standoff between China and the five claimant states, especially Vietnam and the Philippines, has cast a shadow of great concern for security and peace not only over the SCS but beyond in the Asia-Pacific. The western Pacific is once again a zone of much tension and therefore cause of concern not only to the littoral states but to the neighbouring countries like India which has huge political, strategic and economic interests in the stability of the region.

How does India look at the situation in the SCS and what are India's plans and strategies to help maintain security in this area? The SCS is a waterway of critical importance. An estimated US$5 trillion of international trade passes through this water body. It is a vital sea-lane for India as well as over 50 per cent of its seaborne trade passes through this sea. In view of this a situation of tension in the SCS acquires significance even as the global centre of gravity is seen to be steadily shifting to the East and India's own presence in the newly designated Indo-Pacific is being increasingly recognised and respected. The topicality and anxiety that the developments in the region evoke have therefore a clear bearing on India's own policy to the East and inevitably profound implications. This has very aptly led the scholars, Prof. Tridib Chakraborti and Dr. Mohor Chakraborty from Kolkata to come up with a detailed analysis of the whole issue and a discussion on the possible strategic response and policy options for India. As described by them it is indeed a case study of the challenges to the liberal rules-based maritime order for which no ready solution seems in sight. A comprehensive discussion on the subject was therefore a timely need which happily the two experienced academics have taken up.

The issue, namely, the claims of individual states on the littoral of the SCS, China's aggressive and assertive stand of declaring the whole water body as its own (in open defiance of world opinion) and consequent reclamation and militarisation of the islands is outlined in full detail. The political fall-out within ASEAN is already manifest in a serious threat to the unity and centrality of this regional grouping, which the authors have highlighted in their book. How this delicate question can impact on India's own geostrategic and economic interests and what strategies India needs to adopt to deal with this challenge needs careful examination. In analysing India's position, it is also instructive to see whether there is any scope for a broad consensus with ASEAN, the US or Japan. The Indo-US Joint Statement in 2014, the US National Defence Strategy (2018) and the re-designation of the Asia-Pacific as Indo-Pacific, the Japanese Free and Open Indo-Pacific Strategy (2016), the explicit reference to the SCS issue in the India-US-Japan Trilateral (2015) and the India-ASEAN Joint Statement at the Commemorative Summit in January, 2018 all seem to point towards it.

The vast asymmetry between India and China as indeed between ASEAN and China in their gross domestic product or defence spending poses the question whether India or ASEAN can adopt a strategy to deal with China's defiant and arbitrary stand on the SCS issue and equally importantly will be able to sustain it. Despite their economic or military weakness *vis-à-vis* China a number of countries in Southeast Asia have voiced their strong opposition to the latter on the SCS issue. Indonesia has declared a 200-mile Exclusive Economic Zone north of their Natuna Islands as the North Natuna Sea. India, which believes that it can act as a security provider and a responsible player in the Indo-Pacific, will have to find various ways in which to address the challenge of China's claim. The authors have referred to India's possible approaches of "external balancing" and "internal balancing". External balancing is suggested to involve forging regional security mechanisms with regional navies and strengthening and supporting relevant institutions such as the ASEAN Regional Forum (ARF), the ASEAN Defence Ministers' Meeting (ADMM+), the East Asia Summit (EAS), the ASEAN Maritime Forum, etc. as well as regular maritime and Coast Guard multilateral meetings like MILAN, MALABAR, etc.

The "internal balancing" on the other hand would involve building India's defence capabilities including implementing the Make in India programme with regard to defence equipment and weaponry.

India's response and strategy to the SCS issue could take into account the following.

1   India's maritime security has come into greater and sharper focus in recent years. During the time of Prime Minister Vajpayee's term, the arc of India's maritime security was defined as the one extending from the Gulf of Aden in the west to the Strait of Malacca in the east. The Naval Doctrine brought out in this regard affirms it. This arc has now been further extended to include the SCS in the east and the Persian Gulf and the southern Indian Ocean including the east African coast. For the Indian Navy this whole region is of direct and utmost consequence. The maritime activities of the Navy, including visits to the countries on the littoral, exercises with the navies of these countries and overall cooperation and friendly relations with these countries are therefore an essential part of their natural responsibility.

2   The Chinese position on the SCS of declaring a nine-dash line in the SCS and calling the entire sea and the islands in it their own has been strongly contested by the claimant states. The Philippines took the case of the Chinese intransigence on the issue to the UN. Even after the verdict of the UN-sponsored Permanent Court of Arbitration (PCA) in July 2016 China has refused to give up its assertion of the nine-dash line and the ownership of the entire Sea. This is seen by the claimant states (as well by most ASEAN members) as an open threat to the freedom of navigation and overflights in clear violation of the international law on the seas. For India, which believes in open navigation and uninterrupted trade in the seas and which has had joint venture oil and natural gas projects with Vietnam in the SCS for nearly two decades, the Chinese arbitrary contention cannot be acceptable. India's decision to join with the US, Japan and Australia in setting up the Quadrilateral Security Dialogue (QUAD) clearly reflects its assessment and future approach towards freedom of navigation and adherence to the international norms in the SCS. This grouping is not a military alliance or a confrontational outfit of any kind but essentially the coming together of like-minded countries which subscribe to the principle of open seas to establish a cooperative response.

3   India's strategic view of the SCS issue also needs to keep in mind the pressures that the dispute has brought upon the member-states of ASEAN and how the very basis of ASEAN unity and its centrality in the ASEAN-led dialogue processes in the East is being eroded. It was noteworthy that in 2012 the ASEAN Foreign Ministers' Meeting ended without even a communiqué on this issue. For India the very core of its engagement and Act East policy is the strength and integrity of ASEAN. India can ill-afford to see ASEAN weakening on account of the differences within ASEAN on the SCS question. India should therefore welcome the ongoing negotiations between ASEAN and China to evolve a Code of Conduct (COC) to replace the Declaration of Conduct (DOC). The negotiations which started in August 2017 following a framework agreement are now believed to have arrived at a draft text though there is no indication if and when the CoC will be concluded.

4   The recent re-designation of the Asia-Pacific Ocean as the Indo-Pacific Ocean should be seen as a development with a clear meaning for most countries bordering this vast oceanic space. The recognition of the strategic integrity of the Pacific and Indian Oceans brings in its wake the need for countries to resolve their disputes through discussions and negotiations. It is also hoped that the East Sea, the SCS and the Indian Ocean will see greater exchanges and cooperation in the future. As a centrally located maritime state, India should be playing a direct and major role as expressed in the Indian Prime Minister's concept of SAGAR (Security and Growth for All in the Region). It is for this reason India's approach of "inclusiveness" for dealing with the maritime issues of the Indo-Pacific was projected at the Shangrila Dialogue in Singapore in 2018.

5   India's primary response to the SCS issue should be in the form of its enhanced cooperation with ASEAN – in the three areas identified by both, namely, commerce, connectivity and culture. A stronger India-ASEAN relationship would enable ASEAN states to deal with the SCS issue with greater confidence and effectiveness.

In the six chapters that, Prof. Tridib Chakraborti and Dr. Mohor Chakraborty have included in their book they have covered all aspects of the issue, namely, the genesis and canvas of the issue, China's intractable stand, India's interests, India's strategy and military response and the positions of President Trump and Prime Minister Abe.

India's foreign policy will be strongly influenced by the developments in the Indo-Pacific in the coming years in which the SCS issue could be a dominant aspect. It is therefore essential to have an in-depth study of the Indian perspective on the subject. This book will be an excellent and extremely useful reference or textbook for students, research scholars, practitioners of international relations and all those interested in India's profile abroad, especially in the Indo-Pacific.

Sudhir T. Devare
Former Secretary,
Ministry of External Affairs,
Government of India
May 17, 2019

Glossary

A&N	Andaman and Nicobar
A2/AD	Anti-access, Area Denial
ACSA	Acquisition and Cross Servicing Agreement
ADIZ	Air-Defence Identification Zone
ADMM	ASEAN Defence Ministers' Meeting
AEP	Act East Policy
AMM	ASEAN Ministerial Meeting
AOIP	ASEAN Outlook on the Indo-Pacific
APSARA	Authority for the Protection and Management of the Angkor Region
ARF	ASEAN Regional Forum
ASEAN	Association of Southeast Asian Nations
ASI	Archaeological Survey of India
ASW	Anti-Submarine Warfare
AUSINDEX	Australia-India Exercise
BECA	Basic Exchange and Cooperation Agreement
BRI	Belt and Road Initiative
C4ISR	Command, Control, Communications, Computers, Intelligence, Surveillance, Reconnaissance
CENTRIXS	Combined Enterprise Regional Information Exchange System
CISMOA	Communications and Information Security Memorandum of Agreement
CMS	China Maritime Surveillance
CMS	Combat Management System
COC	Code of Conduct
COMCASA	Communications Compatibility and Security Agreement
CORPAT	Coordinated Patrol
CPC	Communist Party of China
DOC	Declaration on the Conduct of the Parties in the South China Sea
DPP	Defence Procurement Procedure
DProP	Defence Production Policy
DRDO	Defence Research and Development Organisation
DTTI	Defense Technology and Trade Initiative

EAS	East Asia Summit
EEZ	Exclusive Economic Zone
FDI	Foreign Direct Investment
FENC	Far East Naval Command
FLEC	Fisheries Law Enforcement Command
FOIP	Free and Open Indo-Pacific
FY	Financial Year
GDP	Gross Domestic Product
GNP	Gross National Product
GSMIA	General Security of Military Information Agreement
HADR	Humanitarian Assistance and Disaster Relief
HDW	Howaldtswerke-Deutsche Werft
IAC	Indigenous Aircraft Carrier
IDMM	Indigenously Designed, Developed and Manufactured
IFC–IOR	Information Fusion Centre for the Indian Ocean Region
IMBL	International Maritime Boundary Line
IMCOR	Indo-Myanmar CORPAT
IMMS	India's Maritime Military Strategy
IMNEX	India-Myanmar Naval Exercise
IMO	International Maritime Organisation
IMSS	Indian Maritime Security Strategy
IMT	India-Myanmar-Thailand
IND-INDO CORPAT	India-Indonesia Coordinated Patrolling
INIP	Indian Naval Indigenisation Plan
INS	Indian Naval Ship
IONS	Indian Ocean Naval Symposium
IOR	Indian Ocean Region
IORA	Indian Ocean Rim Association
IRRC	India Rapid Reaction Cell
ISL	International Shipping Lines
ISR	Intelligence, Surveillance and Reconnaissance
JAI	Japan-America-India
JIMEX	Japan-India Maritime Exercise
JMSU	Joint Seismic Maritime Undertaking
JWG	Joint Working Group
KMMTT	Kaladan Multimodal Transit and Transport
LCU	Landing Craft Utility
LEMOA	Logistics Exchange and Memorandum of Agreement
LEP	Look East Policy
LRSAM	Long Range Surface to Air Missiles
MCPP	Maritime Capability Perspective Plan
MDP	Major Defense Partner
MEA	Ministry of External Affairs
MF-STAR	Multi-function Active Phased Array Radar

MIPP	Maritime Infrastructure Perspective Plan
MoU	Memorandum of Understanding
MSR	Maritime Silk Road
MSSI	Malacca Strait Security Initiatives
MTDP	Medium Term Defense Programme
NAS	Naval Air Station
NDA	National Democratic Alliance
NDPG	National Defense Programme Guidelines
NDS	National Defense Strategy
NEO	Non-combatant Evacuation Operations
NM	Nautical Mile
NSS	National Security Strategy
OEM	Original Equipment Manufacturers
OVL	ONGC Videsh Limited
PASSEX	Passage Exercise
PCA	Permanent Court of Arbitration
PLA – AF	People's Liberation Army – Air Force
PLAN	People's Liberation Army – Navy
PMC	Post Ministerial Conference
PRC	People's Republic of China
QUAD	Quadrilateral Alliance Dialogue
R&D	Research and Development
RCEP	Regional Comprehensive Economic Partnership
ReCAAP	Regional Cooperation Agreement on Combating Piracy and Armed Robbery of Ships in Asia
RIMPAC	Rim of the Pacific
SAARC	South Asian Association for Regional Cooperation
SAGAR	Security and Growth for All in the Region
SAR	Search and Rescue
SCS	South China Sea
SDF	Self-Defence Forces
SDNT	Single Draft Negotiating Text
SIMBEX	Singapore-India Maritime Bilateral Exercise
SLOC	Sea Lanes of Communication
SOM	Senior Officials' Meeting
SP	Strategic Partnership
SQ KM	Square Kilometre
SREB	Silk Road Economic Belt
STA	Strategic Trade Authorization
TAC	Treaty of Amity and Cooperation
UAV	Unmanned Aerial Vehicle
UN	United Nations
UNCLOS	United Nations Convention on the Law of the Sea
UPA	United Progressive Alliance
US	United States

USINDO PACOM	US Indo-Pacific Command
USPACOM	US Pacific Command
VCLM	Vietnam, Cambodia, Laos, Myanmar

1 India and the South China Sea

A strategic mirror of Chinese hegemony

The South China Sea (SCS), stretching over 3.5 million square kilometres (sq km), is a strategic gateway serving a third of international maritime traffic. It has been mired in a protracted conflict stemming from overlapping claims to sovereignty over disputed islets, island regimes and its impact on maritime demarcation between China, Brunei, Indonesia, Malaysia, the Philippines, Taiwan and Vietnam. The SCS is dotted with numerous islands, islets, reefs, shoals and rocks among which, four island groups, namely, the Paracel Islands (Xisha), the Spratly Islands (Nansha), the Pratas Islands (Dongsha) and the Macclesfield Bank (Zhongsha) are the most pertinent. China claims sovereignty over the island groups encompassed and represented by the "nine-dash" line, a maritime delimitation synonymous with its claim of sovereignty over the island groups, in addition to its claim of historical rights of fishing, navigation and other maritime activities on the islands and adjacent waters (Gao and Jia, 2013: 99). In 1992, further clarifying and affirming its territorial sovereignty and maritime rights and interests over all the islands in the SCS, China enacted its Law of the People's Republic of China on the Territorial Sea and Contiguous Zone, specifying its claims over the features of all of the four island groups encompassed by the "nine-dash line" (Law of the People's Republic of China on the Territorial Sea and Contiguous Zone, 1992: Art. 2). Although China's claims to the Paracel Islands clash with those of Taiwan and Vietnam, the whole of this chain has been under China's occupation since the Sino-Vietnam skirmish in 1974. The Spratly Islands are contested by China, Taiwan and Vietnam (wholly) and Brunei, the Philippines and Malaysia (partially). The SCS is a salient navigational junction between the Indian and Pacific Oceans through which international trade worth US$3.5 trillion ("How Much Trade Transits the South China Sea?", 2016) transits annually. Connecting the Indian Ocean through the Malacca Strait to the southwest and commanding access to the East China Sea to the northeast, the strategic location of the SCS and its bounty of natural resources[1] have catapulted it to the core of the global geopolitical computations. In view of its significance as a "global commons" site, it has been rightly acknowledged that a situation of volatility or instability would trigger serious consequences for global trade and commerce, in addition to dismantling the ambience of peace, security and stability in the Indo-Pacific region.

1 Understanding the context of the problem: situating the rationale of India's response

Set in this backdrop, the present book scrutinises the rationale and implications of India's strategies and responses pertaining to the SCS dispute over chequered claims to sovereignty that has emerged as a major bone of geostrategic contention in the region. The study brings into focus the impact of India's strategies and responses on its Southeast Asia policy, presently christened the Act East Policy (AEP) (formerly the Look East ASEAN Policy/LEP), since five member-states of the Association of Southeast Asian Nations (ASEAN), namely Brunei, Indonesia, Malaysia, the Philippines and Vietnam are embroiled in protracted territorial disputes with China in the SCS. Throughout its constituent six chapters, this book anchors its analysis on the tension-fraught littorals, which emerges as a classic case-study of the challenges posed to the rules-based liberal international maritime order, by a hegemonic state, China. Acknowledged as an integral part of its "core interests", China avers its uncompromising stance on the question of indisputable sovereign rights and jurisdiction over the islands in the SCS, adjacent waters, as well as the seabed and subsoil thereof and its adherence to protect the domain militarily (Bingguo, 2009). The underpinning philosophy fuelling this quest is borne in its motivation, intent and capacity to transcend the experiences of the "Century of Humiliation" and move towards realising the "Chinese Dream" of national rejuvenation. The emphasis on reviving this "Chinese Dream", particularly since President Xi Jinping assumed the helm in 2012, fundamentally alludes to the "great rejuvenation of the Chinese nation", or put otherwise, its return to greatness, with strong foundational roots seeped in historical, philosophical (Confucian) and national experience, which have provided the nation's modern identity and purpose (Wang, 2013). The objective of pushing through and sustaining national rejuvenation had its formative roots in the doctrine of "Peaceful Rise", and the re-phrased usage as "Peaceful Development", which reflected China's acknowledgement of the need to balance its domestic reform and development with a peaceful and stable external environment, by following the path of "scientific, independent, open, peaceful, cooperative and common development" (China's Peaceful Development, 2011: 2).

The nomenclature, "Peaceful Development", which supplanted "Peaceful Rise", suggested allaying concerns of a "China threat" among its neighbours and the wider international corpus alike. Under the leadership of Xi Jinping, who has guided Beijing's unapologetic approach to disputes in the SCS since 2012, it has relinquished Deng Xiaoping's stance of hiding its capabilities and biding its time in favour of a more proactive, assertive and even confrontational policy, insofar as safeguarding its territorial claims in general and core interests in particular, is concerned. Besides, the Chinese Premier, Li Keqiang's espousal of the resolve to "respond firmly to provocation" ("Any Provocation on the South China Sea will Meet a Decisive Response", 2014) demonstrates the uncompromising, non-concessionary posture towards issues pertaining to sovereignty, security and overall development. The present foreign policy stature exhibited by China, also popularised as its

"Peaceful Rise 2.0" is anchored on three principal attributes including greater determination to forcefully protect its national interests; seeking reciprocal strategic reassurance from other countries *vis-à-vis* their reciprocal commitments to peace; and adopting a top-level design, indicative of the need to envisage strategic visions, planning and implementation, with the objective of creating and sustaining a stable external environment. It also provides the podium for the execution of China's peripheral or regional diplomacy (Zhang, 2015: 9). The first principle could be traced to Xi Jinping's articulation of a holistic national security outlook, unveiled in 2014, which underscored the imperative of tethering development and security, encompassing both the domestic and external spheres, to foster "development, reform and stability" (Yunbi, 2014). By linking the imperative of securing national interests to those of development and security, the strategy implied that issues impinging on China's economic development, such as resource management or maritime security, would receive top priority and evoke proportionate response by exercising the option of first use of military force, through "Preparation for Military Struggle".

This concern was subsequently institutionalised in its active defence Military Strategy (2015), which unified active strategic defence with operational and tactical offence, in the context of safeguarding China's "national unification, territorial integrity and development interests". It also entailed the realisation of the "Chinese Dream" of great national rejuvenation. Furthermore, by attaching importance to "managing the seas and oceans and protecting maritime rights and interests", falling within its "critical security domain", the Strategy justified the development of a "modern maritime military force structure commensurate with its national security and development" as a means to

> safeguard its national sovereignty and maritime rights and interests, protect the security of strategic Sea Lanes of Communication (SLOC) and overseas interests, and participate in international maritime cooperation, so as to provide strategic support for building itself into a maritime power.
>
> (China's Military Strategy, 2015)

Axiomatically, the Strategy not only reversed China's "traditional mentality" of territorial concerns outweighing the maritime, by catapulting the latter to the crux of its security strategy, but also scripted the People's Liberation Army –Navy's (PLAN's) gradual shift in focus from "offshore waters defense" to the combination of "offshore waters defense" and "open seas protection", and laid threadbare its intention to pursue a more proactive maritime policy. The innovation addressed China's perceived "grave concerns" stemming from the "provocative actions" of offshore neighbours, on the one hand, and the "rebalance" in the Indo-Pacific by the United States (US), in consonance with its military allies, or through the conduct of close-in air and sea surveillance and reconnaissance operations, on the other (China's Military Strategy, 2015: 13–16). Its concerns and proactive strategic intentions were reiterated in "China's Policies on Asia-Pacific Security Cooperation" (2017), as it alluded to undertaking "necessary responses to the provocative actions which infringe on China's territorial sovereignty and maritime rights and interests, and undermine peace and stability in the South China Sea". It further expressed China's uncompromising stance with a caveat that "no effort to internationalize and judicialize the South China Sea issue will be of any avail for its resolution". It would, on the contrary, "endanger regional peace and stability", by complicating the path to resolving the issue (China's Policies on Asia-Pacific Security Cooperation, 2017: Cl. IV).

Under the present circumstances, as Xi Jinping heralds the dawn of a "new era" of politics and power and enthusiastically embarks upon writing a new chapter in the pages of "diplomacy with Chinese characteristics", intended to transform the nation "into a mighty force that could lead the world" ("Secure a Decisive Victory in Building a Moderately Prosperous Society in All Respects and Strive for the Great Success of Socialism with Chinese Characteristics for a New Era", 2017: 2, 6) there is unlikely to be any basic change in China's overall policy stance on territorial issues following the same. Echoing the Party propaganda that preceded the 19th Congress of the Communist Party of China (CPC) of October 2017, Xi counted SCS reef and island construction among his top accomplishments and appreciated the successful prosecution of maritime rights (Doshi, 2017). Therefore, it may be apprehended that while, on the one hand, Beijing is believed to continue to voice support for a peaceful resolution of the territorial disputes as well as the conclusion of a Code of Conduct (COC), through the conduct of negotiations with those states directly involved, on the basis of respecting historical facts and international law, it will sustain efforts to beef up its military and diplomatic activities in the SCS, on the other (China's National Defense in the New Era, 2019: 7). China's dedicated "terraclaims", land reclamation and island-building spree, enhanced with military surveillance, communication and logistics infrastructure-building in the form of port facilities, military installations and airstrips, have heightened since 2012 and further compounded the situation. Additionally, its substantial and progressive ability to monitor and project outreach throughout the SCS by initiating and sustaining construction of dual civilian-military bases at outposts in several disputed islands has generated disquiet among regional and extra-regional stakeholders. In its "Annual Report to the Congress on Military and Security Developments Involving the People's Republic of China" (PRC), released in May 2017, the US Department of Defense estimated that China had added at least 3,200 acres of land to the seven outposts[2] under its occupation in the Spratly Islands. This was in glaring contrast to 50 acres of land reclaimed by all other claimants over the same period. The report also highlighted that in December 2016 China installed anti-aircraft and anti-missile weapons on its artificial islands. Satellite images confirmed that three new air bases built on artificial islands were nearing completion in Fiery Cross, Mischief and Subi Reefs in the Spratlys. Beyond the hangars and air defence systems, three naval bases readying for operation, including large berthing facilities and harbours for the PLAN, the Coast Guard and other maritime law enforcement agencies were also visible. In addition, it was reported that the bases would be capable of hosting Chinese strategic bombers, early warning and surveillance aircrafts and long-range transport and tanker jets, while anti-aircraft guns and close-in weapons systems designed to guard against missile attacks had been placed on all seven of China's artificially constructed islands (Annual Report to Congress: Military and Security Developments Involving the People's Republic of China in 2017, 2017: 12). In May 2018, the People's Liberation Army – Air Force (PLA – AF) declared its successful landing of bombers, including the H6-K on an outpost in the Woody Island in the Paracels. The Woody Island doubles as the military and administrative capital of China's claimed territories in the SCS as well as acting as a listening and surveillance station, thereby safeguarding its expanding military bases in the nearby Hainan Island.[3] The spree of unrestrained construction was attested to by aerial surveillance photographs taken between June and December 2017 of runways, hangars, control towers, helipads, radar domes, antenna arrays and a series of multi-storey buildings constructed on most of its Spratly outposts (Phillips, 2018).

As of mid-2018, China mounted wave-monitoring devices on Woody Island and conducted scientific surveys in the contested regions. The expeditious expansion in the number of buildings (1,652; as of 2017) across the Spratly and Paracel Islands has evoked much concern since it exceeds those of all other claimants combined.[4] ("Concrete and Coral – Tracking Expansion in the South China Sea", 2018) In its bid to justify the construction of artificial islands in the SCS, China's decision to permanently station a large and advanced rescue vessel, the *Nanhaijiu 115* at Subi Reef in July 2018, has been an exemplary demonstration of its intention not only to establish its entrenchment, but also to possibly consolidate its jurisdiction in the region, following in the footsteps of the Sansha-like civilian administrative establishment (Neill, 2018). Notwithstanding Beijing's justification of its outposts being employed for the purposes of improving marine research, safety of navigation and the living and working conditions of personnel stationed therein, the available facilities including aviation, port and communications, fixed-weapons positions, barracks and administrative buildings provide it with an edge in promoting its "active defense" strategy, by maintaining a strong military and paramilitary presence in the SCS (Annual Report to Congress: Military and Security Developments Involving the People's Republic of China in 2019, 2019: 74–75). Furthermore, Beijing's rejection of the verdict of the tribunal established under Art. VII of the 1982 United Nations (UN) Convention on the Law of the Sea (UNCLOS) for dispute resolution under the auspices of the Permanent Court of Arbitration (PCA) of July 2016, which ruled that its claims to "historic rights" over the SCS encompassed by the "nine-dash" line could not exceed its maritime rights under the UNCLOS provisions, has perplexed the international community at large. It has also raised serious questions pertaining to maintaining the freedom, security and the notion of the Grotian common right (*res communis*) of all nations to use the seas for the purposes of trade, navigation and scientific endeavour. On the basis of this introductory analysis, the following sub-sections will enumerate the rationale of India's response to the SCS issue and outline the theoretical framework underlying the book as its anchor.

1.1 India's strategy in the South China Sea: understanding the rationale

Although India is neither a SCS state, nor claimant to any territory therein, there are a host of factors and concerns that determine and stimulate its "genuine and legitimate interests in the peace, stability and predictability of access to the major waterways in the region" (Media Briefing by the Official Spokesperson of the Ministry of External Affairs of India, Raveesh Kumar, 2019).

- First, as a rational actor, India's policy is aimed at safeguarding and maximising regional security and stability, underscored by its vision of realising and upholding "a free, open, inclusive and rules-based Indo-Pacific" (Opening Remarks by External Affairs Minister of India at the ASEAN-India Ministerial Meeting, 2019). The theoretical underpinning of this outlook stems from the logic of sustaining a regional balance of power and order, aimed at deterring China's hegemonic ambitions in the SCS.
- Second, the SCS is a crucial naval artery for India, accounting for the transportation of more than 55 per cent of its sea-borne trade (Answer of the Minister of State in the Ministry of External Affairs, Gen. V. K. Singh (Retd.) to Unstarred Question No. 808 in Rajya Sabha, 2017; Media Briefing by the Official Spokesperson of the Ministry of External Affairs of India, Raveesh Kumar, 2019). In addition to significant trade and economic interests, India's engagement with Vietnam for oil exploration is another substantive issue, highlighting its stakes in the littorals, as it facilitates securing the nation's energy requirements in the face of burgeoning demands. ONGC Videsh Limited/OVL, one of the pioneering Indian investors in the oil and gas sector, accounts for investments worth almost US$430 million since the early 1990s (Vietnamese President, Tran Dai Quang's Interview with Roy Chaudhury, Dipanjan, 2018). OVL and Petro-Vietnam had signed an Agreement of Cooperation in 2011 to conduct joint oil drilling exercises in two Vietnamese blocks in the Phu Kanh Basin of the SCS. The Agreement, aimed at developing long-term bilateral cooperation in the oil and gas industry, primarily focused on the following: new investments, expansion and operations of oil and gas exploration and production including refining, transportation and supply in Vietnam, India and third countries according to the laws and regulations of their countries; exchange of information on the petroleum industry and exchange of working visits of authorities and specialists in various domains of the petroleum industry ("Text of the Agreement of Cooperation between ONGC Videsh Limited and Vietnam Oil and Gas Group/Petro-Vietnam", 2011). However, Beijing voiced its vehement opposition to India's engagement with Vietnam. In this context, the then Chinese Foreign Ministry spokesperson, Jiang Yu, while asserting China's "indisputable sovereignty" over the SCS and its islands, also added: "Our consistent position is that we are opposed to any country engaging in oil and gas exploration and development activities in waters under China's jurisdiction." (Krishnan, 2011) Notwithstanding China's opposition, New Delhi responded that its engagement

with Hanoi for oil and gas exploration activities in the SCS served commercial purposes and "China's objection to OVL's explorations in South China Sea has no legal basis as the blocks belonged to Vietnam." (Media Briefing by the Official Spokesperson, Vishnu Prakash, 2011) Subsequently, amid tensions emanating from the call from China's state-owned oil firm, China National Offshore Oil Corporation, for bids from foreign companies offering exploration of oil in nine blocks in the SCS in June 2012, Vietnam decided to extend the contract for exploration of hydrocarbons in a crucial oil block, 128 to OVL in July. From the Vietnamese standpoint, this gesture followed its desire to hold on to Indian presence in the resource-rich littorals, defying increasing Chinese assertiveness therein ("Vietnam Extends Contract: Wants India's Presence in 128 Block", 2012). Against this backdrop, the then Chief of the Indian Navy, Admiral D.K. Joshi described India's position as follows: "It is not that we expect to be in those waters very frequently, but whenever the situation required, with the country's interests at stake – we will be required to go there and we are prepared for that." (Kumar, 2012) The Indo-Vietnamese collaborative endeavour scaled yet another height, when, in 2013, Vietnam offered seven oil blocks in the SCS to OVL, including three on an exclusive basis and joint prospecting in some Central Asian countries on a nomination basis to OVL. The very next year, OVL and Petro-Vietnam agreed to "enhance mutual cooperation in the hydrocarbon sector" and further expand OVL's presence in Vietnam in two other blocks (Agreement between ONGC Videsh Limited and PetroVietnam and Memorandum of Understanding between OVL and PetroVietnam, 2014: Cl. 7). In 2017, OVL received a two-year extension[5] to explore the 7058 sq km. Block 128 in Phu Kanh Basin, clearly indicating Hanoi's commitment to its engagement with India, despite Beijing's discomfiture and vocal assertions repudiating the extension. As the latest records indicate, OVL has invested US$50.88 million in the block (Nguyen, Verma and Miglani, 2017). Thus, India naturally nurtures legitimate interests in ensuring freedom of navigation, overflight, commercial activities and peaceful settlement of maritime disputes in accordance with international law in the SCS.

• Third, through the successful execution of the LEP/AEP, India has played and intends to continue playing a more direct role in the dynamics of the SCS littorals. With the objective of emerging as the net security provider to render "unstinted support for the security and economic prosperity" of its maritime neighbours ("Indian Navy – Net Security Provider to Island Nations in Indian Ocean Region: Anthony", 2011) the Indian Navy's intention to act as the first responder in the region has been highlighted in various editions of its Indian Maritime Doctrine (2004, 2007, 2009 and 2015). It has observed that the "Indian maritime vision for the first quarter of the twenty-first century must look at the arc from the Persian Gulf to the Straits of Malacca as a legitimate area of interest", in conformity with the Navy's potential to emerge as an "anchor of stability and security" (Indian Maritime Doctrine 2004, 2004: 56). The Doctrine provides an insight and rationale for the resurgence of India's naval power and postulates the various ways in which the Indian Navy could serve as a catalyst for peace, security and stability in the Indian Ocean Region (IOR). Moving ahead from its preceding versions, the 2009 edition of the Maritime Doctrine specifically mentioned the choke points, leading to and from the Indian Ocean[6] and their littoral regions within the Navy's primary area of interest (Indian Maritime Doctrine 2009, 2009: 67–68). The latest maritime guidance document, Ensuring Secure Seas: Indian Maritime Security Strategy (IMSS) unveiled in 2015, stresses the need to bolster the Navy's operational sphere and influence. The IMSS has consolidated the rationale and expectations of the Indian Navy as a net security provider to encompass the ability to balance "against prevailing threats, meeting risks and rising challenges through continuous monitoring, and a containment strategy for non-traditional challenges". The five-pronged strategy for realising this vision embraces the strategies for Deterrence, Conflict, Shaping Favourable and Positive Environment, Coastal and Offshore Security and Maritime Force and Capability Development. On the whole, the IMSS validates the employment of the Indian Navy as the primary instrument for securing and safeguarding the vital sea-lanes and addressing both traditional and non-traditional maritime challenges with a seamless and holistic approach (Ensuring Secure Seas: Indian Maritime Security Strategy, 2015: 8–9).

• Fourth, the enhanced stature of India in the Indo-Pacific region may be viewed in consonance with the convergence of the policies of the US, Japan and Australia towards ensuring its freedom and openness, reiterated *ad nauseam* in official declarations. In particular, India's Indo-Pacific policy, as enumerated by the Prime Minister of India, Narendra Modi in 2018, is premised on inclusiveness, without intending to single out any country as inimical; openness and ASEAN centrality and unity. The term "Indo-Pacific" deems some explanation in this context. The "Indo-Pacific", a term representing the Indian Ocean – Pacific Ocean combined, is construed as a singular and integrated geopolitical construct, fraught with security challenges, on the one hand, and containing huge geo-economic opportunities, on the other. "Indo" implies the Indian Ocean (not connoting India) and acknowledges the inadequacy and ambiguity of the "Asia-Pacific", a term traditionally representing the Asian littoral of the Pacific construct in terms of incorporating India in the affairs of the region (Khurana, 2007: 140). The official usage of "Indo-Pacific" may be traced back to the figurative anointment of the Japanese Premier, Shinzo Abe's address to the Indian Parliament in August 2007, when he regarded the "confluence of the Indian and Pacific Oceans" as "the dynamic coupling as seas of freedom and of prosperity" in the "broader Asia" (Speech by the Prime Minister of Japan, H.E. Mr. Shinzo Abe at the Parliament of the Republic of India, 2007) It subsequently found niche in official reference by the former US Secretary of State, Hillary Clinton in October 2010 and in Australia's Defense White Paper: 2013, prior to its usage in India and the more recent popularisation, led by the President of the US, Donald Trump's administration, particularly in the context of his first sojourn in Asia in

November 2017. Although the central actor in the Indo-Pacific podium, ASEAN had initially been averse to the articulation, apprehending such an idea would compel smaller countries to take sides, consequently resulting in the weakening of ASEAN (Khurana, 2019: 27), the present circumstances indicate a reversal of such an understanding and greater amenability of the organisation towards the "Indo-Pacific" reference. The most recent exposition of this acknowledgement is contained in the *ASEAN Outlook on the Indo-Pacific* (AOIP), which refers to the "wider Asia-Pacific and the Indian Ocean regions" as the Indo-Pacific, "not as contiguous territorial spaces but a closely integrated and interconnected region" with ASEAN adorning its central and strategic position therein (*ASEAN Outlook on the Indo-Pacific*, 2019: 1–2). India's perspective and official use of the term "Indo-Pacific", a region expanding from the "shores of Africa to that of the Americas", has been evident in Prime Minister, Narendra Modi's reference to the "Indo-Pacific" neither as a "strategy or as a club of limited members, nor as a grouping that seeks to dominate", directed against any particular country. On the contrary, India's espousal of the Indo-Pacific is infused with positivity, representing a "free, open, inclusive region, which embraces us all in a common pursuit of progress and prosperity". It primarily seeks to promote, safeguard and evolve a common rules-based regional order, which "equally appl[ies] to all individually as well as to the global commons", ensuring the prospects of "equal access as a right under international law to the use of common spaces on sea and in the air that would require freedom of navigation, unimpeded commerce and peaceful settlement of disputes in accordance with international law" (Narendra Modi's Keynote Address at the 17th Asia Security Summit at Singapore, 2018: 5). With the expanded domain of India's LEP in its second phase of integrating the countries of East Asia, Japan and Australia within the policy architecture, the converging strains towards maintaining a free and open Indo-Pacific have eventually synchronised with the US Pivot to Asia policy, unveiled by President Barack Obama in 2009. It gained momentum by accommodating the evolving concert of "like-minded" partners, as they tended to be "ambitious together" in providing a cooperative response to the challenges in the region ("Raisina Dialogue Remarks by Admiral Harry B. Harris, Jr.", 2016). Such a strategy demonstrated the selective engagement of the US with its key allies through the establishment of priorities, simultaneously assuring the security of its vital and important international interests (Art, 2003: 9). Washington identified India and Japan as solid pillars of its strategic pivot in the Indo-Pacific, while trying to undertake more concrete and decisive efforts to "constrain" China by a burgeoning counter-alliance. As part of its anti-China "pivot", Washington had been pushing for increased cooperation with India and Japan, as indicated by the maiden Trilateral Dialogue (2015), the subsequent induction of Japan as a permanent participant in the MALABAR exercises (in 2015) and the revival of the Quadrilateral Dialogue (QUAD 2.0) between Australia, India, Japan and the US (in 2017). This may also be viewed in the context of India's strides towards assuming a more significant role in the Indo-Pacific region, thus providing ample opportunities for buttressing the dimensions of multilateral cooperation with Australia, Japan and the US. Incidentally, the deepening quadrangular strategic bonhomie is reminiscent of Shinzo Abe's concept of the "Democratic Security Diamond", which envisioned the formation of a virtual security "diamond" by Australia, India, Japan and the US, and collectively embarking on securing regional peace and stability (Abe, 2012). Furthermore, President Donald Trump's emphatic use of the term "Indo-Pacific", acknowledged as the "priority theatre" of the US, not only reverberates the "importance of India's rise", but also acknowledges the vital role it envisages playing in the region. Washington's Indo-Pacific strategy is poised to catapult India to the centre of the regional security dynamics, facilitating and encouraging greater and sustainable coordination among the littoral powers within and even outside the ASEAN domain. As the US National Security Strategy (NSS) (December 2017) and the National Defense Strategy (NDS) (January 2018) highlight, strengthening Indo-Pacific alliances and partnerships is an imperative for Washington, for which India acts as the conduit. The US seeks to develop a collective response with partners that uphold a shared respect for sovereign, fair and reciprocal trade and rule of law, as a counter to Chinese dominance which "risks diminishing the sovereignty of many states in the Indo-Pacific". Therefore, its emphasis on reinforced commitment to freedom of the seas and the peaceful resolution of territorial and maritime disputes in accordance with international law underscores Washington's stance of safeguarding a Free and Open Indo-Pacific (National Security Strategy of the United States of America, 2017: 45–46). Additionally, identifying China as a revisionist power, intent on overtly challenging the free and open international order, the NDS underscored Beijing's pursuit of "Indo-Pacific regional hegemony in the near-term and displacement of the United States to achieve global pre-eminence in the future". In this context, the Strategy acknowledged the need for maintenance of a favourable balance of power in the region, as well as ensuring the freedom and openness of global common domains as primary defence objectives. For its execution, the Strategy prioritised the endurance and elevation of long-term security partnerships and alliances in the Indo-Pacific "to a networked security architecture capable of deterring aggression, maintaining stability, and ensuring free access to common domains". As the US embarks on the path of coordinating and assembling "key countries in the region" through bilateral and multilateral security relationships to preserve the free and open international system (Summary of the 2018 National Defense Strategy of the United States of America: Sharpening the American Military's Competitive Edge, 2018: 9), the dovetailing of its defence strategies, Japan's Free and Open Indo-Pacific Strategy with India's AEP provides the rationale and unveils the possibility of balancing China's ambitions, which seek to jeopardise the peace and stability of the region. India has hitherto seldom experienced the centripetal pull towards synchronisation of interests of this magnitude and it pragmatically intends to seize the moment.

- Fifth, as China expands its political and economic influence in India's immediate neighbourhood over a string of sub-continental states including

Bangladesh, the Maldives, Nepal, Pakistan and Sri Lanka, the LEP/AEP facilitates India's policy of containing China's footprints in its "extended" neighbourhood by rallying weight behind countries caught in the dispute over overlapping claims to sovereignty with Beijing. Furthermore, these countries are stakeholders in China's grand geostrategic initiative termed the Belt and Road Initiative (BRI). The 21st Century Maritime Silk Road (MSR), the maritime component of BRI, complemented by its overland counterpart, the Silk Road Economic Belt (SREB) is envisioned to run through the continents of Asia, Europe and Africa, connecting the vibrant East Asian economic circle, at one end, and the European economic circle, at the other. The SREB focuses on bringing together China, Central Asia, Russia and the Baltic by linking China with the Persian Gulf and the Mediterranean Sea through Central Asia and West Asia, on the one hand, and connecting China with Southeast Asia, South Asia and the Indian Ocean, on the other. The MSR is designed to stretch from China's coast to Europe through the SCS and the Indian Ocean via one route and from China's coast through the SCS to the South Pacific via the other ("Vision and Actions on Jointly Building Silk Road Economic Belt and 21st-Century Maritime Silk Road", 2015). The initiative, therefore, poses a direct challenge to India's stature as a security provider in the IOR, particularly with China's "benevolent entry" into the region through its spree of building infrastructure, ports, deep water ports and container terminals and connecting these with the mainland through a string of road and railway corridors, logistical stations, storage facilities and free-trade zones in India's primary area of interest. In sum, through the BRI, China engineers and sustains heavy investments across strategic locations, pursuing not only the expansion of the web of its entrenchment and control, but also attempting to circumvent its "Malacca Dilemma". Under such circumstances, India finds it a strategic necessity to explore the advantages of its geographical location and potential in the Indo-Pacific domain to balance China.

- Finally, the manifestation of India's concerns in the context of the unfolding events in the SCS gains currency when compared to China's not too dissimilar aggressive and expansionist strategy adopted in the Sino-India binary.[7] Beijing practises the classic "salami slicing tactic",[8] a practice of slow accumulation of small actions, culminating incrementally in a major strategic change over time (Haddick, 2012) of being non-committal of territorial demarcation and employing it as a means of further expansion and claim. Such a consideration is borne out by their historical legacy, recently refreshed by the Doklam standoff in 2017.

Having analysed the rationale of India's policy and responses in the SCS, which justify the logic of embarking on the present academic discourse, the following subsection attempts to situate the book in its theoretical framework.

1.2 India's strategy and responses to actions in the South China Sea: through the theoretical lens

A single theory is inadequate in explaining the underpinnings and arguments that form the building blocks of the book. Therefore, a blend of two principal theoretical frameworks, realism and neoliberalism has been employed in analysing the same. A discerning analysis reveals two distinct components by disintegrating the basic premise of the book: first, to identify and explain the implications of India's strategies and responses pertaining to the SCS dispute and the impact on its Southeast Asia policy (LEP/AEP) and, second, to evaluate ASEAN's stance and posture with respect to India's policy in the SCS and weigh the extent of India's potential to act as a significant balancer to China. With respect to the first component, taking cognisance of the history of Sino-India relations as well as in view of the contemporary circumstances, a realist approach is perhaps the most appropriate template for analysis. A realist perception is tempered with strains of tangible, critical geopolitical imperatives, and the constructivist logic of intangibles, namely images and perceptions in state-level interactions and policy-making, which have impressed upon the Sino-India binary. For instance, the scars of the limited but intense war of 1962 have passed down generational veins, leading to a psychological osmosis of un-recuperated mutual suspicion and discomfiture. The 1962 war, experiences of occasional border transgression and the claim of Arunachal Pradesh as a part of China have been predominantly responsible for generating a security dilemma syndrome in the Indian psyche, as it shares a majority of its Southeast and East Asian neighbours' apprehension pertaining to a hegemonic China's expansionist trajectory. This geopolitical angle has subsequently been emboldened by ground realities represented by incidents like the Depsang (April 2013), Chumar (September 2014) which incidentally coincided with Xi Jinping's Presidential visit to India and the Doklam incursions (July 2017); China's unrelenting patronage of Pakistan and stringent opposition to India's permanent membership of the UN Security Council and of the Nuclear Suppliers' Group, thus triggering questions about China's "peaceful" intentions in the Indian psyche. These responses from China have stimulated counter-responses from India, manifest in its LEP/AEP and burgeoning role as a net security provider in the Indo-Pacific. The Sino-India binary mirrors the classic illustration of synergising the historical vestiges of threat perceptions emanating from China with defensive realism, which implies that the means employed by a state to enhance its security proportionately decrease the security of the other states, thus giving rise to a security dilemma. This dilemma is motivated by the considerations of territorial expansion and absolute gains, which prompt apprehensions in one regarding the relative power and future intentions of the other. Consequently, states step into a downward spiral of mutual hostility. Similarly, China's policy in the SCS manifests the offensive realist rationale of a power-maximiser, aspiring regional hegemony, as opposed to maintaining a balance or equality. Although the security dilemma does not, as a rule, engulf the concerned states into severe competition and war, it introduces a downward spiral in their relations and may be mitigated through signalling, balance and differentiation of offensive and defensive means (Jervis, 1978: 178).

In accordance with the classical concept of security dilemma, the interest-max-imisation logic of China's expansionist policies in the SCS poses an inverse effect not only on the security domain of its neighbours in Southeast Asia, but also on India. As an emerging maritime power in the Indo-Pacific, having high stakes in maintaining the international maritime liberal order in a strategically high priority region like the SCS, India construes China's assertiveness as jeopardising its national and regional interests. The book does not suggest that India's enhanced engagement in the region would trigger Sino-India military conflict in the SCS. This hypothesis may be explained in light of regulatory "structural modifiers" (Taliaferro, 2000–2001: 131) or the relative distribution of capabilities that enables states to undertake particular diplomatic and military strategies, and primarily include the offence-defence balance in military strength, technology and capacity. Prompted by the understanding that the "best way to ensure their survival is to be the most powerful state in the system" (Lobell, 2017: 2), ambitious states like China are believed to adopt competitive, offensive and expansionist policies, thus provoking a security dilemma and counterbalancing behaviour. On the other hand, India's policy in the SCS, explained by the defensive realist logic of security max-imisation, seeks to maintain the status quo through defensive strategies, and this echoes the classical posture of "states balancing against hegemons" (Layne, 1993: 6) or deterring them in order to guarantee the region's balance of power.

With respect to the second component, prior to analysing ASEAN's stance and posture pertaining to India's policy in the SCS, it would be contingent to dwell upon ASEAN's perceptions and policy *vis-à-vis* China. This may be explained in the framework of the neoliberal theory of interdependence, particularly the con-cept of interrelation between power and asymmetrical interdependence as a power resource. The theory of interdependence explains politics in terms of political and economic exchanges, characterised by "bargaining", as rational actors pursue their respective national interests by responding to incentives. While liberalism accords equal priority to economic and security concerns, interdependence results in pro-blems of political strategy, particularly in an organisation or system bearing dis-parate members (as in the case of ASEAN as a composite organisation) since the actions or decisions of some of its members have the potential to inflict heavy costs on the other members (Keohane and Nye, 1987: 728–729). The evidence of an intrinsic incongruence in ASEAN's posture towards China is borne in the disarray among its members *vis-à-vis* the stance of containing China's ambitions in the SCS, which has been glaringly evident since 2012 and the manner in which developments have posed a threat to sustaining the solidarity of ASEAN as an organisation. In this context, it is necessary to acknowledge a couple of facts: first, the challenges to ASEAN centrality and leadership test the vitality of its norms and identity, and its ability to reconcile the opposing strains of adherence to the nor-mative motivations contained in the ASEAN Way, on the one hand, and the pri-macy of individual national interests of the member-states, on the other, as they interact with an actor and source of economic and military benefits of asymmetric capabilities; and second, the position and predominance that China enjoys among ASEAN members, notwithstanding their contested and overlapping sovereignty claims in the disputed SCS, propagate the equation of asymmetrical inter-dependence. China's spectacular economic success, matched with military pro-wess, along with factors like the presence and influence of overseas Chinese and the benefits that its allies would accrue as part of the BRI have further cemented its legitimacy in the region.

Across the range of ASEAN member-states, not only is there a distinction among those involved in territorial dispute over the SCS and those not involved, but also in terms of their preference for either a policy of pragmatic equidistance or a tight alignment with China. Whether a particular state prefers to maintain a policy of limited alignment or deeper engagement with China varies as a function of the level of economic and military development and capability, threat perceptions and a pragmatic analysis of advantages it accrues from China. This brings to the fore the indeterminacy of realism (Goh, 2007–2008: 116, 121; Laksmana, 2017: 114) in analysing the behaviour of smaller and relatively less-developed ASEAN states, since their decisions are influenced by imperatives of national interest, threat perceptions and vulnerability, thus expressing a high degree of accommodation and amenability to China. Summarily, China, towards which ASEAN nurtures "mixed feelings as both an asset and a liability" (Buzan, 1988: 11) to its security, has been successful in converting its resources into influence over the strategic decisions of the member-states, albeit to varying degrees. This has resulted in outcomes to China's advantage, particularly since the National Security Concept (1997) articulated its rejection of the "old Cold War security outlook", in favour of mutual trust and benefit, equality, interdependence, cooperative security and international norms (Goh, 2014: 838–839) bolstered subsequently by attempts to counter the "China threat" thesis with the tenets of "Peaceful Rise" and "Peaceful Development".

Reverting to the question of ASEAN's stance and posture with respect to India's policy in the SCS, it is imperative to mention the two-pronged approach embarked upon by India, to begin with. India, as a responsible regional power, espouses the importance of maintaining and promoting peace, stability, maritime safety and security, freedom of navigation and over-light and other lawful uses of the seas and unimpeded lawful maritime commerce, in keeping with universally recognised principles of international law (Closing Remarks by the Minister of State for External Affairs, Dr. V.K. Singh at the 14th ASEAN-India Foreign Ministers' Meeting, 2016: Cl. 16). Additionally, it resorts to faith in ASEAN centrality to promote peaceful resolution of disputes in the region. This has been manifested in India welcoming the

> collective commitment by the concerned countries to abide by and implement the 2002 Declaration on the Conduct of Parties in the South China Sea and to work towards the adoption of a Code of Conduct in the South China Sea on the basis of consensus.
>
> (Answer of the Minister of State in the Ministry of External Affairs, Gen. V. K. Singh (Retd.) to Starred Question No. 568 in Lok Sabha, 2016)

India's approach is contingent upon the principles of internal and external balancing, which trail its origin to Kenneth Waltz's espousal of states balancing with
internal and external efforts (Waltz, 1979: 118) and synchronise with the logic of
ensuring cooperative security. With respect to internal balancing, India pursues the
prospect of bolstering its economic and defence capabilities, and raising stronger
forces and weapons procurement, towards which the Make in India initiative,
unveiled by New Delhi under the National Democratic Alliance – II (NDA-II)
government in September 2014 has provided a major boost. Besides, the Indian
Navy plays an effective role in combating both traditional and non-traditional
challenges to security in the arc from the Persian Gulf to the Strait of Malacca,
which is considered a legitimate area of interest, and in shaping a favourable
and positive regional maritime environment. The Indian Navy is also on the
threshold of deploying "mission-ready warships" and aircraft along critical
SLOC and "choke points" ranging from the Persian Gulf and Gulf of Aden to
the Malacca and Sunda Straits.

In terms of external balancing, India has been engaged in forging security
mechanisms with regional navies; participating in relevant institutional mechanisms
like the ASEAN Regional Forum (ARF), the East Asia Summit (EAS), the ASEAN
Defence Ministers' Meeting (ADMM), the ASEAN Maritime Forum; and the
conduct of regular maritime and Coast Guard exercises to facilitate interoperability, at the bilateral, trilateral and multilateral levels. The latter has been
demonstrated by exercises like MILAN and MALABAR, and multilateral institutional linkages fostered through the Indian Ocean Naval Symposium (IONS), the
Indian Ocean Rim Association (IORA) and the rejuvenation of the Quadrilateral
Alliance (QUAD) between Australia, India, Japan and the US. Furthermore, in
the context of vital developments in the SCS like China's island building spree,
enhanced by military surveillance, communication and logistics infrastructure; its
opposition to the US Freedom of Navigation operations; rejection of the July
2016 verdict of the PCA; new fishing rules implemented on the Hainan coast;
PLAN's shadowing of passing vessels and objection to exploration of natural
resources in the disputed littorals have disturbed the liberal maritime order in
the Indo-Pacific, besides raising the possibility of military confrontation among
claimant states.

ASEAN has in general been accommodating of China, evading a direct confrontational posture, while simultaneously welcoming the role of regional littoral
nations like India, Japan, Australia and the most prominent external power, the
US, which have significant geostrategic stakes in the maintenance of peace and
order in the Indo-Pacific in general and the SCS in particular, as potential
balancers in an attempt to deter the aggressive posture of China. This strategy has
been explained in terms of ASEAN's engagement in "double binding" or
consciously enveloping China and other prominent stakeholders, including the
US, in an architecture of regional interdependence and institutions, so as to exert
a moderating effect on China (Acharya, 2003–2004: 153). Acknowledged as the
most viable means of safeguarding a "stable, predictable regional order in which
countries big and small can prosper together", as well as of encouraging them to

develop closer economic and political relationships so as to deepen interdependence and strengthen their sense of sharing a stake in the region's security, ASEAN has emphasised the notion of cooperative security. This has been implemented through the institutionalisation of bilateral and multilateral engagements and erecting a cooperative security framework of dialogue and institutionalised defence/strategic interactions with major stakeholding nations towards indirect balancing of China. It thus envisages a situation in which major powers would be actively and legitimately involved in the security dynamics of the region, through a sustained pattern of mutual engagement and accommodation (Goh, 2007–2008: 129–131). The cooperative security approach, which is non-linear and evolutionary in nature, attempts to deepen comprehension of the mutuality of both traditional and non-traditional security and introduce consistency and coherence to bilateral and multilateral relations between and among regional stakeholders (Snyder, 1997: 12–13).

In tandem with this theoretical string, ASEAN's response towards India's SCS policy and its attempt to weigh the extent of New Delhi's intent and capability to act as a significant balancer and credible deterrent to China, has been viewed from the perspective of the LEP/AEP, which has successfully expanded the scope of strategic cooperation with the ASEAN states as well as non-ASEAN maritime powers like Japan and Australia. The philosophy of India's Look East rests on the realisation and maintenance of "a peaceful, open, equitable, stable and rule-based order in the Indo-Pacific region and beyond" with ASEAN at its fulcrum. The former Prime Minister of India, P.V. Narasimha Rao's seminal "Singapore Lecture", delivered in 1994, rightly acknowledged as the principal architectural beam of the LEP, contained the rationale of this "new relationship" between India and its Southeast Asian neighbours. The relationship was unfolded against the backdrop of the exigencies of the changing global order, made conspicuous by new and emerging challenges, both endogenous and exogenous in nature. This famous "Lecture" identified the LEP as a platform for India and its ASEAN partners to address challenges like the interpretation of sovereignty, security stakes involving the rights of passage through crucial waterways, security of navigation from piracy, claims over disputed lands, maritime zones and resources, among others, and announced India's "commitment to the cause of global peace". In sum, Narasimha Rao envisioned an opportunity in the LEP for India and ASEAN to engage and cooperate, principally in the economic and strategic spheres, by vigorously exploring their mutual potential, premised on the ethos of compassion, harmony and a sense of sharing. This was ultimately aimed at establishing "equal partnership with equal say in the eventual codification of international laws and regulations that will govern international political, economic and social activity in the next century" ("Text of the 12th Singapore Lecture Delivered by the Prime Minister of India, P. V. Narasimha Rao on September 8, 1994", 1994: 1413). Implicitly, LEP was conceived of as a strategic instrument for India to engage with the broader Indo-Pacific region and emerge as a responsible stakeholder in its dynamics and challenges.

ASEAN, being cognisant of India's geographical location athwart the Indian Ocean, welcomed its enthusiasm to play a constructive and positive role in contributing to regional and maritime peace, security and stability, as demonstrated in its acceptance as a Full Dialogue Partner and member of the ARF in 1995 and 1996 respectively. In addition to the strategic rationale, India's emerging profile as a major commercial destination, backed by a strong economy with gross national product (GNP) exceeding US$280 billion, high growth rates and export propensity in consort with the country's commitment to the irreversibility of the economic reform and liberalisation policy, convinced ASEAN of the inevitability of its potential rise as an economic power of substance back in the 1990s. India's Dialogue Partnership with ASEAN constituted a milestone during the First Phase (1991–2001) of LEP, anchoring its incremental leap into the dynamics of the region on a solid foundation. Attesting to its indispensability in providing ASEAN with "vital links to the Indian Ocean", the then Foreign Minister of Singapore, S. Jayakumar hailed India's full dialogue partnership with the organisation as a mutual, enabling means of establishing "a more robust relationship and work[ing] closely together to achieve economic prosperity and a greater security for the Asia-Pacific region" ("Opening Statement of Singapore's Foreign Minister, S. Jayakumar at ASEAN Post Ministerial Conference", 1996: 1532). Overwhelmed by the acknowledgement, his Indian counterpart, I.K. Gujral lauded ASEAN's decision to accord this status to India as a "far-sighted assessment about the political and strategic convergence, acceleration of economic relations and future potential, and complementarities in areas that were hitherto not evident or remained unexploited." Further, he articulated this position "as a political and psychological watershed" aimed at moving over from a period of quiescence into a more activist phase; from an era of borrowed images and refracted perceptions to direct communication and proximate cognition in ASEAN-India relations ("Statement of the Indian Minister of External Affairs, I.K. Gujral at ASEAN Post Ministerial Conference", 1996: 1534). Therefore, with India assuming a full dialogue stature, the collaboration encompassed political and security dimensions, manifested in a series of consultative deliberations including ministerial meetings, Senior Officials Meetings and meetings at experts' level, as well as through dialogue and cooperation frameworks such as ARF, the Post Ministerial Conference (PMC) and the like. Subsequently, Jayakumar, while welcoming India as an ARF member at its Jakarta Ministerial in July 1996, expressed the Forum's collective willingness to forge long-term and comprehensive security linkages with New Delhi, when he acknowledged: "India, given its size and strategic location in the Indian Ocean, can play a constructive and positive role in contributing to the stability of the region. In this regard, we are pleased to have India in the ARF." (Address of Singapore's Foreign Minister, S. Jayakumar at the 3rd Ministerial Meeting, ASEAN Regional Forum, 1996) In this meeting, I.K. Gujral described India's ARF membership as a "manifestation of our Look East destiny" (Address of the Indian Minister of External Affairs, I. K. Gujral at the 3rd Ministerial Meeting, ASEAN Regional Forum, 1996).

It follows from the discussion above that the timely convergence of strategic and economic interests between India and ASEAN, institutionalised within the Look East rubric, not only facilitated India's relations with ASEAN, but also served as a threshold to embarking on the wider security dynamics of the Indo-Pacific region, embedded in its commitment to play a commensurate and responsible role in securing peace and stability. The confidence that the deft execution of the LEP had generated over a decade resulted in the elevation of India to the status of the coveted Summit-level or ASEAN+1 partner in 2002, as India and ASEAN charted the future road-map of cooperation, with the emphasis on working together towards the preservation of regional peace and stability and promoting development of the region (Joint Statement of the 1st ASEAN-India Summit, 2002). India's ascendance within the ASEAN matrix was officially celebrated as "a significant development in our relations with ASEAN countries, as India joined the ranks of a handful of countries with which ASEAN has summit dialogues, namely, China, Japan, and South Korea". Furthermore, this up-gradation was acknowledged to be a "natural culmination of ten years of progressive engagement with ASEAN" in addition to vindicating the LEP's success in building "on our historical and cultural ties with the region to create a mutually beneficial strategic and economic relationship" (Annual Report: 2002–2003, 2003: 17). In this context, New Delhi's sincere urge towards the development of a better understanding with ASEAN received a major boost when the then Indian Minister of External Affairs, Yashwant Sinha, officially pronounced the Second Phase (Phase II) of LEP in September 2003. He declared that:

> India's Look East Policy has now entered its Phase II. Phase I was focused primarily on the ASEAN countries and on trade and investment linkages. Phase II is characterized by an expanded definition of "East" extending from Australia to China and East Asia with ASEAN as its core. Phase II marks a shift in focus from exclusively economic issues to economic and security issues including joint efforts to protect sea-lanes, coordination on counter terrorism etc. On the economic sphere, Phase II is also characterized by arrangements for Free Trade Agreements and establishment of institutional economic linkages between the countries of the region and India.
>
> (Statement of the Indian Minister of External Affairs, Yashwant Sinha, at the Plenary Session of 2nd ASEAN-India Business Summit, 2003)

India's steady graduation from a Full Dialogue Partner to attaining the membership of ARF and subsequently becoming a "Plus One" (Summit-level) associate, followed by its inclusion within the EAS and ADMM+8 in 2005 and 2010 respectively, constituted an adroit edifice for the future development and entrenchment of India-ASEAN ties, as well as its greater participation and responsibility in Indo-Pacific affairs. The ASEAN-India Summit was regarded as a framework that would "add some sheen to the organisation". It was also strongly felt by ASEAN that "associating with India at the summit level at this point of time will be beneficial to the ASEAN as well a vindication for India's 'Look East' policy" (Press Statement by the Chairman of the 7th ASEAN Summit, 2001). Besides, the establishment of India's new space in the regional dynamics as a member of EAS was likened to the engine of the "East Asian" aircraft by the former ASEAN Secretary General, Ong Keng Yong. He applied the "aircraft analogy", portraying India as the engine of the aircraft, of which ASEAN was the "pilot". The fact that ASEAN could bank on India as a possible balancer of China could have been a definite consideration guiding its inclusion within the ASEAN orbit, which was made all the more evident with the apparent and approximate synchronisation of extending to India admission into the ARF, EAS, ADMM+ and accession to the Treaty of Amity and Cooperation (TAC) with that of China. An explicit reference to it was contained in the Secretary General's portrayal of India and China as the twin "engines" of the figurative "aircraft" of which ASEAN was the "pilot" (Address of the Secretary-General of ASEAN, Ong Keng Yong at the 2nd East Asia Summit, 2007). In addition, a host of factors like its evolving economic and military prowess, its sincere drive to attain blue-water naval status and strategic autonomy as a nuclear power state, coupled with the harbouring of no territorial or belligerent regional ambitions and the acceptance of the policy of ASEAN centrality, featured as significant pointers for ASEAN to enthusiastically explore the whole range of strategic, economic and cultural ties with India. On the whole, the extended institutional mechanism of ASEAN, whether in the form of Full Dialogue, Summit-level or EAS partnership generated "tremendous goodwill for India in South East and East Asia", and opened up the proverbial "sky" as the "limit for our engagement with this region" (Prime Minister of India, Manmohan Singh's Statement at the 7th India-ASEAN Summit, 2009).

As India adorned the status of ASEAN's Strategic Partner in 2012, it marked the successful culmination of two decades of its Look East odyssey and bore testimony to its responsible "role in ensuring regional peace and stability through India's accession to the TAC in 2003" and its "active contribution" in the ASEAN+1, ARF, EAS and ADMM+ architecture. During the second phase of the Look East, generally considered to start with India's Summit-level partnership resulted in the extension of its diplomatic and strategic footprints into East Asia, or its "extended neighbourhood'" including the fellow EAS members, viz. China, Japan, South Korea, Australia and New Zealand, with ASEAN as its core. It further paved the way for mutual coordination on regional and international issues of concern, aimed at bolstering cooperation in ensuring "maritime security and freedom of navigation, and safety of sea lanes of communication for unfettered movement of trade in accordance with international law, including UNCLOS"; and promoting engagement in the ASEAN Maritime Forum and its expanded format. These efforts were aimed at jointly addressing maritime challenges pertaining to sea piracy, search and rescue at sea, maritime connectivity and freedom of navigation, among others (Vision Statement: ASEAN-India Commemorative Summit, 2012).

Thus, it may be contended from the discussion above that ASEAN's acknowledgement and acceptance of India's role as a responsible actor in the Indo-Pacific has a lineage to its substantiation. India's graduation from "looking" to "acting" East, reciprocated by ASEAN welcoming its steady ascendance within the regional architecture since the days of Dialogue Partnership, substantiates the claim considerably. Historically and going by its foreign policy philosophy, India is anti-expansionist and respects the need for securing a rules-based international order. These traits have attracted ASEAN to India ever since the LEP was inaugurated officially. Under the present circumstances, the possibility of greater mutual engagement in an array of spheres as diverse as trade, services and investment, defence, energy, connectivity, knowledge-base, culture and restoration activities, etc., particularly within the Make in India ambit, fosters convergence between India and ASEAN. This has the potential to not only bolster India's stature within ASEAN, but also to catapult it to the position of a potential balancer in the region. As a predominant maritime power in the Indo-Pacific region, the Indian Navy has stepped up its reassuring role in safeguarding against both traditional and non-traditional threats to security. Further, its interaction with the ASEAN navies through the regular conduct of joint exercises (at bilateral and multilateral eche-lons), embarking on exercises towards mutual understanding and inter-operability in a plethora of situations ranging from Non-combatant Evacuation Operations (NEO), Humanitarian Assistance and Disaster Relief (HADR) operations to intelligence-sharing have encouraged the prospects of confidence-building and Maritime Domain Awareness. With security and defence cooperation constituting the major agenda in the "Plan of Action of India-ASEAN Cooperation: 2016–2020", the Indian Navy is bolstering cooperation with member-states through a series of exercises, coordinated patrols, training exchanges as well as supply of equipment. With the objective of remaining outcome-oriented in both onshore and offshore endeavours, coupled with the impressive features of combat-readi-ness, pace of modernisation and progressive acquisitions, the Indian Navy's status as a "responsible" naval power has enhanced its acceptability among the ASEAN states. New Delhi's role as a net security provider becomes more critical in shaping the regional strategic discourse that has been drifting towards uncertainty and militarisation. ASEAN and India are on the same page regarding the full and effective implementation of the Declaration on the Conduct of the Parties in the South China Sea (DOC) and expectations for the early conclusion of the COC reveal their shared vision for ensuring a rules-based maritime order in the SCS, where the hegemony of any power would not go unchallenged. On the other hand, as the Indian Navy sincerely and vigorously pursues the vision of SAGAR (Security and Growth for All in the Region) through security cooperation and capacity-building initiatives with the ASEAN, the perception that economic development and security are complementary and interlinked is finding deeper roots in their dynamics as well.

Having provided the rationale, theoretical groundwork and pivotal arguments which help in erecting the framework of the study, it also attempts to identify certain blind spots, often overlooked while addressing ASEAN's response to India's policies relating to China in the SCS. Insofar as the question of whether ASEAN acknowledges India as a commensurate balancer to China is concerned, references to New Delhi's tight-rope walk are put forward by its asymmetric eco-nomic and military capabilities when compared to Beijing. Besides, it is equally important to underscore the position and predominance that China enjoys among the ASEAN members, as mentioned above. Additionally, ASEAN and China have been creeping forward, subsequent to the conclusion of the framework agreement, or outline, on the COC in August 2017; have agreed on initiating negotiations for the text of a binding document on the SCS in November 2017, followed by the declaration of a shared commitment to promote peace and stability in the region at the ASEAN Retreat of February 2018 and the most recent signing of the Single Draft Negotiating Text (SDNT) to provide the basis for further negotiations on specific provisions of the COC exactly a year later. ASEAN has acknowledged "substantive progress" on the SDNT negotiations (Chongkittavorn, 2019) and appears optimistic with respect to its future trajectory, welcoming "the completion of the first reading of the Single Draft COC Negotiating Text ahead of schedule" (Chairman's Statement of the 26th ASEAN Regional Forum, 2019: Cl. 7). Simultaneously, it has underscored the imperative of maintaining an ambience conducive to expedited negotiations on the COC and confidence-building among the parties concerned (Chairman's Statement of the 34th ASEAN Summit, 2019: Cl. 53). Under these circumstances, ASEAN, wary of disturbing the evolving alchemy with China, will be intent on maintaining the precarious balance in its relations with India and China.

With this background in place, the book is an attempt to identify and analyse the following objectives in the course of its six chapters:

- First, to identify the implications of India's strategies and responses *vis-à-vis* the SCS dispute and their impact on LEP/AEP.
- Second, to analyse the basis and structural intractability of territorial claims of the states involved in the dispute, in light of international legal interpretations and the manner in which ASEAN addresses the issue.
- Third, to discuss ASEAN's stance with respect to India's policy in the SCS and weigh the extent of its acceptability as a counterweight or deterrent to China.
- Fourth, to discuss India's strategies of internal and external balancing as pragmatic responses to the SCS conundrum.
- Fifth, to study the implications of great power shifts in priorities for Indian policy, with particular reference to the positions of President Donald Trump and Prime Minister Shinzo Abe.
- Finally, to conclude with a summary of the trajectory of recent developments in the SCS, their implications for Indian policy responses and for the stability of the region.

The reference time-frame encompasses the administrative tenures of the two governments in India: United Progressive Alliance (UPA: May 2004–April 2014) and National Democratic Alliance (NDA: May 2014–May 2019), with a brief background study of the issue and its importance in Indian foreign policy computations. The uniqueness of the book lies in its attempt to bridge the gap in existing literature pertaining to the Indian perspective, responses and policy options on the SCS conundrum and ASEAN's stance in this respect. Herein is the novelty and contribution of this book to the existing pedagogy on the scenario in the SCS.

Notes

1 This includes both organic and inorganic natural resources – minerals, marine livestock/ flora and fauna and energy reserves
2 Cuarteron Reef, Fiery Cross Reef, Gaven Reef, Hughes Reef, Johnson Reef, Mischief Reef (North and South) and Subi Reef
3 Beijing has created the Sansha City in 2012 in the Woody Island as the civilian administrative hub for its claims in the South China Sea
4 Vietnam: 338, the Philippines: 100, Taiwan: 37 and Malaysia: 28 – concentrated in the Spratlys
5 Fifth extension valid till June 2019
6 The choke points include the Six-degree Channel; Eight/ Nine-degree Channels; Strait of Hormuz, Bab-el-Mandeb, Malacca, Singapore, Sunda and Lombok; the Mozambique Channel and the Cape of Good Hope
7 The un-demarcated Line of Actual Control on the Sino-India border is a case in point
8 Salami Slicing tactic refers to the "taking over territory in a very gradual manner", quoted by the Indian Army Chief, Gen. Bipin Rawat (in Dutta, 2017)

References

Abe, Shinzo. (2012, December 27). "Asia's Democratic Security Diamond", Project Syndicate, www.project-syndicate.org/commentary/a-strategic-alliance-for-japan-and-india-by-shinzo-abe?barrier=accesspaylog (accessed on 2019, June 23)

Acharya, Amitav. (2003–2004). "Will Asia's Past be its Future?". *International Security*, 28(3)

Address of Singapore's Foreign Minister, S. Jayakumar at the 3rd Ministerial Meeting, ASEAN Regional Forum. (1996, July 23). Jakarta: ASEAN Secretariat, www.asean regionalforum.asean.org/about.html (accessed on 2019, May 12)

Address of the Indian Minister of External Affairs, I. K. Gujral at the 3rd Ministerial Meeting, ASEAN Regional Forum. (1996, July 23). Jakarta: ASEAN Secretariat, www. aseanregionalforum.asean.org/about.html (accessed on 2019, May 12)

Address of the Secretary-General of ASEAN, Ong Keng Yong at the 2nd East Asia Summit. (2007, January 15). Jakarta: ASEAN Secretariat, www.aseansec.org/21924.htm (accessed on 2019, May 12)

Agreement between ONGC Videsh Limited and PetroVietnam and Memorandum of Understanding between OVL and PetroVietnam. (2014, October 27–28). List of Documents Signed during the State Visit of Prime Minister of Vietnam to India. New Delhi: Ministry of External Affairs, www.mea.gov.in/incoming-visit-detail.htm?24144/List+of+documents+signed+during+the+State+Visit+of+Prime+Minister+of+Vietnam+to+India+October+2728+2014 (accessed on 2019, February 18)

Annual Report to Congress: Military and Security Developments Involving the People's Republic of China in 2017. (2017, May 15). Washington, DC: Office of the Secretary of Defense, www.defense.gov/Portals/1/Documents/pubs/2017_China_Military_Power_Report.PDF (accessed on 2018, February 18)

Annual Report to Congress: Military and Security Developments Involving the People's Republic of China in 2019. (2019, May 2). Washington, DC: Office of the Secretary of Defense, https://media.defense.gov/2019/May/02/2002127082/-1/-1/1/2019_CHINA_MILI TARY_POWER_REPORT.pdf (accessed on 2019, May 20)

Annual Report: 2002–2003. (2003). New Delhi: Ministry of External Affairs

Answer of the Minister of State in the Ministry of External Affairs, Gen. V. K. Singh (Retd.) to Starred Question No. 568 in Lok Sabha. (2017, April 27). New Delhi: Ministry of

External Affairs/Lok Sabha, www.mea.gov.in/lok-sabha.htm?dtl/26684/QUESTION_ NO568_SOUTH_CHINA_SEA (accessed on 2019, January 20)

Answer of the Minister of State in the Ministry of External Affairs, Gen. V. K. Singh (Retd.) to Unstarred Question No. 808 in Rajya Sabha. (2017, February 9). New Delhi: Ministry of External Affairs/Rajya Sabha, www.mea.gov.in/rajya-sabha.htm?dtl/28041/QUESTION_ NO808_TRADE_THROUGH_SOUTH_CHINA_SEA (accessed on 2019, January 20)

"Any Provocation on the South China Sea will Meet a Decisive Response". (2014, April 14). *People's Daily Online,* http://en.people.cn/98649/8597386.html (accessed on 2018, September 12)

Art, Robert J. (2003). *A Grand Strategy for America,* Ithaca, NY: Cornell University Press

ASEAN Outlook on the Indo-Pacific. (2019, June 23). Jakarta: ASEAN Secretariat, https://asean.org/asean-outlook-indo-pacific (accessed on 2019, July 19)

Bingguo, Dai. (2009, August 7). "The Core Interests of the People's Republic of China", *China Digital Times,* https://chinadigitaltimes.net/2009/08/dai-bingguo-%E6%88%B4% E7%A7%89%E5%9B%BD-the-core-interests-of-the-prc (accessed on 2018, August 30)

Buzan, Barry. (1988, June). "The Southeast Asian Security Complex". *Contemporary Southeast Asia,* 10(1)

Chairman's Statement of the 26th ASEAN Regional Forum. (2019, August 2). Jakarta: ASEAN Secretariat, https://asean.org/storage/2019/08/26th-ARF-Chairmans-Statement_FINAL. pdf (accessed on 2019, August 15)

Chairman's Statement of the 34th ASEAN Summit. (2019, June 23). Jakarta: ASEAN Secretariat, https://asean.org/chairmans-statement-34th-asean-summit/ (accessed on 2020, January 3)

China's Military Strategy. (2015, May 26). Beijing: The State Council Information Office, http://eng.mod.gov.cn/Press/2015-05/26/content_4586805.htm (accessed on 2018, September 16)

China's National Defense in the New Era. (2019). Beijing: The State Council Information Office. *Xinhua,* www.xinhuanet.com/english/2019-07/24/c_138253389.htm (accessed on 2019, July 26)

China's Peaceful Development. (2011, September). Beijing: Information Office of the State Council, www.gov.cn/english/official/2011-09/06/content_1941354.htm (accessed on 2018, September 12)

China's Policies on Asia-Pacific Security Cooperation. (2017, January 11). Beijing: Ministry of Foreign Affairs, www.fmprc.gov.cn/mfa_eng/zxxx_662805/t1429771.shtml (accessed on 2018, September 16)

Chongkittavorn, Kavi. (2019, May 28). "More 'Substantive' Deal on S. China Sea". *Bangkok Post,* www.bangkokpost.com/opinion/opinion/1684972/more-substantive- deal-on-s-china-sea (accessed on 2019, July 19)

Closing Remarks by the Minister of State for External Affairs, Dr. V. K. Singh at the 14th ASEAN-India Foreign Ministers' Meeting. (2016, July 25). New Delhi: Ministry of External Affairs, www.mea.gov.in/Speeches-Statements.htm?dtl/27140/Closing_Remarks_by_ Minister_of_State_for_External_Affairs_Dr_VK_Singh_at_the_14th_ASEANIndia_Foreign_ Ministers_Meeting_in_Vientiane_July_25_2016 (accessed on 2019, July 19)

"Concrete and Coral – Tracking Expansion in the South China Sea". (2018, May 24). *Interactive Graphic Preview,* http://pictures.reuters.com/archive/CHINA-SOUTHCHINA SEA-BUILDING-ET1EE5N1RY4KR.html (accessed on 2018, September 12)

Doshi, Rush. (2017, October 25). "Xi Jinping Just Made it Clear where China's Foreign Policy is Headed". *The Washington Post,* www.washingtonpost.com/news/monkey-cage/

wp/2017/10/25/xi-jinping-just-made-it-clear-where-chinas-foreign-policy-is-headed/? utm_term=.f699e6994297 (accessed on 2018, March 20)

Dutta, Prabhash K. (2017, July 7). "What is China's Salami Slicing Tactic that Bipin Rawat Talked About?", *India Today*

Ensuring Secure Seas: Indian Maritime Security Strategy. (2015). New Delhi: Ministry of Defence (Navy), www.indiannavy.nic.in/sites/default/files/Indian_Maritime_Security_ Strategy_Document_25Jan16.pdf (accessed on 2019, April 2)

Gao, Zhigou and Jia, Bing Bing. (2013, January). "The Nine-Dash Line in the South China Sea: History, Status and Implications". *The American Journal of International Law*, 107(1)

Goh, Evelyn. (2007–2008). "Great Powers and Hierarchical Order in Southeast Asia: Analyzing Regional Security Strategies". *International Security*, 32(3)

Goh, Evelyn. (2014, September–October). "The Modes of China's Influence: Cases for Southeast Asia". *Asian Survey*, 54(5)

Haddick, Robert. (2012, August 3). "Salami Slicing in the South China Sea", https://for eignpolicy.com/2012/08/03/salami-slicing-in-the-south-china-sea (accessed on 2019, July 19)

"How Much Trade Transits the South China Sea?" (2016). Washington: Center for Strategic and International Studies, https://chinapower.csis.org/much-trade-transits-south-china-sea/?utm_content=buffer2dfa4&utm_medium=social&utm_source=twitter.com& utm_campaign=buffer (accessed on 2018, August 15)

Indian Maritime Doctrine, 2004. (2004). New Delhi: Ministry of Defence (Navy)

Indian Maritime Doctrine, 2009. (2009). New Delhi: Ministry of Defence (Navy), www. indiannavy.nic.in/sites/default/files/Indian-Maritime-Doctrine-2009-Updated-12Feb16. pdf (accessed on 2019, May 12)

"Indian Navy – Net Security Provider to Island Nations in Indian Ocean Region: Anthony". (2011, October 12). Press Information Bureau. New Delhi: Ministry of Defence, http://pib.nic.in/newsite/PrintRelease.aspx?relid=76590 (accessed on 2019, May 12)

Jervis, Robert. (1978, January). "Cooperation under the Security Dilemma". *World Politics*, 30(2)

Joint Statement of the 1st ASEAN-India Summit. (2002, November 5). Jakarta: ASEAN Secretariat, www.aseansec.org/13198.htm (accessed on 2019, May 12)

Keohane, Robert O. and Joseph S. Nye (Jr.). (1987). "Power and Interdependence Revisited". *International Organization*, 41(4)

Khurana, Gurpreet S. (2007, January). "Security of Sea Lines: Prospects for India-Japan Cooperation". *Strategic Analysis*, 31(1)

Khurana, Gurpreet S. (2019). "What is the Indo-Pacific? The New Geopolitics of the Asia-Centred Rim Land", in Berkofsky, Alex and Sergio Miracola (eds), *Geopolitics by Other Means – the Indo-Pacific Reality*, www.ispionline.it/en/pubblicazione/geopolitics-other-means-indo-pacific-reality-22122 (accessed on 2019, July 19)

Krishnan, Ananth. (2011, September 17). "China Warns India on South China Sea Exploration Projects", *The Hindu*

Kumar, Vinay. (2012, December 4). "We'll Protect Our Interests in South China Sea: Navy Chief", *The Hindu*

Laksmana, Evan A. (2017). "Pragmatic Equidistance – How Indonesia Manages its Great Power Relations", in Denoon, David B.H. (ed.), *The United States and the Future of Southeast Asia*, New York: New York University Press

Law of the People's Republic of China on the Territorial Sea and Contiguous Zone. (1992, February 25). Beijing: The National People's Congress, www.npc.gov.cn/englishnpc/ Law/2007-12/12/content_1383846.htm (accessed on 2018, February 18)

Layne, C. (1993). "The Unipolar Illusion: Why New Great Powers Will Rise". *International Security*, 17

Lobell, Steven E. (2017). "Structural Realism – Offensive and Defensive Realism". *Oxford Research Encyclopaedia of International Studies*, http://internationalstudies. oxfordre.com/view/10.1093/acrefore/9780190846626.001.0001/acrefore-978019084 6626-e-304?print=pdf (accessed on 2019, May 12)

Media Briefing by the Official Spokesperson of the Ministry of External Affairs of India, Raveesh Kumar, quoted in "India Wary over China-Vietnam Standoff in the SCS". (2019, August 1), *The Statesman*

Media Briefing by the Official Spokesperson, Vishnu Prakash. (2011, September 15). New Delhi: Ministry of External Affairs, http://mea.gov.in/in-focus-article.htm?2951 (accessed on 2018, April 2)

Narendra Modi's Keynote Address at the 17th Asia Security Summit at Singapore. (2018, June 1), www.narendramodi.in/pm-%20modi-%20to%20-deliver%20-keynote-%20address%20-at% 20-shangri-la-%20dialouge-%20in%20-singapore-540324 (accessed on 2018, September 16)

National Security Strategy of the United States of America. (2017, December). Washington, DC: The White House, www.whitehouse.gov/wp-content/uploads/ 2017/12/NSS-Final-12-18-2017-0905-2.pdf (accessed on 2019, May 24)

Neill, Alexander. (2018, August 3). "China's Creeping Saturation of the South China Sea". www.iiss.org/blogs/analysis/2018/08/china-saturation-south-china-sea-subi-reef (accessed on 2018, September 12)

Nguyen, Mai, Verma, Nidhi and Miglani, Sanjeev. (2017, July 6). "Vietnam Renews Indian Oil Deal in Tense South China Sea". *Reuters*, www.reuters.com/article/us-southchinasea-viet nam/vietnam-renews-india-oil-deal-in-tense-south-china-sea-idUSKBN19R25P (accessed on 2019, February 18)

Opening Remarks by External Affairs Minister of India at the ASEAN-India Ministerial Meeting. (2019, August 2). New Delhi: Ministry of External Affairs, www.mea.gov.in/ Speeches-Statements.htm?dtl/31709/Opening_Remarks_by_External_Affairs_Minister_ at_the_ASEANIndian_Ministerial_Meeting (accessed on 2019, August 8)

"Opening Statement of Singapore's Foreign Minister, S. Jayakumar at ASEAN Post Ministerial Conference". (1996, July 24). ASEAN Post Ministerial Conference Documents, *Strategic Digest*, 26(10)

Phillips, Tom. (2018, February 6). "Photos Show Beijing's Militarisation of the South China Sea in New Detail", *The Guardian Weekly*, www.theguardian.com/world/2018/ feb/06/photos-beijings-militarisation-south-china-sea-philippines (accessed on 2018, February 18)

Press Statement by the Chairman of the 7th ASEAN Summit. (2001, November 5). Jakarta: ASEAN Secretariat, www.aseansec.org/532.htm (accessed on 2019, May 12)

Prime Minister of India, Manmohan Singh's Statement at the 7th India-ASEAN Summit. (2009, October 24). New Delhi: Ministry of External Affairs, https://mea.gov.in/ outoing-visit-detail.htm?1243/Prime+Ministers+Statement+at+the+7th+IndiaASEAN+ Summit (accessed on 2019, May 12)

"Raisina Dialogue Remarks by Admiral Harry B. Harris, Jr.". (2016, March 2). *Speeches/Testimony*. Hawaii: U.S. Pacific Command, www.pacom.mil/Media/Speeches-Testimony/ Article/683842/raisina-dialogue-remarks-lets-be-ambitious-together (accessed on 2019, May 12)

"Secure a Decisive Victory in Building a Moderately Prosperous Society in All Respects and Strive for the Great Success of Socialism with Chinese Characteristics for a New Era". (2017, October 18). Xi Jinping's Report at 19th National Congress of the Communist

Party of China. *Xinhua*, www.xinhuanet.com/english/download/Xi_Jinping's_rep ort_at_19th_CPC_National_Congress.pdf (accessed on 2018, March 20)

Snyder, Craig A. (1997). "Building Multilateral Security Cooperation in the South China Sea". *Asian Perspective*, 21(1), http://iproxy.inflibnet.ac.in:2060/stable/42704117 (accessed on 2019, July 19)

Speech by the Prime Minister of Japan, H.E. Mr. Shinzo Abe at the Parliament of the Republic of India. (2007, August 22). Tokyo: Ministry of Foreign Affairs of Japan, www.mofa.go.jp/region/asia-paci/pmv0708/speech-2.html (accessed on 2019, May 12)

"Statement of the Indian Minister of External Affairs, I.K. Gujral at ASEAN Post Ministerial Conference". (1996, July 24). ASEAN Post Ministerial Conference Documents, *Strategic Digest*, 26(10)

Statement of the Indian Minister of External Affairs, Yashwant Sinha, at the Plenary Session of 2nd ASEAN-India Business Summit. (2003, September 4). New Delhi: Ministry of External Affairs, http://meaindia.nic.in/mystart.php?id=53016849 (accessed on 2019, May 12)

Summary of the 2018 National Defense Strategy of the United States of America: Sharpening the American Military's Competitive Edge. (2018). Washington: Department of Defense, https:// dod.defense.gov/Portals/1/Documents/pubs/2018-National-Defense-Strategy-Summary. pdf (accessed on 2019, May 30)

Taliaferro, Jeffrey W. (2000–2001). "Security Seeking under Anarchy: Defensive Realism Revisited". *International Security*, 25(3)

"Text of the 12th Singapore Lecture Delivered by the Prime Minister of India, P. V. Narasimha Rao on September 8, 1994". *Strategic Digest*, 14(10)

"Text of the Agreement of Cooperation between ONGC Videsh Limited and Vietnam Oil and Gas Group/Petro-Vietnam". (2011, October 12), ONGC Videsh, www.ongcvidesh. com/NewsContent.aspx?ID=893 (accessed on February 18, 2019)

Vietnamese President, Tran Dai Quang's Interview with Roy Chaudhury, Dipanjan. (2018, March 1). "Welcome India's Efforts in Act East Policy: Tran Dai Quang, Vietnamese President", *Economic Times*

"Vietnam Extends Contract: Wants India's Presence in 128 Block". (2012, July 15), *Business Standard*

"Vision and Actions on Jointly Building Silk Road Economic Belt and 21st-Century Maritime Silk Road". (2015, March 28). News Release. Beijing: National Development and Reform Commission, http://en.ndrc.gov.cn/newsrelease/201503/t20150330_ 669367.html (accessed on 2019, May 12)

Vision Statement: ASEAN-India Commemorative Summit. (2012, December 21). New Delhi: Ministry of External Affairs, https://asean.org/vision-statement-asean-india-commemora tive-summit/ (accessed on 2019, May 12)

Waltz, Kenneth. (1979). *Theory of International Politics*, New York: McGraw Hill

Wang, Zheng. (2013, February 5). "Not Rising, but Rejuvenating: the Chinese Dream", https://thediplomat.com/2013/02/chinese-dream-draft/3 (accessed on 2018, September 9)

Yunbi, Zhang. (2014, April 16). "Xi Outlines New Strategy to Protect Nation", *China Daily*, www.chinadaily.com.cn/china/2014-04/16/content_17436806.htm (accessed on 2018, September 16)

Zhang, Jian. (2015, January 28). "China's New Foreign Policy under Xi Jinping: Towards 'Peaceful Rise 2.0?'". *Global Change, Peace and Security*, 27(1)

2 The structural intractability of rival claims to sovereignty in the South China Sea

The saga of disputes and conflicting claims to sovereignty in the SCS is a manifestation of the interplay between maritime nationalism and geostrategic rivalry among claimant nations. Often described as a potential tinderbox, the conundrum has resulted in bringing about two principal shifts in the Indo-Pacific region: first, it has stimulated the transition of the region from a hegemonic logic to that of balance of power logic of international relations, supplanting the hitherto ubiquitous US presence in the region with the highly animated forays of China. Second, it has expanded the ambit of participatory geopolitical equations from being the exclusive preserve of ASEAN to include other competent regional actors such as India, Japan and Australia (Ikenberry, 2014: 52–53). The complex character of the lingering dispute in the SCS is a function of several factors, prominent among which are: the chequered nature of claims to sovereignty, generating complications for the applicability and interpretation of international law over jurisdiction and access to natural resources; the spree for territorial reclamation and island-building, enhanced by military surveillance, communications and logistics infra-structure-building; and the inability of ASEAN as a regional organisation to unite its members on this issue and present a concerted challenge to China's hegemonic ambitions.

Given this backdrop, the first section of the present chapter attempts to offer a retrospective of the dispute against the premise of the following determinants that have contributed to its intractability: the chequered nature of claims to sovereignty among the claimant nations in the SCS; the quest for access to the oil and hydrocarbon resources; ASEAN's ineptitude in conflict resolution; and the ener-vated pace of the institutional mechanism, as manifested in the progression of negotiations between ASEAN and China since the adoption of the Spratly Declaration in July 1992. The second section of the chapter introduces a back-ground study of the circumstances that catapulted the dynamics of the region into the core of India's policy calculus in the post-Cold War years. It concludes with a brief analysis of certain significant developments that prompted the flaring up of the SCS issue and evoked a more direct and involved response from India. Thus, this chapter attempts to erect the prelude to studying the impact of the dynamics in the SCS and ASEAN's response to it on India's interests and strategy, as envi-saged in the succeeding chapter.

1 Bolstering the quotient of intractability of the South China Sea dispute: an analysis of the prominent determinants

The four identified aspects responsible for sustaining and exacerbating the intractable nature of the SCS dispute may be classified under two broad categories: legal/jurisdictional and organisational/institutional. Of the twin categories, the chequered nature of claims to sovereignty among the claimant nations and the quest for access to the oil and hydrocarbon resources in areas of overlapping and contested claims may be regarded as constitutive of the first. On the other hand, ASEAN's ineptitude in conflict resolution and the enervated pace of the institutional mechanism, i.e., the progression of negotiations between ASEAN and China since the adoption of the Spratly Declaration in July 1992 and the limitations of the principal documents or agreements are integral to the second.

1.1 An overview of legal/jurisdictional aspects to interspersing claims to sovereignty in the South China Sea

The first and the most significant factor that determines the quotient of intractability of the SCS conundrum is the chequered nature of claims to sovereignty, thereby generating complications for the applicability and interpretation of international law. The delimitation of maritime boundaries is extremely problematic and complex, primarily stemming from the intersection of conflicting historical and legal evidence provided by the claimants in support of sovereignty. This affects the delimitation of jurisdictional boundaries between neighbouring sea zones, including Exclusive Economic Zones (EEZs) and continental shelves. The two main sources of jurisdictional disputes in the SCS are the boundaries of the various national EEZs and continental-shelf zones over which each state may exercise its authority. The jurisdictional claims of China (and Taiwan) in the SCS, however, remain ambiguous (Dutton, 2011: 49, 53). Generally, the territorial disputes have been categorised into two types: first, the claims of sovereignty over the individual land features, based on the historical presence or occupation and administration of the islands of the respective countries, as well as cartographic evidence; and second, concerning the size of the maritime zones that can be awarded to the different features. While China, Taiwan and Vietnam base their assertion on historical grounds (prior discovery, occupation and inheritance from colonial powers) the Philippines and Malaysia recognise international law, including the provision of the natural prolongation of the continental shelf as the premise of their claims (Chakraborti, 2001: 174). The Philippines' claims over the Spratlys were initiated in 1956, following the discovery of a group of islands by adventurer Tomas Cloma and its christening as Kalayaan or "Freedomland". Since 1962 (then) South Vietnam occupied several islands such as Nanzi Cay (South West Cay), Dunqian Cay (Sandy Cay), Hongxiu Island (Namyit Island), etc., which was strongly objected to and protested against. Subsequently, the discovery of rich oil and gas reserves on the continental shelves of the SCS by the US and UN survey agencies in the 1970s and 1980s stimulated further claims as exemplified by the Philippine official declaration of the Kalayaan as part of its national territory in 1978; Malaysia's extension of the continental shelf in 1979 to include features in the Spratlys within its territory; Vietnam's claim of the Spratlys since 1975 and its establishment of 200 nautical miles (nm) of EEZ in 1977; and Brunei's establishment in 1988 of an EEZ extending to 200 nm to the South of the Spratlys (Emmers, 2007: 3–4). In 1992, further clarifying and affirming its territorial sovereignty and maritime rights and interests over all the islands in the SCS, China enacted its Law of the People's Republic of China on the Territorial Sea and Contiguous Zone, specifying its claims over the features of all of the island groups encompassed by the nine-dash line, namely the Pratas Islands (Dongsha), the Paracel Islands (Xisha), the Macclesfield Bank (Zhongsha) and the Spratly Islands (Nansha) (Law of the People's Republic of China on the Territorial Sea and Contiguous Zone, 1992: Art. 2).

UNCLOS 1982, a significant confidence building measure itself, which provides for the littoral states to assert sovereignty claims up to 12 nm of territorial limits or contiguous zones of the same width and 200 nm of EEZ from the national baseline, have led to complications as well. Adopted on April 30, 1982, the Convention regulates provisions related to internal waters, archipelagic waters, territorial seas, contiguous zones, EEZs, continental shelves and high seas. It provides coastal states with the authority to extend their sovereign jurisdiction under a specific set of rules. The EEZ regime reflects a careful balance between the rights and duties of coastal states and those of user states. Under Article 121, the islands in the SCS that are above sea level at high tide and capable of supporting human habitation or independent economic activity are either given an EEZ or a continental shelf, which can extend up to several hundred nm from the coast. Within this area, the country with sovereignty over such islands has exclusive rights to the natural resources they contain, such as fish and hydrocarbons (Dutton, 2011: 51). However, on the legal front, UNCLOS 1982 has been debilitated by its inapplicability in solving existing territorial disputes, since it leaves overlapping claims unresolved, has no binding enforcement features and is often overshadowed by the dynamics of politics (Scott, 2012: 1021). It is indeed true that the use of the words "should co-operate" and "shall endeavour" (Article 123); provisions like a coastal state should have "due regard" to the rights and duties of other states in its EEZ [Article 56(2)]; and that other states should have "due regard" to the rights and duties of the coastal state in exercising their rights and duties in the EEZ [Article 58(3)] pose a strong obligation and responsibility on littoral states to cooperate towards maintaining security, safety and law and order at sea. Nevertheless, it stops short of providing any guidance on what constitutes "due regard". Furthermore, the existence of several "grey areas" in the Law of the Sea, particularly with respect to the EEZ regime, is a major limitation of UNCLOS itself (Bateman, 2013: 7–8). The situation has been further compounded by China's recalcitrance towards renouncing its potential "historical rights" within its nine-dash line as well as its rejection of the mechanisms for international arbitration and adjudication provided by UNCLOS upon ratification, citing its right in the Convention to opt out of such procedures ("Stirring up the

South China Sea (II): Regional Responses", 2012: 30). Moreover, since sovereignty claims are an integral part of the national consciousness in claimant countries, the ability of policy-makers to negotiate even the slightest compromise required for a legal solution has been constrained by national sentiments. Consequently, a legal approach has been plagued with its share of failures in resolving the dispute.

Second, the quest for access to the oil and hydrocarbon reserves that the seabed is home to has emerged as another factor fuelling the intractability of the conflict. Although a precise estimation of the amount of oil and natural gas reserves in the SCS is difficult owing to under-exploration and territorial disputes, it is widely acknowledged that the region has approximately 11 billion barrels of oil reserves and 190 trillion cubic feet of natural gas (including both proved and probable reserves) ("South China Sea", 2013). Similarly, one of the key innovations of UNCLOS was that it specified coastal-state authority in the water space beyond the territorial sea, a concept that had been steadily developing over the course of the twentieth century. As discussed above, UNCLOS – Part V established coastal-state jurisdiction over a vast littoral swathe of water space or EEZ, which may extend to 200 nm from the coastal state's baselines (specified coastal boundaries), and in which the coastal state has "sovereign rights" to the resources plus related jurisdictional authorities (exclusive state power over the specified resource-related matters) for the purpose of managing those resources (United Nations Convention on the Law of the Sea, 1982: Part V, Arts. 56–57). Thus, UNCLOS completed the creation of jurisdictional regimes over resources in littoral waters. Therefore, this particular aspect is at its core a disagreement over jurisdictional authority in the SCS to explore and exploit the resources on and under the sea's continental shelf and in its water column (Dutton, 2011: 50).

With the accentuated need for energy resources to meet the demands of the regional states, China's burgeoning spree towards expanding its domain of unilateral exploration, while simultaneously preventing those of other claimants (particularly the Philippines and Vietnam), posing the precondition that its sovereignty be recognised over the areas concerned, has further exacerbated the situation in the SCS. The significance of the potential resources, therefore, is principally political, as entitlement to them derives from sovereignty over land, according to the principles of UNCLOS. For instance, Beijing's justification for commissioning the Haiyang Shiyou (Offshore Oil) 981 rig in 2012 well within Hanoi's EEZ as a "mobile national territory" to help "ensure our country's energy security, advance maritime-power strategy and safeguard our nation's maritime sovereignty" (Zhu, 2012); its deployment 17 nm from the Paracels, whose sovereignty Vietnam also claims; and the launch of a series of offshore nuclear power platforms to promote the development of heavy oil reserves, to support development in remote deep-water zones, such as deep-sea production bases with control centres and living space for workers (Umbach, 2017: 3) are demonstrative of its escalating and incremental assertive presence in the SCS. Furthermore, Beijing's discomfiture and stern protest in the face of Vietnam's partnership with Indian or Spanish companies for joint exploration is registered on the ground of infringement of China's sovereignty. Other incidents like the confrontation of Vietnam's seabed survey ships by Chinese law enforcement vessels and fishing boats have been major stumbling blocks as well. Similar experiences of Chinese law enforcement vessels forcing a Philippine survey ship undertaking seismic studies away from the Reed Bank in 2011 had prompted Manila to take legal recourse. Interestingly enough, there has been a pronounced dichotomy with respect to Beijing's unrelenting attitude insofar as Vietnam and the Philippines are concerned, on the one hand, and that of greater "toleration" and conciliation towards Malaysia and Brunei, on the other. Beijing's apparent flexibility towards the latter could be attributed to their downplaying of differences with China, unlike the Philippine and Vietnamese opposition veering on rallying international support on the issue.

Additionally, the consequent failure of joint development as a confidence-building measure has been manifested by the non-renewal of the Joint Seismic Maritime Undertaking (JMSU) in 2008. Initiated as a bilateral agreement between China and the Philippines in 2004 to survey the seabed for hydrocarbon deposits in some disputed areas, it was extended to Vietnam in 2005. The incompatibility was generated by Beijing's imposition of preconditions and claim to sovereignty, which urged Hanoi and Manila to "recognise hereto unrecognised claims of China". It naturally spurred apprehension in the psyche of the Philippines and Vietnam that embarking upon joint development of the region before agreeing on the disputed areas according to the UNCLOS provisions would be tantamount to legitimising the nine-dash line ("Stirring up the South China Sea (IV): Oil in Troubled Waters", 2016: 16–17). As present circumstances reveal, the aggravated political and strategic ambience in the SCS is hardly the perfect template for joint development and exploration to act as a panacea.

1.2 An overview of organisational/institutional factors perpetuating the intractability of the conflict in the South China Sea

The intersection of claims to sovereignty in the SCS has resulted in three major conflicts and a few military skirmishes spread over the last three decades of the twentieth century. Two major clashes broke out between Vietnam and China: first, Vietnam (South) and China were engaged in a naval standoff over the Paracel Islands in 1974, wherein the latter's naval and military superiority was distinctly established as it gained control over the island chain. This was followed by the second Sino-Vietnam spat in 1998 in the Spratlys, leading to China's control of six islands (Chakraborti, 2012: 287). The third conflict broke out in 1995 between China and the Philippines at Mischief Reef, a shoal in the Spratlys, located well within the 200-nm EEZ claimed by Manila. As a regional organisation, though ASEAN was concerned about hostile developments in the SCS, it did not emerge as the principal security issue throughout the 1970s and 1980s. Probably, the more pressing stimuli like the Vietnamese invasion of Cambodia in December 1978 and the Sino-Vietnam War of February 1979, unfolding in the shadow of the Cold War, relegated the maritime dispute to the backburner. Moreover, deliberations on the SCS conundrum were limited to the Sino-Vietnam "misadventures" and the Soviet Navy's burgeoning activities in the region. As a result, the threat that China could pose to the regional status quo, though palpable, was not manifested in ASEAN dialogue and debate. This was facilitated by the tenor of improving ties between China and ASEAN in the early 1980s, as they converged on rescinding Vietnam out of Cambodia. However, the scenario was transformed by the mid-1980s, precisely after 1985, prior to which, China, notwithstanding its claim over the whole of the Spratlys, had not physically occupied any of the islands. Besides, there was a shift in China's attitude towards the Soviet Union, as the former embarked upon a radical change in its defence policy with the new focus on fighting local and limited wars around its periphery. In this context, the PLAN was tasked with a review of its naval requirements, befitting the defence of its territorial claims in the SCS. Towards this end the PLAN set the target of developing an offshore naval capacity by the year 2000 and a blue-water navy by 2050. In exhibiting its expanding physical presence in the Spratlys, the PLAN carried out the first large-scale patrol of these islands (May 16–June 6, 1987) and conducted the longest reported cruise from Qingdao through the western Pacific to James Shoal in October–November, 1987. Subsequently, in 1988, a major naval exercise code-named "Guangzi-15" was conducted to assess PLAN's ability to defend both the coastal territorial waters as well as islands that China claimed in the SCS (Guan, 1999: 1–4). As China's force projection in the SCS became more prominent in the 1990s, the binary nature (Sino-Vietnam) of dispute began to erode and Beijing's passage of the Law of the People's Republic of China on the Territorial Sea and Contiguous Zone in February 1992 supplanted its erstwhile claim of indisputable sovereignty over the Spratly Islands and the adjacent waters (from the mid-1970s through the 1980s) with its assertion of sovereignty over the whole of the SCS. The law further authorised the PLAN to evict trespassers by force. The incongruity between China's commitments and action also became prominent. Notwithstanding the then Chinese Premier, Li Peng's announcement during his visits to Singapore and Malaysia in August and December 1990 respectively that he would discuss joint efforts to develop the Spratlys and shelve the question of sovereignty, the aforesaid law had been passed by Beijing. Moreover, China occupied the Da Lac Reef, claimed by Vietnam, almost on the heels of the Third Workshop on "Managing Potential Conflicts in the South China Sea", organised by Indonesia (June 29–July 3, 1992) which emphasised prospects of transforming the region into a zone of cooperation on the basis of common interests and mutual benefits (Chakraborti, 2001: 197–198).

In 1993, Beijing published a map that depicted its territorial waters extending into part of the Natuna's EEZ. The concern reached its zenith in 1995, with China's occupation of the Mischief Reef, also claimed by the Philippines. The significance of this incident lay in the fact that this was the first time that China had occupied a reef claimed by an ASEAN member-state (since Vietnam was not a member of the organisation yet). The occupation was interpreted as a likely first step towards the "Tibetisation" of the SCS (Kreuzer, 2016: 260). In its wake, the ASEAN Foreign Ministers issued a statement on the SCS, expressing "serious concern" and urging the concerned parties "to refrain from taking actions that destabilize the situation". The situation also prompted the Philippines to lobby its fellow members to adopt a COC that would constrain China from further encroachment. Subsequently, in 1999, the ASEAN member-states officially converged on a draft ASEAN COC. Incidentally, China had also drawn up its COC by that time (Thayer, 2013: 76).

Another factor that aggravated Sino-centric concerns pertained to China's adoption of a method of measurement that was reserved for archipelagic countries to calculate her territorial waters. As a consequence, both the Philippines and Vietnam[1] were provoked and goaded ASEAN's discomfiture regarding China's regional ambitions and intentions (Guan, 1999: 8). In the wake of China's passage of the Law of the People's Republic of China on the Territorial Sea and Contiguous Zone, at the 25th ASEAN Ministerial Meeting (AMM) and the PMC in Manila (July 1992), for the first time ASEAN adopted a common stance *vis-à-vis* the SCS issue in the 1992 ASEAN Declaration on the South China Sea (Spratly Declaration). The Declaration called on the concerned parties to settle the dispute by peaceful means, exercise restraint and cooperate in applying the principles enshrined in the Treaty of Amity and Cooperation (TAC) (1976) as a basis for establishing a code of international conduct (1992 ASEAN Declaration on the South China Sea, 1992: Art. 4). Following the AMM, the then Foreign Minister of China, Qian Qichen exchanged views with six of his ASEAN counterparts and reaffirmed his country's proposal for "setting aside dispute and pursuing joint development" and the intention to seek settlement of disputes with countries concerned when conditions were ripe. The draft Spratly Declaration was essentially based on Article 2 of the TAC, premised on the "fundamental principles" of respect for independence, sovereignty, equality, territorial integrity and national identity of all ASEAN member-states; non-interference in the internal affairs of ASEAN member-states and enhanced consultations on matters seriously affecting the common interests of ASEAN (Treaty of Amity and Cooperation in Southeast Asia, 1976: Art. 2). In other words, the ASEAN members agreed on multilateralism, as opposed to bilateralism, for negotiating the dispute. Although Qian Qichen assured ASEAN that China would abide by the Manila Declaration, on the issue of the level of consultation, the incongruity between ASEAN's emphasis on multilateral negotiations, on the one hand, and bilateralism, on the other, as professed by China was evident. It may be argued that China's unwillingness to address issues concerning its "core interests" multilaterally stems from apprehension that the involvement of a multiplicity of actors would lead to the internationalisation of such issues. In that case, China would face the greater possibility of relenting under pressure and compromising on its sacrosanct "core national interests". This divergence on the level of negotiation between ASEAN and China is yet to be reconciled.

The late 1990s was dominated by a tumultuous phase as Southeast Asia was engulfed in the throes of the Asian Financial Crisis (1997–1998) and Indonesia, Malaysia and the Philippines experienced seismic political transitions. The immediate concern of ASEAN centred on addressing the economic maelstrom that the region had plunged into. Under such circumstances, though China continued its territorial assertion, renovating structures in the Mischief Reef in 1998 (July), ASEAN was not in a position to propose an organisational stand against it, considering the consequences that would befall the region, if China devalued its currency. ASEAN's response was limited to the then Secretary-General, Domingo Siazon's commitment at the Hanoi Annual Meeting to holding further talks "when conditions are right", thereby sending a signal of the organisation's willingness to have "improved relations with China". It is pertinent to note at this juncture that, though the Philippines had suggested US mediation in lieu of its hosting a meeting among the rival claimants, it was strongly opposed by both China and Malaysia. The Chinese Ambassador to the Philippines, Guang Dengming unequivocally reiterated the official position of addressing the issue bilaterally, fearing that external interference would only complicate matters (Lim, 2000: 93–94).

Furthermore, certain developments, such as the normalisation of Sino-Vietnam diplomatic relations in 1994, the induction of Vietnam as a member of ASEAN in 1995, China's assumption of the status of ASEAN's Full Dialogue Partner in 1996, its responsible role in tiding over the Asian Financial Crisis and pursuit of a policy of "strategic pause" with respect to physical confrontation over the Spratly Islands roughly from the late 1990s till 2007, led to a transformation in Sino-ASEAN ties, in addition to enhancing ASEAN's trust and confidence in Beijing. During this period, Beijing offered ASEAN greater opportunities for regional political and economic integration, through programmes of economic, commercial, and infrastructure development that were received warmly by the ASEAN member-states. Significantly, Sino-ASEAN trade figures soared from US$8 billion in 1991 to US$106 billion in 2004 and further to US$231 billion in 2008 (superseding the amount of US-ASEAN trade in 2008). China's support for major infrastructure projects, like the Nanning–Singapore economic corridor, and the Greater Mekong Sub-region, connecting China to Laos, Myanmar, Thailand and Vietnam, not only represented its initiatives for bolstering regional integration, but also were construed as constitutive of a "ripe fruit" strategy, designed to freeze the disputes and create favourable political conditions and wider acceptability among the ASEAN member-states, which it successfully garnered (Dutton 2011: 55–56).

Second, the languid pace with which negotiations have progressed between ASEAN and China, ever since ASEAN's adoption of a common stance on the issue in terms of the Spratly Declaration in July 1992 was registered, has compounded the situation in the SCS. The present section traces the chronological trajectory of the negotiations towards the resolution of the dispute, simultaneously identifying the limitations of the principal documents/agreements that emerged as stumbling blocks on the path of the deliberations. Following the adoption of the Spratly Declaration, five years elapsed before the inaugural China-ASEAN Meeting of the Heads of State was held in Kuala Lumpur, in December 1997, at which both sides converged on the establishment of "a 21st century-oriented partnership of good neighbourliness and mutual trust" (1997 Joint Statement of the Meeting of Heads of State/Government of the Member States of ASEAN and the President of the People's Republic of China, 1997: Cl. 12). As a means of preventing the dispute from spilling over into the matrix of the emerging cooperative ambience, both sides consciously resorted to a series of diplomatic efforts on consultation, with emphasis on Vietnam, Malaysia and the Philippines. These confidence-building endeavours, in tandem with China's proposal to "[set] aside dispute and pursuing joint development" for the sake of cooperation and regional stability formed the edifice for future consensus between China and ASEAN. With the foundations having been laid, at the 1998 ASEAN Summit, the Hanoi Plan of Action proposed that efforts should be made to "establish a regional code of conduct in the South China Sea among the parties directly concerned" (1998 Ha Noi Declaration, 1998: Cl. 7.16). However, it was another two years before an informal meeting was held in Thailand, in March 2000, wherein ASEAN and China agreed to exchange their respective draft COCs, and consolidate them into a final agreed-upon text. The consultations hit a roadblock as divergences cropped up with respect to its binding powers as well as to Sino-Vietnam differences on its geographical scope and provisions concerning detainment of fishermen found in disputed waters, thus putting a question mark on the future course of the negotiations (Thayer, 2013: 77). Amidst these differences, a fresh lease of life was received at the 35th AMM held in Brunei in July 2002, when Malaysia's proposal to replace the "code of conduct" with a compromising and non-binding "declaration" was approved and the Joint Ministerial Statement raised hopes that ASEAN and China would work in coordination to make "the declaration" a reality (2002 Joint Communiqué of 35th ASEAN Minister Meeting, 2002). This led to a consultation on the DOC, following which both sides engaged in many rounds of negotiations that led to the signing of the DOC between ASEAN and China at the 8th ASEAN Summit convened in Cambodia on November 4, 2002.

The DOC constitutes a significant and affirmative political document for enhancing mutual trust and minimising the risk of future crises among the parties concerned. Recognised as a guideline for confidence-building and conflict resolution, the ten provisions of the DOC outline three major purposes: to enhance favourable conditions for a peaceful and durable solution of differences and disputes among countries concerned; to formulate trust and confidence among the claimants; and to lead to the establishment of a regional COC in the SCS. Through the signing of the DOC, China and ASEAN reaffirmed their commitment to the purposes and principles of the UN Charter, the 1982 UNCLOS, TAC and the Five Principles of Peaceful Coexistence (2002 Declaration on the Conduct of Parties in the South China Sea, 2002: Art. 1). Unfortunately, the signing of the DOC was not successful in generating the desired result due to a host of factors, some of which are discussed below:

- First, it was argued that the DOC itself was intrinsically flawed because it did not provide for the legal power to restrain belligerent behaviour of any party in the SCS. The DOC lacked the mechanism to monitor, let alone enforce, compliance. As addressed by Article 9 of the DOC, "The Parties encourage other countries to respect the principles contained in this Declaration." (2002 Declaration on the Conduct of Parties in the South China Sea, 2002: Art. 9).

This was quite contradictory given the fact that states not involved in the negotiation process of the future COC could not be expected to be constrained by a mechanism that they could never explicitly accept (Chang, 2015).

- Second, the ambiguous and overlapping concepts of "disputes over islands" and "maritime disputes" compounded the problem. It was argued that the negotiations focused more on the disputes over the sovereignty of the islands and reefs in the Spratlys, with the purpose of preventing further acts of occupying and controlling islands.
- Third, on the operational front, except for the Sino-Vietnamese negotiation to demarcate the waters outside the Gulf of Tonkin, there had not been any discussions to resolve the jurisdictional disputes, let alone the territorial ones. Subsequently, there had been a constant stream of incidents relating to maritime space that the DOC was completely ineffectual in preventing. This failure stemmed from its inability to specify the "activities that would complicate or escalate disputes and affect peace and stability" (2002 Declaration on the Conduct of Parties in the South China Sea, 2002: Art. 5) rendering this phrase meaningless rhetoric that the claimants could use to their interests to accuse others of violating the DOC (Duong, 2015).
- Finally, the text of the DOC provided scant information on the specific implementation of confidence-building measures and other forms of cooperation in the SCS. The understanding was restricted to the provision that all relevant parties would have to follow up with further discussion on the scope, specific modalities and policy measures to push for future cooperation (Li, 2014).

Notwithstanding its limitations, the DOC bolstered the avenues of cooperation and confidence-building between ASEAN and China. Since Art. 10 reaffirmed the commitment of the concerned parties to a COC aimed at furthering peace and stability in the region on the basis of consensus, the DOC could be acknowledged as a reference point and the guiding document for framing the COC. It is also contended that the DOC, embodied as a moral constraint on claimant states in the SCS, has been a milestone in emerging as a common platform to exchange views as well as maintaining considerable stability in the littorals. Significantly, since 2002, none of the claimants has inhabited previously uninhabited features. The 36th AMM held in June 2003 in Phnom Penh stressed the need for observance of the provisions of the DOC and urged concerned parties to undertake the confidence-building and cooperative measures called for in accordance with the Declaration (2003 Joint Communiqué of the 36th ASEAN Ministerial Meeting, 2003: Cl. 26). As important steps towards the implementation of the DOC, the proposal for convening a Senior Officials' Meeting (SOM) and establishing an ASEAN-China Joint Working Group (JWG) to oversee the implementation mechanism in spirit and letter were well received (2004 Chairman's Statement of the 11th Meeting of ASEAN Regional Forum, 2004: Cl. 14). The JWG, tasked to study and provide specific policy measures for the implementation of the DOC, was expected to identify actions that caused dispute complication or escalation, as well as areas of cooperation including marine environmental protection, marine scientific research, safe maritime navigation, search and rescue (SAR) and anti-transnational crime operations. Furthermore, the Vientiane Plan of Action (2004) embodied the promotion of trust and confidence-building through cooperative activities, in accordance with the principles of the DOC. It particularly focused on consultations and consensus among the concerned parties in the SCS, pending the peaceful settlement of the territorial and jurisdictional issues (2004 Plan of Action to Implement the Joint Declaration on ASEAN-China Strategic Partnership for Peace and Prosperity, 2004: Cl. 1.5.5). At the maiden JWG meeting, held in Manila in August 2005, ASEAN proposed a draft document of seven-point guidelines for the implementation of the DOC. The second point stated, "ASEAN will continue its current practice of consulting among themselves before meeting China." China's objection to this clause emerged from the argument that since the SCS issue did not concern ASEAN as a whole, it preferred to discuss with the "relevant parties" bilaterally, rather than with the organisation as a collective entity. It thus adhered to its position of resolving issues relating to sovereignty and jurisdictional disputes bilaterally with the parties directly concerned (Li, 2014).

The period of relative calm was sustained for about five years following the signing of the DOC and the re-detonation was fuelled by Sino-Vietnamese tensions, culminating in dividing the opinion of ASEAN member-states on the issue. Three major incidents strained the situation:

- First, in April 2007, China accused Vietnam of violating its sovereignty by allowing a consortium of energy companies led by British Petroleum to develop two gas fields in the Con Son Basin, 230 nm off Vietnam's southeast coast. Vietnam negated the allegation on the basis that the project was within the domain of its EEZ.
- Second, the firings by Chinese patrol vessels on a Vietnamese fishing boat in July 2007, which cost a Vietnamese sailor's life. The very next month, China announced its plans to begin tourist cruises to the Paracels, prompting Vietnam to reaffirm its sovereignty claims over the archipelago.
- Finally, in December 2007, the passage of a law by the Chinese National People's Congress, providing for the creation of a county-level city in Hainan Province to administer its contested claims in the SCS, including the Paracel and Spratly Islands, evolved as a stimulant in disturbing the regional dynamics (Storey, 2008).

Furthermore, tensions were spurred by China's policy shift on the SCS to a more active and aggressive posture, against the backdrop of its increasing military and economic sinews. China's escalating assertiveness was particularly prominent from 2007 onwards. On the military front, it increased the number of submarines and surface vessels, besides rapidly strengthening its naval power, including the construction of submarine bases and aircraft carriers. Simultaneously, it bolstered its patrols and exercises and beefed up the deployment of China Maritime Surveillance (CMS) and the Fisheries Law Enforcement Command (FLEC) as key players for protecting China's rights and interests in the SCS. In addition, PLAN officers clarified their intention to deploy the navy to the Persian Gulf and the Strait of Malacca to stabilise energy transportation and secure Chinese interests in the East and South China Seas. On the political front, the precariousness of the situation was exacerbated by China's assertion in March 2010, that it would not tolerate any interference in the SCS. This statement sparked intense international reaction, as it was the first time that China had identified the SCS as a "core interest" domain on a par with Taiwan and Tibet. The assertion was reflected upon as China's expression of expanded interests leveraging its capabilities in the SCS spread security concerns not only among the countries sharing sovereignty claims, but also ASEAN as a whole. The concern was extrapolated at the Second Round of the US-China Strategic and Economic Dialogue, which was held in May 2010 in Beijing, when State Councillor, Dai Bingguo informed the then US Secretary of State, Hillary Clinton that China viewed its rights and interests in the SCS as a "core national interest" (Swaine, 2010: 8; Shoji, 2012: 7).

It was after six years of intermittent negotiations and the exchange of 21 drafts since the signing of the DOC that the "Guidelines for the Implementation of the DOC" was signed by ASEAN and China on July 20, 2011. A significant compromise that ASEAN was required to undertake was the dropping of the clause on prior consultations and amending Clause 2 with the words, "to promote dialogue and consultation among the parties" (Guidelines on the Implementation of the DOC, 2011: Cl. 2). Additionally, the Chinese Assistant Foreign Minister, Liu Zhenmin reiterated China's active support for cooperation in the SCS and proposed a shift in focus towards conducting practical cooperation within the framework of the DOC. Several other proposals like the convening of a symposium on free navigation in the SCS and the establishment of three special committees on marine scientific research and environmental protection, navigation safety and SAR operations and combating transnational crimes on the sea were also tabled by him, which received a positive response from ASEAN ("China, ASEAN Nations Agree on Guidelines for Implementation of DOC in South China Sea", 2011). The signing of the "Guidelines" raised hope that the COC would be adopted the following year at the Phnom Penh Summit of ASEAN, which incidentally, coincided with the tenth anniversary of the signing of the DOC. However, circumstances belied this hope and five more years lapsed before the two sides could converge on adopting a framework of the COC that "will facilitate the work for the conclusion of an effective COC on a mutually agreed timeline" in August 2017 and a SDNT, to provide the basis for further negotiations on specific provisions of the COC exactly a year later. It is true that the negotiation process has moved at a lethargic pace, often blemished by China's recalcitrance with respect to the modalities of deliberation, among others factors. As the present situation stands, one hopes that expedited negotiations, facilitated by pragmatic political will, on a legally binding and enforceable COC between ASEAN and China will be successful in tiding over the technical and institutional encumbrances in the near future.

It emerges from the analysis above that the complex and intertwined nature of the four determinants under review, viz. the chequered nature of claims to sovereignty among the claimant nations; the quest for access to the oil and hydrocarbon resources; ASEAN's ineptitude in conflict resolution; and the languid pace of China-ASEAN negotiations, has bolstered the intransigence of the SCS conundrum. The strain of interrelations running through the jurisdictional and institutional factors has further complicated and retarded the cadence of dispute resolution, since the factors tend to be complementary to each other. Above all, it is contingent on ASEAN to exert its consensual, organised weight *vis-à-vis* China in dealing with the issue, such that the holistic interests of the organisation are no longer sacrificed at the altar of the priorities, interests and equations of individual member-states.

2 Setting the promenade for India's South China Sea policy: through the "Look East" prism

Prior to embarking on the analysis of India's responses towards the SCS dispute, it would be pertinent to introduce a background study of the circumstances that catapulted the dynamics of the region into the kernel of India's policy prerogative. Although India's direct interactions within the framework of a "declared" policy towards Southeast Asia and the Indo-Pacific were initiated with the inauguration of the LEP in 1991, the foundations had already been laid by the Indian Prime Minister, Rajiv Gandhi's success in mediating the Indochina crisis during the twilight years of the Cold War. The sincerity and responsibility exhibited by him had spawned ASEAN's confidence in New Delhi's capabilities, following which, it was accorded Sectoral Dialogue Partnership of ASEAN in 1993. This inclusion happened quite early, precisely within two years of India unveiling its ambitious programme of economic liberalisation, christened the "New Economic Policy". India's elevation of status from Sectoral Dialogue Partner to a Full Dialogue Partner of ASEAN followed in quick succession, and at the Jakarta PMC (July 1996), India's maiden participation as a Full Dialogue Partner heralded the beginning of a "new era in ASEAN-India relations". The faith reposed by ASEAN in the indispensability of India in securing and sustaining the future dynamics of the Asia-Pacific region was expressed by the then Foreign Minister of Singapore, S. Jayakumar, when he acknowledged:

> ASEAN leaders recognized India's growing political, economic and strategic importance and the mutual benefits to be gained by both India and ASEAN through closer cooperation. You can provide ASEAN, with vital links to the Indian Ocean. ASEAN, on the other hand, can be India's springboard into the Asia-Pacific. It would be hard to imagine an Asia-Pacific Century without India's participation .... This next phase in ASEAN-India ties will enable us to establish a more robust relationship and work closely together to achieve economic prosperity and a greater security for the peoples of our two regions.
> ("ASEAN and India: A New Partnership", 1996: 1532–1533)

The Joint Statement issued at the conclusion of the PMC identified economic development and preservation of regional peace and stability as the two principal pillars of ASEAN-India cooperation. Therefore, India's graduation to a Full Dialogue Partner of ASEAN manifested a "far-sighted assessment" about political and strategic convergence, acceleration of economic relations and their future potential, and complementarities in areas that were hitherto opaque or remained unexploited between the two sides. This was the much-needed giant step taken by India to "move from derivative to direct relationship" ("Statement of the Indian Minister of External Affairs, I. K. Gujral", 1996: 1535) with ASEAN and thereby, to have a greater stake in the unveiling dynamics of the region at that point in time.

The next milestone of the LEP was India's elevation to the Summit-level or ASEAN+1 partner in 2002. Hailed as a significant development since India joined the ranks of a handful of countries with which ASEAN has summit dialogues, namely, China, Japan and South Korea, this up-gradation was a natural culmination of ten years of progressive engagement with ASEAN. In the context of its elevation to a Summit-level partner of ASEAN, New Delhi's drive towards the development of greater strategic and economic convergence with the region received a major boost, when the Second Phase (Phase II) of the LEP was officially announced on September 4, 2003. The operational domain of Phase II of this policy was not only characterised by "an expanded definition of 'East' extending from Australia to China and East Asia with ASEAN as its core", but also was marked by a shift in emphasis from "exclusively economic issues to economic and security issues including joint efforts to protect sea-lanes, coordination on counter terrorism, etc." (Statement of the Indian Minister of External Affairs, Yashwant Sinha, 2003) This transition in impetus on the strategic component of the policy made it plain that India would have a more direct responsibility and stake in the regional security domain, and the maritime sphere was integral to it. Although ASEAN, cognisant of spiralling Chinese influence in the region, perceived India as an ideal strategic partner to balance its overtures, the Indian response was articulated by the then Prime Minister, Manmohan Singh:

> As far as our overall defence policy is concerned, we are essentially a status quo power and harbour no extra-territorial ambitions. However, we have island territories in the Bay of Bengal as well as the Arabian Sea. We also have friends in the Indian Ocean Region, whose security is our concern. Therefore, contingencies can be envisioned where we may be compelled to cross the seas to protect our own island territories, or even reach "out of area" to safeguard the interests of our friends.
>
> ("Shaping India's Maritime Strategy: Opportunities and Challenges", 2005)

Furthermore, India's willingness to accede to the TAC and its endorsement of the Southeast Asia Nuclear Weapons Free Zone went a long way in assuring the region of its peaceful intent and commitment. Subsequently, ASEAN perceived India's security imperatives more as a factor emanating from the compulsions of its geostrategic location, rather than a derivative of any hegemonic design (Sundararaman, 2003).

Over the next few years, India charted a steadily upward trajectory in its relations and assimilation not only with ASEAN, but also with its other dialogue partners. This was facilitated by its membership of the EAS in 2005 and the ADMM+8 in 2010. India explored the ADMM platform to unequivocally assert the "paramount importance" of the safety and security of the sea lanes of communication, in addition to reaffirming the importance of unimpeded right of passage and other maritime rights in accordance with the accepted principles of international law. In keeping with the developments on this front, India exhorted all parties to disputes in the SCS to "abide by the 2002 Declaration on Conduct in the South China Sea and work together to ensure peaceful resolution of disputes, in accordance with international law, including the UNCLOS". Its position reiterated a call to all parties concerned to "take forward these discussions towards adoption of a Code of Conduct in the South China Sea on the basis of consensus" (Chaturvedy, 2015: 363). Associated factors like the signing of the ASEAN-India Free Trade Agreement in Goods in August 2009, in addition to a host of bilateral Comprehensive Economic Cooperation/Partnership Agreements with individual ASEAN members (including Singapore, Thailand, Malaysia) and other regional partners (South Korea and Japan) fortified India's presence and priority. The emerging strategic and economic complementarities necessitated an "open, balanced and inclusive regional architecture", encompassing the Indian Ocean region stretching from the East African coast to the SCS as a crucial conduit for foreign trade, energy and national security interests ("Security Dimensions of India's Foreign Policy", 2011).

As India embarked upon playing a more direct and responsible role in the littoral dynamics of the region, its emphasis on bolstering naval capabilities with the objective of emerging as the net security provider and first responder became pronounced. Its quest for evolving from "brown water" to a "blue water" naval power, seeking increasingly to safeguard its coastlines and simultaneously enhance the maritime domain of interests and outreach was envisaged in various editions of the *Indian Maritime Doctrine* (2004, 2007, 2009, 2015). In April 2004, the Government of India enunciated a Maritime Doctrine stressing the need for a submarine-based credible Minimum Nuclear Deterrence capability that was "inexorably linked" to its pursuit of an independent foreign policy posture, "if India is to exude the quiet confidence of a nation that seeks to be neither deferential nor belligerent". Through this Doctrine, the Indian Navy acknowledged the establishment of its naval outreach and sustainability across the "legitimate area of interest", extending from the Persian Gulf to the Strait of Malacca (Indian Maritime Doctrine, 2004: 65). The LEP was an important edifice of this Doctrine since it highlighted the imperative of building cooperative maritime security linkages with the littoral countries of the Indo-Pacific, with regard to common aspirations and challenges manifested through expanding bilateral and multilateral interactions, confidence-building and interoperability like joint exercises, patrolling, humanitarian and anti-terror operations.

Furthermore, the revised version of the above Doctrine (2009) clearly spelt out the Indian Navy's key role "in meeting the maritime components of these challenges, which have been increasing in both scale and scope in recent years"

(Indian Maritime Doctrine, 2009: v–vi). Towards this end, India's significant naval build-up in the Andaman and Nicobar (A&N) Islands and the establishment of a Far Eastern Naval Command (FENC) based in these Islands manifested a more strategically pragmatic and vision-oriented LEP (Chakraborti, 2009: 466). This endeavour was bolstered by the commissioning of the Indian naval ship (INS) INS *Baaz* at the Great Nicobar's Campbell Bay in August 2012 allowing India to assert itself more forcefully and keep a hawk-like eye on the strategically important Strait of Malacca. Although viewed as a strategy to balance the PLAN's assertiveness in the regional waters, especially in the context of China's entry into the South Asian Association for Regional Cooperation (SAARC) in 2007 and its strategic calculations in South Asia and Myanmar, the Indian Navy was successful in upholding New Delhi's benign and humanitarian face in the wake of its whole-hearted response to the ruinous tsunami (December 2004) and sporadic cyclonic and environmental disasters in Southeast Asia (particularly in Indonesia, Laos, Myanmar and the Philippines) as well as in its sincere efforts to ward off the menace of piracy in the Gulf of Aden and neighbouring Sea Lanes of Communication (SLOCs). The Indian Navy's emphasis on the all-encompassing concept of security, embracing the entire gamut of national and human interests, not only catapulted it to the centre of gravity of interaction with regional navies in the traditional sphere, but also provided it with a platform to collaborate in the non-traditional security domain.

2.1 Towards a more enthusiastic Indian response vis-à-vis the dynamics of the South China Sea

In addition to the dynamics of the LEP and India's burgeoning naval presence in the Indo-Pacific region that have facilitated its strategy in the SCS, a host of significant developments have evoked a more direct and involved response. A summary of these developments follows in the present sub-section.

- First, since 2009, the former US President, Barack Obama's "Pivot to Asia" policy articulated an integrated diplomatic, military, economic and leadership strategy stretching across from the Indian subcontinent through Northeast Asia. With respect to the SCS, though the Obama administration had formally affirmed its neutrality in territorial disputes, it had, in practice, adopted substantive positions that ruffled China's feathers (Lieberthal, 2011). India's rationale of greater strategic coordination with the regional navies received impetus with the "Obama Doctrine" or "Pivot to Asia" policy, which had identified India, Japan and Australia as solid pillars of its strategic pivot in the Indo-Pacific, while attempting to undertake more concrete and decisive efforts at "constraining" China by a resonating counter-alliance. As part of its anti-China "pivot", Washington patronised increased cooperation with India and Japan, as the inauguration of the Trilateral Dialogue and the subsequent induction of Japan as a permanent participant in the trilateral MALABAR naval exercises indicated.

- Second and closely related to the first stimulus pertained to Beijing's rebuke in response to Hillary Clinton's ARF Address in July 2010, wherein she apprehended that Washington might step into a long-simmering territorial dispute between China and its neighbours in the SCS. This unambiguously suggested that the US had a "national interest" in seeking to mediate the dispute. The statement was responded to with contempt and concern by the then Chinese Foreign Minister, Yang Jiechi's reiteration that "China will never waive its right to protect its core interest with military means". Furthermore, he warned the US against intervening in the dynamics of the regional conflict, since it would "only make matters worse and the resolution more difficult". Secretary Clinton, however, clarified at this ARF meeting that Washington would not accept China's limitations on freedom of navigation for military purposes in the SCS, further asserting that the US, like all nations, had "a national interest in freedom of navigation, open access to Asia's maritime commons, and respect for international law in the South China Sea" (Landler, 2010). The US emphasis and support for safeguarding freedom of navigation and overflight in the SCS had inherent tones coinciding with India's interests and declarations in defence of a rules-based order.
- The third factor related to China's "harassment" of the Indian naval assault vessel, INS *Airavat* in July 2011, during its scheduled visit to Vietnam. Describing the incident as "very unusual", the Indian Ministry of External Affairs strongly criticised the Chinese "harassment", and voiced support for freedom of navigation in international waters, including in the SCS and the right of passage in accordance with accepted principles of international law ("Incident Involving 'INS Airavat' in the South China Sea", 2011).
- Fourth, the development which perturbed China enough to have qualms and assert its "sovereignty" over the disputed littorals was the signing of an Agreement between OVL and Petro-Vietnam in October 2011, to conduct joint oil drilling exploration in two blocks in the Phu Kanh Basin of the SCS. Although claimed by Vietnam as its sovereign territory, in keeping with UNCLOS provisions, China's resistance was premised on the ground of infringement on its sovereignty. In this context, Beijing not only voiced its vehement opposition to India engaging in oil and gas exploration projects in the blocks, but also warned Indian companies against entering into any agreements with Vietnam. This was in addition to China's harassment of Petro-Vietnam oil survey ships in quest of oil and gas deposits in Vietnam's EEZ and the deliberate severing of the cables of its survey vessels. In response to China's posture, the then spokesman of the Indian Ministry of External Affairs, Vishnu Prakash highlighted that its engagement with Vietnam for oil and gas exploration activities served commercial purposes and "China's objection to OVL's explorations in South China Sea has no legal basis as the blocks belonged to Vietnam" (Media Briefing by the Official Spokesperson, Vishnu Prakash, 2011). He underscored India's financial stakes in the blocks, citing an investment of US$400 million in Vietnamese hydrocarbons sectors, further to OVL having invested US$500 million in oil exploration projects. Such an essentially pragmatic stance not only

exhibited new dynamics in India's China policy, but also manifested New Delhi's greater assertiveness in its neighbouring maritime domain.

- Finally, China's grandiose MSR project, the maritime component of the BRI, unveiled in 2013, has also been a significant stimulus to India's enhanced interests in the SCS. Served by a network of roads, high-speed railways, fibre-optical lines, transcontinental submarine optical cables and satellite information passageways, the initiative is poised to shift the centre of geo-economic power towards Eurasia, and challenge the US "Asia Pivot" strategy ("Vision and Actions on Jointly Building Silk Road Economic Belt and 21st-Century Maritime Silk Road", 2015). The project is also aimed at alleviating what Chinese strategists identify as the "Malacca Dilemma", viz. the vulnerabilities resulting from having to ship much-needed energy imports through the SCS and up the east coast of China, where the US and other regional players have the capacity to threaten or block maritime traffic. Notwithstanding its projected role in delivering the economic promises, the initiative poses a direct challenge to India's stature as a security provider in the IOR. Ironically, as the MSR initiative exhibits, connectivity that was once the leitmotif of aiding countries transcend the barriers posed by geopolitics, has "emerged as a theatre of present day geopolitics" (Speech by Indian Foreign Secretary at Raisina Dialogue, 2016).

Therefore, in response to China's increasing force projection and strategic entrenchment in India's neighbourhood, the least that New Delhi can do is strike a balance and safeguard its interests and geo-economic stakes in the SCS. India has been slowly, but steadily, rather incrementally, leaving its footprints in the affairs of the SCS and the reciprocation by ASEAN, the regional fulcrum, has been more than welcome. India's credentials as a peaceful, responsible stakeholder in the Indo-Pacific, in conjunction with its emphasis on the safeguarding of the norms of freedom of navigation, overflight, unimpeded commerce and adherence to the principles of a rules-based maritime order have exceeded rhetoric and found expression in practice. Its focus on a collaborative and consultative approach to the maritime domain has been borne out by the Indo-Bangladesh Agreement on the maritime boundary, which serves as an exemplar in the history of peaceful resolution of disputes with neighbours. Under the present circumstances, as the region drifts towards uncertainty and militarisation, New Delhi's role as a net security provider has become increasingly critical in shaping the strategic discourse in the Indo-Pacific.

Note

1 Vietnam was inducted as a member of ASEAN in 1995

References

1992 ASEAN Declaration on the South China Sea. (1992, July 22), SCRIBD Inc., www.scribd.com/Document/355737404/1992-ASEAN-Declaration-on-the-South-China-Sea (accessed on 2018, March 10)

1997 Joint Statement of the Meeting of Heads of State/Government of the Member States of ASEAN and the President of the People's Republic of China. (1997, December 16). Jakarta: ASEAN Secretariat, http://asean.org/?static_post=joint-statement-of-the-meeting-of-heads-of-stategovernment-of-the-member-states-of-asean-and-the-president-of-the-people-s-repub lic-of-china-kuala-lumpur-malaysia-16-december-1997 (accessed on 2018, March 10)

1998 Ha Noi Declaration. (1998, December 16). Jakarta: ASEAN Secretariat, http://asean. org/?static_post=ha-noi-declaration-of-1998-16-december-1998 (accessed on 2018, March 10)

2002 Declaration on the Conduct of Parties in the South China Sea. (2002, November 4). Jakarta: ASEAN Secretariat, http://asean.org/?static_post=declaration-on-the-conduct-of-parties-in-the-south-china-sea-2 (accessed on 2018, March 10)

2002 Joint Communiqué of 35th ASEAN Minister Meeting. (2002, July 29–30). Jakarta: ASEAN Secretariat, http://asean.org/?static_post=joint-communique-of-the-35th-asean-ministerial-meeting-bandar-seri-begawan-29-30-july-2002 (accessed on 2018, March 10)

2003 Joint Communiqué of the 36th ASEAN Ministerial Meeting. (2003, June 16–17). Jakarta: ASEAN Secretariat, http://asean.org/joint-communique-of-the-36th-asean-ministerial-meet ing-phnom-penh/ (accessed on 2018, March 14)

2004 Chairman's Statement of the 11th Meeting of ASEAN Regional Forum. (2004, July 2). Jakarta: ASEAN Secretariat, http://asean.org/?static_post=chairman-s-statement-the-eleventh-meeting-of-asean-regional-forum (accessed on 2018, March 14)

2004 Plan of Action to Implement the Joint Declaration on ASEAN-China Strategic Partnership for Peace and Prosperity. (2004, November 29). Jakarta: ASEAN Secretariat, http://asean. org/?static_post=plan-of-action-to-implement-the-joint-declaration-on-asean-china-strategic-partnership-for-peace-and-prosperity (accessed on 2018, March 14)

"ASEAN and India: A New Partnership". Opening Statement of Singapore's Foreign Minister, S. Jayakumar at ASEAN Post Ministerial Conference. (1996, July 24). ASEAN Post Ministerial Conference Documents, *Strategic Digest*, 26(10)

Bateman, Sam. (2013, September). "Maritime Confidence Building Measures – An Overview", *Special Report*, Barton, Australia: Australian Strategic Policy Institute, www.files. ethz.ch/isn/170342/Maritime%20Confidence%20Building%20Measures.pdf (accessed on 2018, February 24)

Chakraborti, Tridib. (2001). "Territorial Claims in South China Sea: Probing Persistent Uncertainties", in Banerji, A.K., and Purusottam Bhattacharya (eds), *People's Republic of China at Fifty: Politics, Economy and Foreign Relations*, New Delhi: Lancer's Books

Chakraborti, Tridib. (2009, November–December). "India's Look East Policy: Time for Stock-Taking". *World Focus*, 30(11)

Chakraborti, Tridib. (2012, December 3). "China and Vietnam in the South China Sea Dispute: A Creeping 'Conflict – Peace Trepidation' Syndrome", *China Report*, 48(3)

Chang, Ching. (2015, October 20). "Examining the Flaws of the South China Sea Code of Conduct", http://cimsec.org/examining-the-flaws-of-the-south-china-sea-code-of-con duct/19187 (accessed on 2018, March 14)

Chaturvedy, Rajeev Ranjan. (2015). "South China Sea: India's Maritime Gateway to the Pacific". *Strategic Analysis*, 39(4)

"China, ASEAN Nations Agree on Guidelines for Implementation of DOC in South China Sea". (2011, July 20). *People's Daily Online*, http://en.people.cn/90001/90776/90883/7446480.html20 July 2011 (accessed on 2018, March 20)

Duong, Huy. (2015, July 1). "A Fair and Effective Code of Conduct for the South China Sea", https://amti.csis.org/a-fair-and-effective-code-of-conduct-for-the-south-china-sea/1 (accessed on 2018, March 14)

Dutton, Peter. (2011). "Three Disputes and Three Objectives – China and the South China Sea", *Naval War College Review*, 64(4), http://digital-commons.usnwc.edu/cgi/view content.cgi?article=1553&context=nwc-review (accessed on 2018, February 18)

Emmers, Ralf. (2007, June 6). "The De-escalation of the Spratly Dispute in Sino-Southeast Asian Relations", *Working Paper*, 129, Singapore: RSIS, www.rsis.edu.sg/wp-content/uploads/2014/07/WP1296.pdf (accessed on 2018, February 18)

Guan, Ang Cheng. (1999, August). "The South China Sea Dispute Re-visited", *Working Paper*, 4, Singapore: Institute of Defence and Strategic Studies, www.rsis.edu.sg/wp-con tent/uploads/rsis-pubs/WP04.pdf (accessed on 2018, February 28)

Guidelines on the Implementation of the DOC. (2011, July 20). Jakarta: ASEAN Secretariat, www.asean.org/wp-content/uploads/images/archive/documents/20185-DOC.pdf (accessed on 2018, February 18)

Ikenberry, John. (2014). "From Hegemony to the Balance of Power: The Rise of China and American Grand Strategy in East Asia", *International Journal of Korean Unification Studies*, 23(2)

"Incident Involving 'INS Airavat' in the South China Sea". *Media Briefings*. (2011, September 1). New Delhi: Ministry of External Affairs, www.mea.gov.in/media-briefings.htm?dtl/3040/Incident+involving+INS+Airavat+in+South+China+Sea (accessed on 2018, April 2)

Indian Maritime Doctrine, 2004. (2004). New Delhi: Ministry of Defence (Navy)

Indian Maritime Doctrine, 2009. (2009, August). New Delhi: Ministry of Defence (Navy), www.indiannavy.nic.in/sites/default/files/Indian-Maritime-Doctrine-2009-Up dated-12Feb16.pdf (accessed on 2019, May 12)

Kreuzer, Peter. (2016, June 16). "A Comparison of Philippine and Malaysian Responses to China in the South China Sea". *The Chinese Journal of International Politics*, 9(3), https://academic.oup.com/cjip/article/9/3/239/2352046 (accessed on 2018, March 4)

Landler, Mark. (2010, July 23). "Offering to Aid Talks, US Challenges China on Disputed Islands". *New York Times*, www.nytimes.com/2010/07/24/world/asia/24diplo.html (accessed on 2018, April 1)

Law of the People's Republic of China on the Territorial Sea and Contiguous Zone. (1992, February 25). Beijing: The National People's Congress, www.npc.gov.cn/englishnpc/Law/2007-12/12/content_1383846.htm (accessed on 2018, February 18)

Li, Mingjiang. (2014, March). "Managing Security in the South China Sea from DOC to COC". *Kyoto Review of Southeast Asia*, 15, https://kyotoreview.org/issue-15/managing-security-in-the-south-china-sea-from-DoC-to-coc/ (accessed on 2018, March 14)

Lieberthal, Kenneth G. (2011, December 21). "The American Pivot to Asia", Brookings, www.brookings.edu/articles/the-american-pivot-to-asia (accessed on 2018, April 1)

Lim, Benito. (2000). "Tempest over the South China Sea: Chinese Perspectives on the Sprat-lys". *Asian Studies*, 36(2), www.asj.upd.edu.ph/mediabox/archive/ASJ-36-2-2000/lim.pdf (accessed on 2018, March 10)

Media Briefing by the Official Spokesperson, Vishnu Prakash. (2011, September 15). New Delhi: Ministry of External Affairs, http://mea.gov.in/in-focus-article.htm?2951 (accessed on 2018, April 2)

Scott, David. (2012, November/December). "Conflict Irresolution in the South China Sea", *Asian Survey*, 52(6)

"Security Dimensions of India's Foreign Policy". Address by Foreign Secretary of India, Ranjan Mathai at National Defence College, New Delhi. (2011, November 23). New Delhi: Ministry of External Affairs, www.mea.gov.in/Speeches-Statements.htm?dtl/6946/Address+by+For eign+Secretary+at+NDC+on+Security+dimensions+of+Indias+Foreign+Policy (accessed on 2018, March 28)

"*Shaping India's Maritime Strategy: Opportunities and Challenges*". Prime Minister of India, Manmohan Singh's Speech at National Defence College, New Delhi. (2005, October 21), http://indiannavy.nic.in/cns_add2.htm (accessed on 2018, March 28)

Shoji, Tomotaka. (2012, December). "Vietnam, ASEAN and the South China Sea: Unity or Diverseness?". *NIDS Journal of Defense and Security*, 13, www.nids.mod. go.jp/english/publication/kiyo/pdf/2012/bulletin_e2012_2.pdf (accessed on 2018, March 20)

South China Sea. (2013, February 7). Washington, DC: U.S. Energy Information Administration, www.eia.gov/beta/international/regions-topics.php?RegionTopicID=SCS (accessed on 2018, February 24)

Speech by Indian Foreign Secretary at Raisina Dialogue. (2016, March 2). New Delhi: Ministry of External Affairs, http://mea.gov.in/Speeches-Statements.htm?dtl/26433/ Speech_by_Foreign_Secretary_at_Raisina_Dialogue_in_New_Delhi_March_2_2016 (acc essed on 2018, May 12)

"Statement of the Indian Minister of External Affairs, I. K. Gujral, at ASEAN Post Ministerial Conference". (1996, July 24). ASEAN Post Ministerial Conference Documents, *Strategic Digest*, 26(10)

Statement of the Indian Minister of External Affairs, Yashwant Sinha, at the Plenary Session of the Second ASEAN-India Business Summit. (2003, September 4). New Delhi: Ministry of External Affairs, http://meaindia.nic.in/mystart.php?id=53016849 (accessed on 2018, March 28)

"Stirring up the South China Sea (II): Regional Responses". (2012, July 24). *International Crisis Group: Asia Report*, 229, www.files.ethz.ch/isn/151038/229-stirring-up-the-south-china-sea-ii-regional-responses.pdf (accessed on 2018, February 24)

"Stirring up the South China Sea (IV): Oil in Troubled Waters". (2016, January 26). *International Crisis Group: Asia Report*, 275, www.files.ethz.ch/isn/195791/South% 20china%20sea4.pdf (accessed on 2018, February 28)

Storey, Ian. (2008, April 28). "Trouble and Strife in the South China Sea: The Philippines and China". *China Brief,* 8(9), https://jamestown.org/program/trouble-and-strife-in-the-south-china-sea-part-ii-the-philippines-and-china/ (accessed on 2018, March 20)

Sundararaman, Shankari. (2003, November 19). "India and ASEAN", *The Hindu*

Swaine, Michael D. (2010, November 15). "China's Assertive Behavior Part I: On Core Interests". *China Leadership Monitor*, 34, https://carnegieendowment.org/files/ CLM34MS_FINAL.pdf (accessed on 2018, February 18)

Thayer, Carlyle A. (2013, Summer–Fall–Fall). "ASEAN, China and the Code of Conduct in the South China Sea". *SAIS Review of International Affairs*, 33(2), https://muse. jhu.edu/article/527061/pdf (accessed on 2018, March 4)

Treaty of Amity and Cooperation in Southeast Asia. (1976, February 24). Jakarta: ASEAN Secretariat, http://asean.org/treaty-amity-cooperation-southeast-asia-indonesia-24-feb ruary-1976/ (accessed on 2018, March 10)

Umbach, Frank. (2017, May 4). "The South China Sea Disputes: The Energy Dimensions". *Commentary*, 85, Singapore: RSIS, www.rsis.edu.sg/wp-content/uploads/ 2017/05/CO17085.pdf (accessed on 2018, February 28)

United Nations Convention on the Law of the Sea. (1982, December 10). "Part V, United Nations: Oceans and Law of the Sea", Geneva: United Nations, www.un.org/Depts/ los/convention_agreements/texts/unclos/part5.htm (accessed on 2018, March 20)

"Vision and Actions on Jointly Building Silk Road Economic Belt and 21st-Century Maritime Silk Road". (2015, March 28). *News Release.* Beijing: National Development and Reform Commission, http://en.ndrc.gov.cn/newsrelease/201503/t20150330_669367.html (accessed on 2019, May 12)

Zhu, Charlie. (2012, June 21). "China Tests Troubled Waters with $1 Billion Rig for South China Sea". *Reuters*, www.reuters.com/article/us-china-southchinasea-idUS BRE85K03Y20120621 (accessed on 2018, February 28)

3 ASEAN–China diplomatic dissension and India's interests

The rationale supporting the establishment of ASEAN was contained in its resolve to securitise the Southeast Asian region, conflict management and conflict resolution. ASEAN's formal mechanism for conflict management and resolution is enshrined in the TAC, and premised on basic principles of mutual respect for the independence, sovereignty, equality, territorial integrity and national identity of all nations; the right of every state to lead its national existence free from external interference, subversion and coercion; non-interference in the internal affairs of one another; settlement of differences or disputes by peaceful means; renunciation of threat or use of force; and effective cooperation among member-states (Treaty of Amity and Cooperation in Southeast Asia, 1976: Art. 2; Caballero-Anthony, 1998: 49). True to these foundational tenets, ASEAN's most significant attempt to address the SCS dispute was reflected in its adherence to the TAC, with the introduction of the Spratly Declaration in 1992. The Declaration emphasised the imperative of resolution of all sovereignty and jurisdictional issues by "peaceful means, without using force" and exhorted "all parties concerned to apply the principles contained in the Treaty of Amity and Cooperation in Southeast Asia as the basis for establishing a code of international conduct over the South China Sea" (1992 ASEAN Declaration on the South China Sea, 1992: Art. 4). It not only made its mark as the pivotal ASEAN-China negotiating conduit, but also formally established the converging space for working towards the design of an international code of conduct on the SCS and exercising self-restraint in order to develop an ambience conducive to conflict resolution. It thus echoed the need to subscribe to the TAC's seminal clauses of mutual respect for the independence, sovereignty, equality, territorial integrity and national identity of all nations and non-interference in the internal affairs of one another (Treaty of Amity and Cooperation in Southeast Asia, 1976: Art. 2a, c) These norms, adherence to which has been reiterated in the Preamble of the ASEAN Charter (Charter of the Association of Southeast Asian Nations, 2007: 2) constitute the edifice for the four broad organisational principles of ASEAN, viz. open regionalism, cooperative security, soft rules or a non-legalistic approach to cooperation and consensus-building (Acharya, 1997: 324).

China's initiation of the New Security Concept in 1997–1998, which synchronised with the five principles of peaceful coexistence and mutually beneficial cooperation, formed the key elements of its contemporary foreign policy. It was premised on the strong foundation of equality, mutual respect, non-interference in the internal affairs of other countries and conflict resolution through dialogue, converging with the ASEAN principles as enshrined in the TAC/ASEAN Way. The crux of the New Security Concept resided in China's easing of relations with its immediate neighbours through the propagation of confidence-building measures, dialogue and cooperation for the purpose of ensuring regional peace and security. Furthermore, the evident shift in emphasis from alliance politics to "strategic partnerships", as reflected in the Defence White Paper: 1998, signalled its intent to present a more benign and less threatening face in the region, by debunking the "China threat" theory and positioning itself as a responsible actor (Davison, 2004: 64–65), its assistance to the economically debilitated neighbours of Southeast Asia in the wake of the East Asian Financial Crisis (1997–1998), being the most timely expression.

The Spratly Declaration set the stage for a proposed "regional code" on the SCS put forward by Malaysia and the Philippines at the ASEAN Foreign Ministers' Meeting held in Singapore in July 1999. The regional COC was primarily an intra-ASEAN document, seeking to enlarge its scope and domain by incorporating China's cooperation. It was prepared and accepted by ASEAN in November 1999 with the decision that it should be placed before China for its consideration. For its part, China neither agreed to the Code nor rejected it outright, though it refused to be a signatory to it. In this context, following a meeting with his Singapore counterpart, Goh Chok Tong, the then Chinese Premier, Zhu Rongi added that the COC was a "very serious and important matter to China" and it would not rush to sign it. Nevertheless, Beijing agreed to hold talks with the ASEAN member-states on the same, which ASEAN, as an organisation, pursued in right earnest, with the intention of reducing tensions in the SCS (Chakraborti, 2001: 200). Subsequently, in July 2000, at the 7th ARF Meeting in Bangkok, the then Chinese Foreign Minister, Tang Jaixuan expressed his country's commitment to reaching a COC, though it took another couple of years to ink the same. The signing of the DOC in November 2002, at the 6th China-ASEAN Summit in Phnom Penh emerged as a trailblazer, in addition to assuming niche as the first political document concluded between ASEAN and China pertaining to the dispute. The DOC was acknowledged as a guideline for diplomatic behaviour and restraint, with a twofold rationale of formulating trust and confidence among the claimants as well as paving the way for the establishment of a regional COC in the SCS. It also served as the conduit for China and ASEAN to reaffirm their commitment to the purposes and principles of the Charter of the United Nations, the 1982 UNCLOS and the TAC premised on principles of non-intervention and multilateralism (Chakraborti and Chakraborty, 2011: 227). The signing of the DOC ushered in a temporary thaw in Sino-ASEAN dynamics, at least until the end of the first decade of the twenty-first century, insofar as the SCS issue was concerned. Reflecting China's impetus on shaping and maintaining a stable and peaceful regional environment, amenable to its domestic economic development, this also served as an assurance of confidence-building with ASEAN, against the backdrop of its active involvement in the multilateral ASEAN+ China frameworks, a series of annual summits and PMCs, followed up by its signing of the TAC as the first non-ASEAN member in 2003, thus renouncing its inertia towards multi-lateralism and minimising, if not totally reversing, the perceived "China threat" syndrome among the ASEAN member-states (Saunders, 2008: 131–132).

Given this backdrop of emerging confidence and cooperation in Sino-ASEAN dynamics, the first section of the present chapter will analyse the reasons behind the disarray among the ASEAN members *vis-à-vis* the stance of containing China's ambitions in the SCS, particularly evident since 2012, and the manner in which developments have posed a threat to sustaining the solidarity of ASEAN as an organisation. In sum, the issue seems to challenge ASEAN's underlying, embryonic concept of regional cooperation and integration as an instrument for consolidating Southeast Asia's position in the regional architecture. The second section of the present chapter premises its analysis on the acknowledgement that the challenges to ASEAN centrality and leadership test the vitality of its norms and identity, and its ability to reconcile the opposing strains of adherence to the normative motivations contained in the ASEAN Way, on the one hand, and the primacy of individual national interests of the member-states, on the other. Serving as a background for examining India's military strategy and naval diplomacy in the SCS (as discussed in the next chapter), it identifies the implications of this incongruity for India's policy responses in the region.

1 South China Sea conundrum: ASEAN unity disarrayed

ASEAN has often been brought to the altar for its inability to unite its members on the SCS issue. It has been blamed for its incompetence in challenging China's hegemonic ambitions in the regional littorals, thereby underscoring the limitations of the organisation's role and centrality, further paving the way for the intervention of extra-regional powers, given the high stakes that they share *vis-à-vis* the strategic pertinence of the SCS. ASEAN's dynamics viewed in relation to China require construal perhaps from an understanding of the position and predominance that the latter enjoys among the ASEAN member-states, notwithstanding their contested and overlapping sovereignty claims in the SCS. The ASEAN member-states are seldom comfortable taking China head-on, thus providing it with more credence and acceptability, and often leading to concerns over the organisation's unity regarding the SCS dispute. This tangible rift was succinctly expressed by the Chinese Foreign Minister, Yang Jiechi in 2010, when he underscored: "There are territorial and maritime right disputes between China and some of its neighbors, and those disputes should not be viewed as ones between China and ASEAN as a whole just because the countries involved are ASEAN members." (Xiaokun and Ting, 2010) ASEAN thus exhibits a division into two distinct segments: on the one hand, between four countries engaged in territorial dispute with China in the SCS, viz. Brunei, Malaysia, the Philippines and Vietnam and, on the other hand, Cambodia, Indonesia, Laos, Myanmar, Singapore and Thailand, which do not share such conflicting ties with Beijing. Cognisant of their individual capabilities, national interests and vulnerabilities, the ASEAN member-states have evoked proportional responses to Chinese policies and actions. ASEAN's inability to present a united stance on the issue of China's assertiveness in the SCS has been expounded in the organisation's failure to officially document it in Summit Joint Statements/Communiqués. The same is true with respect to ASEAN's skirting reference to China's setback in the PCA in 2016.

1.1 ASEAN's cleavage vis-à-vis China: analysing the factors

ASEAN, constituted of a motley of diverse sovereign states, with different standards and levels of political, economic and military development, has been tethered by a COC that has manifested itself as the ASEAN Way. The organisation has operated on the basis of ad hoc understandings, consultations, consensus and informal procedures rather than within the framework of binding agreements arrived at through formal processes, while incorporating and respecting the principles of non-interference in domestic affairs, non-use of force, pacific settlement of disputes and respect for sovereignty and territorial integrity of the member-states (Severino, 2001). Thus, while the consensual process of decision-making germane to the ASEAN Way has been hailed as a contributing factor for dispute settlement, veering towards moderation and accommodation, and preventing the escalation of regional tensions, it has, on the other hand, been viewed as a justification for minimalism and conservatism on controversial issues, particularly in those engaging fundamental national interests, sovereignty and territorial integrity. These tenets of soft regionalism and consensus have circumscribed the degree of effectiveness in dealing with the SCS issue, legitimising the inability of the member-states to prioritise the organisation's "collective goals" ahead of individual national self-interests (Acharya, 1997: 342–343). It has often been argued that the principles of sovereignty and non-interference in the internal affairs of member-states that lie at the heart of the ASEAN Way have limited effective cooperation, particularly in the case of relations with non-ASEAN states. However, across the range of ASEAN member-states not only is there a distinction between those involved in territorial dispute over the SCS and those not involved, but also in terms of their preference for either a policy of pragmatic equidistance or a tight alignment with China, also referred to as "omni-enmeshment". The preference for either limited alignment, analysed in terms of maintaining a balance between deeper engagement and strategic autonomy, or "omni-enmeshment", defined as the process of engaging with a state (China, in this case) based on the logic of deeper involvement and enveloping it into a network of sustained exchanges and relations, varies as a function of the level of economic and military development and capability, threat assessment and a pragmatic analysis of advantages the member-states would accrue *vis-à-vis* China (Goh, 2007–2008: 116, 121; Laksmana, 2017: 114). Perceived from this premise, the founding members of ASEAN,[1] characterised by a greater degree of military and economic development *vis-à-vis* their VCLM[2] counterparts, were expected to exercise a higher level of strategic autonomy, higher bargaining power and limited alignment with China. Such a behaviour would also take stock of and be influenced by their historical experiences as well as the imperatives of national interest and pragmatic realism, given the computations of cost-benefit and advantages that could be accrued by aligning with or accommodating China. Thus, China has been successful in converting its resources into influence over the strategic decisions of the ASEAN member-states, albeit to varying degrees, resulting in outcomes that have been to China's advantage.

1.1.1 Interplay of the divisive factors on ASEAN-China relations and manifestations

On the whole, the twin factors discussed above, viz. the limitations of the ASEAN Way and the predominance of individual national interests over those of the organisation as a whole, have explicitly conditioned the conduct of ASEAN's relations with China insofar as the SCS dispute is concerned. The prelude to the present rift among ASEAN member-states with respect to the SCS issue can be traced back to the year 2000, when the Philippines bolstered its push for a COC in order to restrain China's assertiveness in the littoral domain. However, the lack of adequate support from its fellow ASEAN counterparts compelled it to remain content with the non-legally binding document, DOC. The brewing tension among the ASEAN members took a sharp turn in the context of drafting of the COC in 2012, with the differences in accepting certain provisions of the informal working draft put forth by the Philippines in January becoming apparent. It received stiff resistance with respect to the provisions pertaining to the proposal to establish a joint cooperation area in the SCS to promote it as a Zone of Peace, Freedom, Friendship and Cooperation. Subsequently, the draft COC that was submitted to the ASEAN-SOM and passed for the consideration of the ASEAN Foreign Ministers at the 45th AMM in July 2012 deleted these clauses (Arts III–VI). The act of deletion was viewed as a means of accommodating China's interests and entertain its engagement in the deliberations, for which the then ASEAN Chair, Cambodia evinced intent. The Philippines had reacted to the deletion quite exceptionally as the inclusion of the clauses would have added substance in support of restraining China's unilateral assertiveness in the littorals. Another bone of contention that proved to be a cause for internal cleavage among the ASEAN members pertained to the timing of China's inclusion in the drafting process of the COC. While the Philippines and Vietnam opposed China's inclusion before the drafting was completed by the ASEAN members, its counterparts, led by Indonesia and Cambodia, argued to the contrary, leading to a "compromise" on the clause on prior consultation within ASEAN itself, in lieu of ensuring "constant communication through the ASEAN-China framework" (Thayer, 2012a).

The most explicit demonstration of the cleavage within ASEAN came to the fore in the course of the 45th AMM held in Phnom Penh in July 2012, which earned a negative distinction for its inability to release a Joint Communiqué, for the first time, in the history of the organisation. This failure was a clear show of the chink in ASEAN's armour of cohesion and unity. Among the ASEAN members, Thailand spoke in unison with Cambodia, advocating negotiation on territorial claims among the parties concerned, in the interest of safeguarding "excellent relations" between China and ASEAN (Thul and Grudgings, 2012). On the other side of the spectrum, Indonesia, Malaysia and Singapore shared the concerns of the Philippines and Vietnam, acknowledging the imperative of reflecting a "clear expression of our concerns on the SCS in the joint communiqué", in the interest of upholding organisational cohesion. As the then Chair, Cambodian Prime Minister, Hun Sen was resolute on not inserting the clause mentioning China's standoff with the Philippines and Vietnam over the Scarborough Shoal and bidding activities by China within Vietnam's EEZ and continental shelf respectively in the Joint Communiqué, thus ignoring the insistence of their representatives. Cambodia justified its refusal on the basis that since these disputes were bilateral in nature, the inclusion of respective national positions in a joint communiqué in place of a common, organisation's view would further hinder a solution (Thayer, 2012b; Clement, 2012).

Intra-ASEAN division was also demonstrated both prior to and following the PCA judgement of July 12, 2016, which rejected China's sweeping claims to territory in the SCS. Less than a month before the judgement, the Special ASEAN-China Foreign Ministers' Meeting in Kunming, held on June 14, 2016, was marked by ASEAN retracting a strongly worded Statement, issued by the Malaysian Foreign Minister expressing "serious concerns over recent and ongoing developments, which have eroded trust and confidence, increased tensions and which may have the potential to undermine peace, security and stability in the South China Sea", within hours. The withdrawal was explained by the Malaysian Foreign Ministry spokesperson on the ground of requiring "urgent amendment", though no updated version was issued later. It was further clarified by the Indonesian Foreign Ministry that the statement, erroneously issued, was only a "media guideline" for ASEAN ministers, meant for reference at the post-meeting press conference (Latiff, 2016; Potkin, 2016). This diplomatic *faux pas*, though managed subsequently, brought to the fore ASEAN's forced submission to Beijing's heavy-handed attempt towards retraction and deft playing of its Cambodia-Laos card, with the support of Cambodia and, most importantly, Laos, the then ASEAN Chair. Even before the declaration of the PCA ruling, Cambodia had clarified its stand against backing an ASEAN statement on the ruling, since it had no intention of getting embroiled in a dispute over sovereignty with China and any other member of ASEAN. In keeping with this position, much to the Philippines' chagrin, Cambodia not only blocked reference to the PCA verdict, but also pushed for the removal of a previously routine phrase regarding "militarisation" in the SCS, in the Joint Communiqué of the 49th ASEAN Foreign Ministers Meeting at Vientiane on July 24, 2016 (Willemyns, 2016) that was held just a week after the declaration of the ruling. The Joint Communiqué contained a watered-down section on the "South China Sea", expressing concern over "land reclamations" and "escalation of activities" in the littorals, without naming China or making reference to the PCA award (Joint Communiqué of the 49th ASEAN Foreign Ministers' Meeting, 2016: Cl. 174). This alluded to the preference of a majority of ASEAN members, particularly those with no claims in the SCS, to steer clear of upsetting China, apprehending the consequences, much to the displeasure of the Philippines and Vietnam. These were instances of China reaping the dividend of having taken Cambodia, ASEAN's Achilles' heel, into its confidence, and successfully alienating Cambodia, Brunei and Laos from the rest of the ASEAN members in reaching a Four Point Consensus on the SCS in April 2016. The Consensus principally acknowledged that the dispute, not being an issue between China and ASEAN, "should not affect China-ASEAN relations"; and that disputes over territorial and maritime rights and interests "should be resolved through dialogues and consultations by parties directly concerned under Article 4 of the DOC" ("Wang Yi Talks about China's Four-Point Consensus on South China Sea Issue with Brunei, Cambodia and Laos", 2016). Thus, it not only demarcated the three signatories from the rest of the ASEAN members, but also challenged the notion of ASEAN centrality, echoing Beijing's preference for bilateralism, as against the organisation's adherence to multilateralism in dealing with the SCS dispute.

The practical reason for Phnom Penh's action can be explained by its discomfiture in irking Beijing, largely responsible for providing aid and foreign direct investment (FDI), the key driver of Cambodia's economic development, and boosting "excellent diplomatic relationship". In other words, Cambodia was believed to echo China's concern about neither internationalising the issue, nor pushing it too hard or too fast. As Cambodia's largest FDI donor, between 1994 and 2013 Chinese investments had recorded US$10 billion, focused mainly on agriculture, mining, infrastructure projects, hydro-power dams and garment production, in addition to US$3 billion in concessional loans and grants. By 2016, total investments from China in Cambodia had leaped to US$14.7 billion (Vannarith, 2017). Summarily, ASEAN's dismissal of the clauses could largely be explained from the practical viewpoint of safeguarding its overall relations with China, particularly in the sphere of trade and investments, which had almost grown thrice during the period 2005–2014, accounting for US$380 billion in 2014. Furthermore, with the commencement of the ASEAN-China Free Trade Area Agreement in 2010, the two sides had set the ambitious target of enhancing the volume of trade to US$1 trillion, in addition to simultaneously encouraging Chinese FDI flow from US$50 billion to US$150 billion by 2020. Chinese companies are major players and significant financiers in infrastructure projects and mining activities in the majority of ASEAN countries, with their commitment to infrastructure projects being US$50 billion, or an average of US$10 billion annually (ASEAN Investment Report: 2013–14, 2014: 63–64). According to Beijing's Ministry of Commerce data, China continued its position as the largest trading partner of 16 Asian countries in 2017, further strengthening economic and trade integration with its neighbours (Tian, 2018). In 2018, China-ASEAN trade reached a record high of US$587 billion, pitching an increase of 14.1 per cent year on year and sustaining its position as ASEAN's largest trading partner for ten consecutive years ("China-ASEAN Trade Hits Record High in 2018", 2019). By the end of 2018, China's investment in ASEAN and vice versa reached US$89.01 billion and US$116.7 billion respectively, accounting for a 22-fold increase in bilateral investment in 15 years (Xilian, 2019).

Furthermore, in the sphere of defence and military modernisation, China has increased its defence spending by 7.5 per cent (over 2018) to US$177.61 billion in 2019, as it aspires to possess five aircraft carriers, build anti-satellite missiles and stealth fighters and add to its fleet of naval ships and submarines. China's defence expenditure has maintained single-digit growth since 2016, with 2018 recording its largest defence spending increase in three years at 8.1 per cent (Liang, 2019; Martina and Blanchard, 2019). On the whole, China's spectacular economic success, matched by its military prowess, along with factors like the presence and influence of overseas Chinese and the benefits that its allies would accrue as part of the BRI have further cemented China's legitimacy within ASEAN, particularly as President Xi Jinping postulated tying its neighbours into a more closely knit community, sharing common destiny, envisaged in the concept of "community of common destiny" (Chinese President, Xi Jinping's Speech at People's Representative Council of Indonesia, 2013). It thus transpires that China's economic clout, employment of "chequebook diplomacy" and other soft-power based diplomatic endeavours have promoted it to the position of an indispensable and almost invincible neighbour in the psyche of the ASEAN nations.

Following speculations that the Chairman's Statement to be issued at the conclusion of the 31st ASEAN Summit (2017) would exclude the section on the SCS dispute, the Secretary General, Le Luong Minh contended that ASEAN was not the forum to resolve sovereignty claims over the SCS; it was at best, the site to regulate the conduct of all parties in the territorial dispute. He also argued that, since the SCS issue was one aspect of ASEAN-China relations as a whole, it was not necessary for other ASEAN countries to have a position "with regards to the sovereignty claims of the claimants" ("ASEAN Cannot Resolve Sea Disputes", 2017). Although this may have created goodwill for the association by encouraging restraint and conservatism on the dispute, the practice could become counterproductive for two principal reasons: first, it would be a cover for legitimising the failure of the member-states to allow the collective organisational interests to be subsumed by national interests; and second, disillusioning the member-states regarding ASEAN's ability or even interest in addressing regional security issues, which may well include some fellow members of the organisation. The quandary faced by the member-states is perhaps the best exemplified by the "golden cage" analogy, the most relevant in analysing the policies of the Philippines and Vietnam towards China (Dosch, 2007: 222). This scepticism may be enough to prompt respective stakeholding members to seek other alternatives, allow the intervention of external players, both extra-ASEAN and extra-regional, or even find succour in teaming up with the antagonist (China in this case) and prolonging the process of conflict resolution by supporting its policies and speaking in favour of their benefactor. This would ultimately defeat the logic of regionalism and spiral China's unbridled assertiveness in the region and champion the cause of the hegemonic stabiliser, a theory which ordains the dominant state with relatively more economic, military and political power resources to a position wherein it can employ that power to coerce other states, or provide them with incentives and security benefits.

A more recent instance to this effect was borne out by the issuing of the Chairman's Statement at the 30th ASEAN Summit, held in April 2017, bereft of references either to China's setback in the Hague-based arbitration case filed by the Philippines (2016), or its land-reclamation and militarisation of disputed islands in the SCS. The incident was a classic example of a golden opportunity being left unutilised by the Chair, the Philippines, to exercise its Chairmanship in referring to the arbitral victory in the face of Chinese lobbying to avoid tacit references to it. The downplaying of the issue as a "non-issue" by the Philippine President, Rodrigo Duterte, in spite of being ardently urged by some of his ASEAN counterparts, once again displayed the effect that Chinese economic and military power and influence had cast on the visage of ASEAN unity (Placido, 2017). Duterte's soft posture on China was naturally hailed by Brunei, Cambodia and Laos, owing to considerations of economic, trade and commercial prioritisation, while the other members of ASEAN, particularly, Indonesia, Malaysia, Singapore and Vietnam rued the Philippines' soft-pedalling of the issue. Almost reversing the strategic posture of his predecessor, Benigno Aquino III, who had vehemently opposed Beijing's assertiveness and militarisation of the SCS, Duterte's pragmatic policy was construed to be intent upon fostering bonhomie and rapprochement with China. This has been evident in his "setting aside" of the controversy erupting in the wake of the PCA verdict and facilitating steps towards joint exploration and development of maritime resources in the disputed littorals. Although justifying the conciliatory stride in relations with China since he assumed office as President in 2016 as the rational means of avoiding conflict and even expressing his aversion to inviting "trouble", "war" and "massacre of Filipino soldiers" (Romero, 2018) by the regional behemoth, the implicit rationale could be deciphered not only in the attraction of Chinese investments and loan agreements, but also Duterte's scouting for its support in the face of international alienation on account of his administration's abysmal human rights record with respect to the "war on drugs" campaign. China emerged as the topmost trading partner of the Philippines, accounting for US$13.9 billion in trade in the first segment of 2018. This is in addition a huge surge in investments, which rose to 67 per cent in 2017 to the value of US$53.8 million, earmarked for principal infrastructure projects like the Chico River Pump irrigation project, the Kaliwa Dam and the southern railway line from Manila (Zheng, 2018). Furthermore, in a significant coincidence with the Chinese President, Xi Jinping's visit to Manila in November 2018, China is set to invest US$2 billion to build an industrial park at Clark Air Base, the former US military outpost in the Philippines, which is hailed as the biggest investment in the country, fuelling and facilitating Duterte's US$180 billion "Build, Build, Build" plan to rejuvenate the country's infrastructure (Ramos and Reed, 2018).

Viwed from this perspective, perhaps the ASEAN Way or its "normative terrain" requires some degree of flexibility in order to allow the ASEAN member-states to address the issue, provide their respective opinions, guided by a resolute leadership, encouraging the members to take and articulate a "more active interest in one another", which can facilitate the promotion of "ASEAN regionalism in the longer term" (Opening Statement by His Excellency Dr. Surin Pitsuwan, Minister of Foreign Affairs of Thailand at the 31st ASEAN Ministerial Meeting, 1998). Even today, one seems to hear the resonating candour of the former Foreign Minister of Thailand, Surin Pitsuwan, when he spoke in favour of supplanting ASEAN's policy of non-interference with "flexible engagement" or "enhanced interaction". That ASEAN has been rigid in its attitude towards allowing the implementation of any other alternative to the ASEAN Way is perhaps borne out most explicitly by its rejection of the Philippine-led Aquino Way, presented as a proposed alternative to the slow and non-confrontational ASEAN Way (Baviera, 2012) back in 2011. These considerations have often sidelined the much-needed attempts to address the issue on a cooperative and more responsible basis, in the face of China's military–economic sinews.

The emergence of a clear dichotomy among the ASEAN member-states based on their strategic preferences for accommodating and even aligning with China, stemming from considerations of their respective national interests, is debilitating the organisation's capacity to take a coordinated stance against China insofar as the SCS issue is concerned. Consequently, in compliance with the ASEAN Way of conducting business, it is being compelled to adopt a minimalist approach, while maintaining interactions through a high degree of informality, consensus-building and non-confrontation (Acharya, 1997: 332) among the members, which, in turn, serves as a justification for safeguarding their individual national interests, on the one hand, and promoting conservatism and accommodation with respect to China on the controversial issue of the SCS, on the other. In sum, what ASEAN needs most is the successful transformation of its role from a convener of dialogue and consultation to an agenda-setter for regional security concerns, consolidating the organisation's unity and vision (Baviera and Maramis, 2017: 10) pending which the region is compelled to rely on external actors to maintain the regional balance, given the high stakes and concerns that countries like India, Japan and the most significant extra-regional player, the US, share, not only to secure access to the resources, freedom of navigation and overflight in the SCS, but also the holistic peace and stability of the Indo-Pacific.

2 India's policy and official pronouncements on the South China Sea issue

It follows from the discussion above that ASEAN's policy and responses, primarily stemming from its organisational principles and norms of implementation, have served China's interests and bolstered its status as an almost invincible and unchallenged regional power, notwithstanding its aggressive posture in the SCS. Although not a totally mute spectator to its forays in the disputed littorals, ASEAN's placatory and conciliatory policy *vis-à-vis* Beijing has definitely emerged as a challenge to India's interests in the Indo-Pacific region, having a strong influence on its strategies. A scrutiny of official pronouncements by the Indian government since 2012, in the wake of the decisive AMM of July, which exposed ASEAN's irreconcilable stance on the SCS dispute, reveals the emphasis laid on the convergence between India and ASEAN in safeguarding maritime security, leading to the emergence of an "open, balanced, inclusive architecture that promotes peace, stability and prosperity in the Asia-Pacific Region". Although no explicit references were made to Chinese activities in the SCS, it was quite obvious that the security of the littoral architecture impinged considerably on China, which evoked genuine concern and response from India (Response by Prime Minister, Manmohan Singh at the 10th ASEAN-India Summit, 2012). The importance that India attached to its partnership with ASEAN was an intrinsic component of the vision of a stable, secure and prosperous regional landscape referred to in the then Prime Minister of India (heading the UPA government), Manmohan Singh's emphatic acknowledgement of the necessity for a "stable, secure and prosperous Indo-Pacific region for our own progress and prosperity", thus unveiling the mutual benefit of the strategic aspects of engagement. A reading of his opening statement at the Plenary Session of the India-ASEAN Commemorative Summit held in December 2012 provides an insight into the prevalent undercurrents pertaining to several "unsettled questions and unresolved issues" in the region (Opening Statement by Prime Minister of India, Manmohan Singh at Plenary Session of India-ASEAN Commemorative Summit, 2012) that necessitated the development of greater comprehensiveness in India-ASEAN strategic ties for the purpose of shaping an open, balanced, inclusive and transparent regional architecture. In this context, the elevation of India-ASEAN relations to the echelon of a Strategic Partnership and enhanced consultation on a range of issues of regional security concerns formed the converging framework as well.

Furthermore, while identifying the challenges faced by the region "not only from its diversity, but also from differences", the Indian Prime Minister's call to inculcate a "cooperative temper" was perhaps a subtle and implicit reference to the disunity prevalent among the ASEAN member-states regarding the SCS issue. As a reminder of the essence of maintaining a stable maritime environment in the Indo-Pacific region, at the EAS held in Brunei the following year (2013), Manmohan Singh suggested reaffirmation and adherence to the principles of maritime security, including the right to passage and unimpeded commerce, based on the precepts of international law and dispute settlement in a peaceful manner (Prime Minister of India, Manmohan Singh's Statement at 8th East Asia Summit, 2013).

The official verbal tirade of India continued unabated when Prime Minister Narendra Modi (heading the NDA-II government) assumed office in May 2014 and in his maiden participation in the EAS held in November declared his commitment to enhance cooperation with ASEAN "in advancing balance, peace and stability in the region", within the framework of AEP, a more proactive successor of the LEP. In the course of delivering this speech, the Prime Minister of India not only identified the need for "a serious and sustained dialogue" among stakeholders in addressing the variety of "complex and unresolved issues" related to security in the Indo-Pacific region, but he also emphasised adherence to "international law and norms for peace and stability in South China Sea as well" (Prime Minister of India, Narendra Modi's Remarks at the 9th East Asia Summit, 2014). The two salient points were that, on the one hand, it addressed China's unabated aggressive posture in the SCS, particularly against the backdrop of its substantial expansion of its ability to monitor and project power throughout the littorals by initiating and sustaining the construction of dual civilian-military bases at its outposts in several disputed islands. On the other hand, it implied ASEAN's organisational limitations in proposing and presenting a concerted stance *vis-à-vis* China. India's posture was in harmony with ASEAN's bid to consolidate cooperation with it on strategic issues, with greater emphasis on "maritime security and addressing the emerging challenges at sea" (ASEAN Chairman's Statement of the 12th ASEAN-India Summit, 2014). India's allusion to the settled maritime boundary with Bangladesh by applying the UNCLOS mechanism was also presented as a point of reference for ASEAN to follow in resolving the dispute in the SCS, in consonance with the DOC, and in addition to beefing up efforts for early adoption of a COC on the basis of consensus (Remarks by Prime Minister of India, Narendra Modi at the 10th East Asia Summit, 2015).

As the latest declaration unveiled at the India-ASEAN Commemorative Summit (Full Text of Delhi Declaration of ASEAN-India Commemorative Summit to Mark the 25th Anniversary of ASEAN-India Relations, 2018) testifies, the two sides reaffirmed the importance of maintaining and promoting peace, stability, maritime safety and security, freedom of navigation and overflight in the region and other lawful uses of the seas and unimpeded lawful maritime commerce and of promoting peaceful resolutions of disputes, in accordance with universally recognised principles of international law (Full Text of Delhi Declaration of ASEAN-India Commemorative Summit to Mark the 25th Anniversary of ASEAN-India Relations, 2018).

Their support for the full and effective implementation of the DOC and expectations for the early conclusion of the COC reveal a shared vision for ensuring a rules-based maritime order in the Indo-Pacific, where the hegemony of any power would not go unchallenged. Furthermore, it envisaged the forward tread of ASEAN-India cooperation by bolstering all relevant, high-level institutional mechanisms and working towards effective operationalisation of the "Plan of Action to Implement the ASEAN-India Partnership for Peace, Progress and Shared Prosperity (2016–2020)" (Answer of the Indian Minister of External Affairs, Sushma Swaraj to Starred Question No. 175, 2018).

In sum, taking cognisance of the unfaltering and aggressive Chinese pursuits in the SCS, considerably facilitated by a weak ASEAN organisational stance on the issue, India has maintained a coherent posture through the two successive administrative tenures of the UPA and NDA-II governments. It seeks to follow a nuanced and balanced approach in the strategic dynamics of the region. As ASEAN finds itself divided by the opposite pulls of organisational rigour, reflected in the ASEAN Way, on the one hand, and the more pragmatic concerns of accommodating China, on the other, this inherent incongruity not only poses the challenge of eroding the unity and cohesiveness of the organisation, but also provides China with leeway in sustaining its forays in the SCS. Against such a backdrop, India's official policy has acknowledged the importance of maintaining and promoting peace, stability, maritime safety and security, freedom of navigation and overflight and other lawful uses of the seas and unimpeded lawful maritime commerce, in addition to restoring faith in ASEAN centrality to promote peaceful resolutions of disputes, in accordance with the universally recognised principles of international law. This has been manifested in India welcoming the

> collective commitment by the concerned countries to abide by and implement the 2002 Declaration on the Conduct of Parties in the SCS and to work towards the adoption of a Code of Conduct in the SCS on the basis of consensus.
>
> (Answer of the Minister of State in the Ministry of External Affairs, Gen. V. K. Singh (Retd.) to Starred Question No. 568 in Lok Sabha, 2016)

This constitutes one of the core characteristics of the ASEAN mechanism of dialogue and negotiation. As India increasingly sees its strategic stakes hindered and even at the risk of being jeopardised by China's assertiveness in the Indo-Pacific, it aspires to project and equip itself as a balancer to China, in keeping with ASEAN's expectations. With the LEP/AEP forming the fulcrum of India's engagement with Southeast Asia in particular and the greater Indo-Pacific in general, the successful ascendance of India's strategic profile and maritime cooperation with the littoral ASEAN states, non-ASEAN maritime powers like Japan and Australia, and even extra-regional navies, has been demonstrative of its potential for emergence as an "anchor of stability and security" in its "legitimate area of interest" stretching from the Persian Gulf to the Straits of Malacca. Premised on this analysis, the subsequent chapter will discuss India's naval strategy in the Indo-Pacific and its pursuit of both internal and external balancing, as it fortifies itself to play a more pro-active and responsible role in the regional security ambience.

Notes

1 Indonesia, Malaysia, the Philippines, Singapore and Thailand
2 Vietnam, Cambodia, Laos and Myanmar joined ASEAN in the 1990s

References

1992 ASEAN Declaration on the South China Sea. (1992, July 22). San Francisco: SCRIBD Inc., www.scribd.com/Document/355737404/1992-ASEAN-Declaration-on-the-South-China-Sea (accessed on 2018, March 10)

Acharya, Amitav. (1997, January 1). "Ideas, Identity and Institution-building: From 'ASEAN Way' to the 'Asia-Pacific Way?'", *Pacific Review*, 10(3)

Answer of the Indian Minister of External Affairs, Sushma Swaraj to Starred Question No. 175. (2018, March 7). New Delhi: Ministry of External Affairs/Lok Sabha, www.mea.gov.in/lok-sabha.htm?dtl/29543/question+no175+indoasean+summit (accessed on 2019, January 20)

Answer of the Minister of State in the Ministry of External Affairs, Gen. V. K. Singh (Retd.) to Starred Question No. 568 in Lok Sabha. (2016, April 27). New Delhi: Ministry of

External Affairs/Lok Sabha, www.mea.gov.in/lok-sabha.htm?dtl/26684/QUESTION_ NO568_SOUTH_CHINA_SEA (accessed on 2019, January 20)

"ASEAN Cannot Resolve Sea Disputes". (2017, November 14). *Business Standard*

ASEAN Chairman's Statement of the 12th ASEAN-India Summit. (2014, November 12). New Delhi: Ministry of External Affairs, https://mea.gov.in/outgoing-visit-detail.htm?24243/ Chairmans+statement+of+the+12th+ASEANIndia+Summit+in+Nay+Pyi+Taw+Myanmar (accessed on 2019, January 17)

ASEAN Investment Report: 2013–14. (2014, October). Jakarta: ASEAN Secretariat, https:// unctad.org/en/PublicationsLibrary/unctad_asean_air2014d1.pdf (accessed on 2018, November 25)

Baviera, Aileen. (2012, March 6). "The South China Sea Disputes: Is the 'Aquino Way' the 'ASEAN Way'?", www.fairobserver.com/region/central_south_asia/south-china-sea-dis putes-aquino-way-asean-way/ (accessed on 2019, May 12)

Baviera, Aileen and Larry Maramis. (2017). "Building ASEAN Community: Political, Security and Socio-Cultural Reflections". *ASEAN @50* (4), Pasay City, Philippines: Department of Foreign Affairs of the Philippines: Economic Research Institute for ASEAN and East Asia, www.eria.org/ASEAN_at_50_Vol_4_Full_Report.pdf (accessed on 2019, May 12)

Caballero-Anthony, Mely. (1998, April). "Mechanisms of Dispute Settlement: The ASEAN Experience". *Contemporary Southeast Asia*, 20(1)

Chakraborti, Tridib. (2001). "Territorial Claims in South China Sea: Probing Persistent Uncertainties", in Banerji, A.K., and Purusottam Bhattacharya (eds), *People's Republic of China at Fifty: Politics, Economy and Foreign Relations*, New Delhi: Lancer's Books

Chakraborti, Tridib and Mohor Chakraborty. (2011, April). "South China Sea: The Refashioned Conflict and the Road Ahead", *World Focus*, 33(4)

Charter of the Association of Southeast Asian Nations. (2007, November 20). Jakarta: ASEAN Secretariat, www.asean.org/wp-content/uploads/2012/05/11.-October-2015- The-ASEAN-Charter-18th-Reprint-Amended-updated-on-05_-April-2016-IJP.pdf (acces- sed on 2018, December 14)

"China-ASEAN Trade Hits Record High in 2018". (2019, March 13). *Xinhua*, www. xinhuanet.com/english/2019-03/13/c_137892383.htm (accessed on 2019, May 30)

"Chinese President, Xi Jinping's Speech at People's Representative Council of Indonesia". (2013, October 2). *China Daily*, www.chinadaily.com.cn/china/2013xiapec/2013-10/ 02/content_17007915.htm (accessed on 2018, November 23)

Clement, Nicholas. (2012, July 19). "China Trumps ASEAN in the South China Sea", *Atlantic Sentinel*, http://atlanticsentinel.com/2012/.../china-trumps-asean-in-the- south-china-sea (accessed on 2018, November 25)

Davison, Remy. (2004). "China in the Asia-Pacific", in Connors, Michael K., Remy Davison and Jorn Dosch (eds), *The New Global Politics of the Asia-Pacific*, London: Routledge Curzon

Dosch, Jorn. (2007). "Managing Security in ASEAN-China Relations: Liberal Peace of Hegemonic Stability". *Asian Perspective*, 31(1)

Full Text of Delhi Declaration of ASEAN-India Commemorative Summit to Mark the 25th Anniversary of ASEAN-India Relations. (2018, January 25). New Delhi: Ministry of External Affairs, www.financialexpress.com/india-news/full-text-of-delhi-declaration- of-asean-india-commemorative-summit-to-mark-25th-anniversary-of-asean-india-rela tions/1030898 (accessed on 2019, January 17)

Goh, Evelyn. (2007–2008). "Great Powers and Hierarchical Order in Southeast Asia: Analyzing Regional Security Strategies", *International Security*, 32(3)

Joint Communiqué of the 49th ASEAN Foreign Ministers' Meeting. (2016, July 24). Jakarta: ASEAN Secretariat, https://asean.org/storage/2016/07/Joint-Communique-of-the-49th-AMM-ADOPTED.pdf (accessed on 2018, December 20)

Laksmana, Evan A. (2017). "Pragmatic Equidistance – How Indonesia Manages Its Great Power Relations", in Denoon, David B.H. (ed.), *The United States and the Future of Southeast Asia*, New York: New York University Press, 113–135

Latiff, Rozanna. (2016, June 15). "Southeast Asian Countries Retract Statement Expressing Concerns on South China Sea", *Reuters*, www.reuters.com/article/us-southchina sea-asean-idUSKCN0Z10KX (accessed on 2018, December 20)

Liang, Lim Yan. (2019, March 5). "China's 2019 Defence Budget to Rise by 7.5%, Growth Rate Lower than Last Year's 8.1%". *Straits Times*, www.straitstimes.com/asia/east-asia/chinas-2019-defence-budget-to-rise-by-75-growth-rate-lower-than-last-years-81 (accessed on 2019, May 1)

Martina, Michael and Ben Blanchard. (2019, March 5). "Rise in China's Defence Budget to Outpace Economic Growth Target". *Reuters*, www.reuters.com/article/uk-china-paliament-defence/rise-in-chinas-defence-budget-to-outpace-economic-growth-target-id UKKCN1QM036 (accessed on 2019, May 1)

Opening Statement by His Excellency Dr. Surin Pitsuwan, Minister of Foreign Affairs of Thailand at the 31st ASEAN Ministerial Meeting. (1998, July 24). Jakarta: ASEAN Secretariat, https://asean.org/?static_post=opening-statement-by-his-excellency-dr-surin-pitsuwan-minister-of-foreign-affairs-of-thailand-at-the-31st-asean-ministerial-meeting-manila-philippines-24-july-1998-2 (accessed on 2019, May 1)

Opening Statement by Prime Minister of India, Manmohan Singh at Plenary Session of India-ASEAN Commemorative Summit. (2012, December 20). New Delhi: Ministry of External Affairs, www.mea.gov.in/Speeches-Statements.htm?dtl/20981/Opening+Statement+by+Prime+Minister+at+Plenary+Session+of+IndiaASEAN+Commemorative+Summit (accessed on 2019, January 17)

Placido, Dharel. (2017, May 2). "DFA: No Leader Brought Up Sea Row during ASEAN Summit". *ABS-CBN News*, https://news.abs-cbn.com/news/05/02/17/dfa-no-leader-brought-up-sea-row-during-asean-summit (accessed on 2018, November 25)

Potkin, Fanny. (2016, June 16). "The Truth Behind ASEAN's Vanishing South China Sea Statement", *Forbes*, www.forbes.com/sites/fannypotkin/2016/06/16/now-you-see-it-now-you-dont-the-truth-behind-aseans-vanishing-south-china-sea-statement (accessed on 2018, December 20)

Prime Minister of India, Manmohan Singh's Statement at 8th East Asia Summit. (2013, October 10). New Delhi: Ministry of External Affairs, https://mea.gov.in/out oging-visit-detail.htm?22305/Prime+Ministers+Statement+at+8th+East+Asia+Summit+in+Brunei+Darussalam+October+10+2013 (accessed on 2019, January 17)

Prime Minister of India, Narendra Modi's Remarks at the 9th East Asia Summit. (2014, November 13). New Delhi: Ministry of External Affairs, https://mea.gov.in/out oging-visit-detail.htm?24238/Prime+Ministers+remarks+at+the+9th+East+Asia+Summit+Nay+Pyi+Taw+Myanmar (accessed on 2019, January 17)

Ramos, Grace and John Reed. (2018, November 19). "Philippines Tilting to China: Beijing to Invest $2 BN in 'Industrial Park' at Clarke AFB", *Financial Times*, https://fortunascorner.com/2018/11/19/philippines-tilting-to-china-beijing-to-invest-2b-in-industrial-park-at-clark-afb (accessed on 2018, December 1)

Remarks by Prime Minister of India, Narendra Modi at the 10th East Asia Summit. (2015, Novemmber 22). New Delhi: Ministry of External Affairs, https://mea.gov.in/outoging-visit-detail.

htm?26053/Remarks+by+Prime+Minister+at+the+10th+East+Asia+Summit+in+Kuala+Lumpur+November+22+2015 (accessed on 2019, January 17)

Response by Prime Minister, Manmohan Singh at the 10th ASEAN-India Summit. (2012, November 19). New Delhi: Ministry of External Affairs, https://mea.gov.in/outoging-visit-detail.htm?20826/Response+by+Prime+Minister+at+the+10th+ASEANIndia+Summit (accessed on 2019, January 10)

Romero, Alexis. (2018, May 21). "Confronting China Means Trouble: Duterte", *Philstar.* www.philstar.com/headlines/2018/05/21/1817169/confronting-china-means-trouble-duterte (accessed on 2018, December 1)

Saunders, Phillip C. (2008). "China's Role in Asia", in Shambaugh, David and Michael Yahuda (eds), *International Relations of Asia*, Lanham, MD: Rowman and Littlefield

Severino, Rudolfo C. (2001, September 3). "ASEAN Way and the Rule of Law". International Law Conference on ASEAN Legal Systems and Regional Integration, Kuala Lumpur, https://asean.org/?static_post=the-asean-way-and-the-rule-of-law (accessed on 2019, May 3)

Thayer, Carlyle A. (2012a, May 2). "Is the Philippines an Orphan?", *The Diplomat*, https://thediplomat.com/2012/05/is-the-philippines-an-orphan/?allpages=yes (accessed on 2018, December 17)

Thayer, Carlyle A. (2012b, August 19). "ASEAN's Code of Conduct in the South China Sea: A Litmus Test for Community-Building?", *The Asia Pacific Journal: Japan Focus*, 10 (34) (4), https://apjjf.org/2012/10/34/Carlyle-A.-Thayer/3813/article.html (accessed on 2018, November 26)

Thul, Park Chan and Stuart Grudgings. (2012, July 13). "SE Asia Meeting in Disarray over Sea Dispute with China", *Reuters*, www.reuters.com/article/us-asean-summit/se-asia-meeting-in-disarray-over-sea-dispute-with-china-idUSBRE86C0BD20120713 (accessed on 2018, February 18)

Tian, Fang. (2018, January 12). "China Rises to 16 Asian Countries' Biggest Trading Partners", *People's Daily Online*, http://en.people.cn/n3/2018/0112/c90000-9314972.html (accessed on 2018, November 23)

Treaty of Amity and Cooperation in Southeast Asia. (1976, February 24). Jakarta: ASEAN Secretariat, www.asean.org/treaty-amity-cooperation-southeast-asia-indonesia-24-february-1976/ (accessed on 2018, March 10)

Vannarith, Chheang. (2017, July 28). "China and Investments It Has Made in Cambodia", *Khmer Times*, www.khmertimeskh.com/5075376/china-investments-made-cambodia/ (accessed on 2018, November 23)

"Wang Yi Talks about China's Four-Point Consensus on South China Sea Issue with Brunei, Cambodia and Laos". (2016, April 23). Beijing: Ministry of Foreign Affairs, www.fmprc.gov.cn/mfa_eng/zxxx_662805/t1358478.shtml (accessed on 2018, December 20)

Willemyns, Alex. (2016, July 25). "Cambodia Blocks ASEAN Statement on South China Sea", *The Cambodia Daily*, www.cambodiadaily.com/news/cambodia-blocks-asean-statement-on-south-china-sea-115834/ (accessed on 2018, December 20)

Xiaokun, Li and Zhang Ting. (2010, July 26). "Foreign Minister Warns of South China Sea Issue", *China Daily*, www.chinadaily.com.cn/china/2010-07/26/content_11046544.htm (accessed on 2018, December 14)

Xilian, Huan. (2019, January 31). "China and ASEAN Doing Well on Economic, Trade Cooperation". *Jakarta Post*, www.thejakartapost.com/academia/2019/01/31/china-and-asean-doing-well-on-economic-trade-cooperation.html (accessed on 2019, April 30)

Zheng, Sarah. (2018, November 1). "Philippines Must Strike a Balance When China's Xi Jinping Comes to Visit, Analysts Say". *South China Morning Post*, www.scmp.com/news/china/diplomacy/article/2171100/philippines-must-strike-balance-when-chinas-xi-jinping-comes (accessed on 2018, December 1)

4   Indian strategy and the military dimension of the South China Sea dispute

By virtue of its unique geographical location in the Indo-Pacific region, India has historically acted as a passive balancer to China's expansion in Southeast Asia, in the sense that the kingdoms of Kambuja[1] and Champa[2] were credited with "evectional claims to the gratitude of the Indian people" for having barred the land route of Chinese expansion for a thousand years. This claim has been substantiated by the historian, K.M. Panikkar as he contended:

> If ever the expanding Empire of China did not extend its authority to Singapore and if the Indian Ocean remains today what its name indicates, it is due to the resistance which Kambuja and Champa put up against the continuous pressure of China.
>
> (Panikkar, 1960: 96)

Moreover, Panikkar acknowledged the Sailendra Dynasty's role in impeding Chinese hegemonic expansion into Southeast Asia, mainly in the Indonesian Archipelago. From a geostrategic perspective, he portrayed the geographical reach of India as jutting out for a thousand miles into the Indian Ocean, thus constituting an area "walled off" on three sides by land, with the southern part of Asia forming a canopy over it, in a manner in which, whatever angle may be used to view India, the concept of an "Indian security sphere" covering the entire Indian Ocean Region (IOR) was evident. This strategic salience of India's geopolitical situation, acting as a security umbrella over the countries of Southeast Asia, was a vindication of the Viceroy (of British India) Lord Curzon's strategic posturing of India as a "fortress ... if rival and unfriendly influences move up to it and lodge themselves under our walls, we are compelled to intervene, because a danger would grow up that one day might menace our security" (Panikkar, 1943: 70). Thus, the imperative of building and projecting India's naval power and outreach was underscored as an absolute instrument for defending its coastal and oceanic frontiers.

The geopolitical imperative and philosophy underlying India's strategic thinking and policy traces its foundations to Lord Curzon's emphasis on the centrality of India in the Indian Ocean, as he acknowledged in his essay, "The Place of India in the Empire" (1909):

The master of India, must, under modern conditions, be the greatest power in the Asiatic Continent, and therefore, it may be added, in the world .... on the north-east and east it can exert great pressure upon China, and it is one of the guardians of the autonomous existence of Siam. On the high seas, it commands the routes to Australia and to the China Seas.

(Raja Mohan, 2003: 204–205)

Although Lord Curzon had envisaged a role for India within the scaffold of British imperial interests, his ideas bore the seeds of an Indo-centric vision of Southeast Asia and the IOR. His strategic philosophy could be extended to propose that, when India did not dominate the region as Great Britain had done during the colonial era, it had the potential to emerge as a regional nucleus of power by harnessing its geopolitical situation. Thus, the genes of a proactive regional policy for India were inherent in the so-called "forward policy", associated with Lord Curzon which had gained a foothold in Britain's diplomatic vocabulary during the nineteenth century. This "forward" school of thought demanded British imperial control of the maritime routes and key ports en route to India, in order to secure the Crown's territorial sovereignty of its overseas Empire, along with the creation of buffer regions to insulate British-India's direct contact with the other empires. By stretching the analogy of contesting perspectives between the "forward looking" and "closed border"[3] strategies of India's foreign policy, with particular reference to Southeast Asia, the debate impinging on the conceptions of India playing a larger role in the region and securing its own territory was germane in the comprehension and justification of its policy approach towards the Southeast Asian region (Raja Mohan, 2003: 206). Thus, "India's key position – at the head of the Indian Ocean, astride the East-West trade routes – is an asset" (Kohli, 1978: 24), the preservation of which is an absolute strategic imperative. Given this historical premise, the first section and sub-sections of the chapter discuss the philosophy of India's maritime vision and doctrine as the backdrop to adopting its balancing strategy, comprising both internal and external balancing as a means to secure and sustain its role as a responsible maritime actor in the region. With this background, the second section analyses ASEAN's response to India's strategy in the SCS and identifies the blind spots therein.

1 India's maritime vision and doctrinal espousal

With maritime force having evolved as an inextricable part of India's overall policy in the Indo-Pacific region, the vision of transforming the Indian Navy into the "most potent and visible force" was introduced as the mantra of and institutionalised in the inaugural publication in 2004 and successive editions of the Maritime Doctrine, the knowledge-base underpinning the development of the country's maritime strategy. Identifying its legitimate duty of ensuring "good order at sea" and safeguarding the "greatest commons" in terms of the geo-economic arteries of International Shipping Lines (ISL) and SLOC flanking and traversing its primary and secondary areas of interest, the maritime philosophy, envisaged in successive editions of the Navy's capstone espousal, has carved a four-pronged role for it: military, diplomatic, constabulary and benign. Through the responsible execution of this four-pronged role, the Indian Navy has derived sustenance as a "stabilizing force" in the region, in addition to bolstering its geostrategic objectives and securing national interests (Admiral Sureesh Mehta's Interview with Rajat Pandit, 2006). Viewed in its entirety, India's maritime strategy is underpinned by the "freedom to use the seas for our national purposes, under all circumstances" (Prime Minister of India, Manmohan Singh's Message, 2007: iii) emphasizing the importance of the successful execution of sea control and denial or containment, as the predominant determinant and measure for pursuing the higher end of national interest, maritime combat effectiveness and other maritime operations. By virtue of its capability, strategic positioning and robust presence in the IOR, the Indian Navy has carved a niche for itself in executing its role as the "catalyst for peace, tranquility and stability in the region", thus bolstering its peacetime naval aspirations of projecting power and deterring the possibility of conflict. The Navy envisions the objective of developing conventional deterrence by denial and punishment: nuclear deterrence, exhibiting credibility, effectiveness and survivability as imbided in the sea-based segment of the nuclear triad, primarily the nuclear-powered submarine carrying ballistic missiles in adherence to the Indian Nuclear Doctrine's commitment to "No First Use"/"retaliation only"; and focusing on bolstering its robust capability to convince potential adversaries of the high costs and limited gains of aggression *(Ensuring Secure Seas: Indian Maritime Security Strategy, 2015: 80–81)*.

1.1 India's maritime vision: through the lens of the four editions of its Maritime Doctrine

The vision of India's emergence as "a core state" whose role would be crucial for long-term peace, stable balance of power, economic growth and security in the Indo-Pacific region, though in the offing since the 1990s, was officially envisaged in the *Indian Maritime Doctrine*, first propounded in 2004 and followed up in its 2007, 2009 and 2015 editions. In 2004, the Government of India, in its first enunciation of the Maritime Doctrine, underscored the need for a submarine-based credible Minimum Nuclear Deterrence capability, "inexorably linked" to the country's pursuit of an independent foreign policy posture, bolstering it with "the quiet confidence of a nation that seeks to be neither deferential nor belligerent". Through this doctrine, the Indian Navy endeavoured to project its power and sustain it across "its legitimate areas of interest stretching from the Persian Gulf to the Malacca Straits" *(Indian Maritime Doctrine, 2004, 2004: 56)*. In 2007, the subsequent version of the Doctrine, viz. *Freedom to Use the Seas: India's Maritime Military Strategy (IMMS-2007)* provided an overarching architecture for the effective exercise of maritime power and employment of its primary instruments, especially the Navy and Coast Guard, by emphasising the growing importance of the maritime environment and the centrality of maritime security for national development.

The Doctrine provided an insight and rationale for the resurgence of India's naval power and postulated the various ways in which the Indian Navy could serve as a catalyst for peace, security and stability in the IOR, including both the traditional and non-traditional constituents. It identified four important passages and choke points leading to and from the Indian Ocean, principally the Strait of Malacca, falling on the shortest sea route connecting the Persian Gulf with East Asia and the US; the Strait of Hormuz, which links the Arabian Sea with the Gulf of Oman and the Persian Gulf; the Strait of Bab-el-Mandeb and the Cape of Good Hope[4] and other principal ISL crossing the IOR among its primary areas of interest, choking or disruption of which impede sea-borne trade, prompting uncontrolled volatility in global oil and commodity prices. India's energy security has a vital role in national development, and is highly dependent on the seas. Nearly 80 per cent of the country's crude oil requirement is imported by sea, using the ISL across the Indian Ocean, while 11 per cent of national crude oil requirement is met from offshore energy sources within the Indian EEZ. The Indian Ocean serves as the "host to the world's busiest waterways" and almost 75 per cent of its traffic is headed for destinations beyond the region, thus transporting half the world's container shipment, one-third of its bulk cargo traffic and two thirds of oil shipment ("Remarks by External Affairs Minister of India, Sushma Swaraj at the 3rd Indian Ocean Conference", 2018). Therefore, the imperative of securitising the SLOC and principal ISL passing through India's areas of maritime interest is a primary responsibility of the Navy. Axiomatically, the doctrinal emphasis on securing chokepoints and the command of the sea, as a means of keeping the SLOC free and open, reflects on the geo-economic focus of safeguarding the "global commons", in consonance with the norms of a liberal, rules-based maritime order.

The Doctrine also identified SCS as its secondary area of interest, a domain having direct connection with areas of primary interest impinging on future deployment, along with the Southern IOR, Red Sea and East Pacific Region (Freedom to Use the Seas – India's Maritime Military Strategy, 2007: 27, 59–60). The 2009 edition of the Maritime Doctrine added two other prominent choke points, Singapore and the Mozambique Channel within its primary area of interest, in addition to extending the status of its secondary area of interest to the East China Sea, Western Pacific Ocean and their littoral regions based on diaspora, overseas investments and political relations. Furthermore, moving on from its preceding edition, it specifically mentioned all the choke points, leading to and from the Indian Ocean[5] within the Navy's primary area of interest (Indian Maritime Doctrine, 2009, 2009: 67–68). Sustaining its spree of working towards the development of a "modern and multi-dimensional navy" (United Through Oceans – International Fleet Review, 2016: 126) the most recent operational blueprint, in the form of a maritime guidance document, has been christened *Ensuring Secure Seas: Indian Maritime Security Strategy (IMSS – 2015)*. In keeping with the principles and concepts of national security and maritime power, enunciated in the Joint Doctrine (Indian Armed Forces) and the Indian Maritime Doctrine, it builds upon the Indian Navy's Vision Statement and Guiding

Principles, formulated in 2014, which highlight the strategic "way points" for the next decade. It reviews the key maritime strategic imperatives and influences, articulates the national maritime interests and defines related maritime security objectives, in addition to deriving corresponding strategies for their attainment. On the one hand, while acknowledging the hybrid nature of maritime challenges, exacerbated by the almost overlapping nature of traditional and non-traditional threats, the document emphasises the imperative of envisaging a seamless and holistic approach, advocating greater coordination between and among different maritime agencies. On the other hand, it justifies the significance of the Indian Navy as the primary instrument to secure the oceanic neighbourhood for economic purposes, given India's centrality in the IOR. To this end, the *IMSS – 2015* recommends a four-pronged approach for the Indian Navy under the present and emerging circumstances:

- First, it advocates a steady increase in the Indian Navy's operational footprints across its areas of maritime interest, with a growing cooperative framework and contribution as a net security provider. The term "net security provider" refers to the state of actual security available in an area, to balancing prevailing threats, inherent risks and rising challenges in a maritime environment against the ability to monitor, contain and counter these impulses in the neighbourhood, including deployments for anti-piracy, maritime security, NEO and HADR operations.
- Second, an expansion in maritime operational engagements, with an increased number and complexity of exercises with foreign navies, coordinated mechanisms for maritime security operations and enhanced training and technical and hydrographic cooperation with friendly maritime forces.
- Third, continued development of regional cooperative approaches to enhance maritime security in the IOR, including operational interactions such as MILAN, IONS and the emergence of maritime security cooperation as a priority area for the IORA.
- Fourth, the growth and development of the Indian Navy's force levels and maritime capabilities, with a steady focus on indigenisation. The revised Doctrine reflects the imperative for substantive enhancement in the Indian Navy's capabilities to exercise deterrence, to project maritime power, to provide maritime security and safeguard India's maritime interests. It advocates reinforcing and complementing the strategy of external balancing for deterrence with that of internal balancing through the development of appropriate force structures and capabilities, conduct of threat assessment and contingency planning, maintenance of strategic situational awareness, Maritime Domain Awareness, preparedness and presence and effective strategic communication (Ensuring Secure Seas: Indian Maritime Security Strategy, 2015: 8, 10–11).

The revised Doctrine advocates reinforcing and complementing the strategy of external balancing for deterrence with that of internal balancing by emphasising the development of appropriate force structures and capabilities, conduct of threat assessment and contingency planning, maintenance of strategic situational awareness and Maritime Domain Awareness, maintenance of preparedness and presence and effective strategic communication. Regarding the outreach of the Indian Navy's areas of interest, it dilates the geographical scope by expanding the two areas of interest southwards and westwards by bringing the South-West Indian Ocean and Red Sea within its primary areas of interest (Ensuring Secure Seas: Indian Maritime Security Strategy, 2015: 10–11, 32). In sum, the Indian Maritime Doctrines have served as the knowledge-base of the Indian Navy and provided the theoretical plank for adopting naval strategies commensurate with the translating nature of geostrategic and geo-economic challenges in the regional seascape, whether in the form of China's twenty-first-century MSR or non-traditional threats emanating from environmental disasters, humanitarian crises, accidents at sea or the menace of piracy, in particular with its offer of implementing the *Eyes in the Sky* programme, as part of the Malacca Strait Security Initiatives (MSSI) for jointly patrolling the Strait of Malacca. It deserves mention that the MSR is an umbrella term referring to China's maritime infrastructure projects in the Indo-Pacific region, including the planned construction of 18 overseas strategic support bases in the IOR, stretching from the Seychelles through Pakistan to Djibouti, with facilities for fuelling and material supply bases for peacetime use; relatively fixed supply bases for warship berthing, fixed-wing reconnaissance aircraft and naval staff ashore rest; and fully functional centres for replenishment, rest and large warship weapons maintenance; deep water ports and container terminals, proposed to connect with the mainland through a string of road and railway corridors, logistical stations, storage facilities and free-trade zones (Singh, 2015). Served by a network of roads, high-speed railways, fibre-optical lines, transcontinental submarine optical cable projects and satellite information passageways, the initiative is poised to shift the centre of geo-economic power towards Eurasia ("Vision and Actions on Jointly Building Silk Road Economic Belt and 21st- Century Maritime Silk Road", 2015). The MSR's principal rationale is the leveraging of China's economic, geostrategic and soft power clout and ensuring the security of SLOC in the Indian and Pacific Oceans, the littorals it passes through. In other words, it is a geostrategic posture to explore, using, protecting and managing the Oceans, involving maritime security, especially the protection of the islands claimed by China in the South and East China Seas, in addition to securing and safeguarding the vast energy and trade lanes, parts of which coincide with India's "areas of maritime interest". Given the nature of myriad challenges, the basic objective underpinning the Indian Maritime Doctrines has been the emphasis on upholding regional peace and tranquillity by engaging with neighbouring littoral states, extending mutual hands of friendship and cooperation, building trust and creating interoperability through joint exercises and maritime assistance, in addition to employing convincing deterrent power when called upon, "whilst maintaining a deterrent posture that ensures peace" (Admiral Sureesh, 2007: iv).

1.2 Practising the doctrinal guidelines: policy of external balancing

The LEP and its successor, AEP have acknowledged the instrumental role played by the Indian Navy in fortifying India's diplomatic outreach to the countries of Southeast and East Asia, thereby serving as the edifice of the policy of external balancing. The fulcrum, thus provided by the LEP and AEP and the Maritime Doctrines, highlights the imperative to build cooperative maritime security linkages with the littoral countries of ASEAN and other East Asian partners, namely Australia, Japan, New Zealand and South Korea, in the sphere of both traditional and non-traditional security echelons. These interactions, whether bilateral or multilateral, including port calls by naval vessels, joint exercises, patrolling, interdiction, anti-piracy operations and naval deployments are aimed at promoting sustained coordination through engagement, security operations, capacity-building and enhancement within the broad spectrum of developing Maritime Domain Awareness. It is aimed at bolstering the Navy's forward presence and capacity to providing rapid response, summarily widening the channels of strategic communication and interoperability with regional stakeholders as a cardinal means of conducting maritime diplomacy. This engagement fulfils the diplomatic role of the Indian Navy as it aspires to build "bridges of friendship", fosters constructive maritime engagement with regional navies, while simultaneously signalling the intent and capability to deter potential adversaries. While the level and intensity of engagement and exchanges with the littoral navies has exhibited variations, the crux of the matter lies in the enhanced visibility of the Indian Navy in the region, which has definitely served to build confidence among its ASEAN and non-ASEAN EAS partners, while simultaneously demonstrating to China the outreach and show of strength and solidarity with the regional navies, across a broad spectrum of conventional and non-conventional security issues. The exercises and war games undertaken by the Indian and regional navies demonstrate the former's capability to play its four-pronged role, viz. military, diplomatic, constabulary and benign, as envisaged in the Naval Doctrines. A brief discussion of the methods of external balancing undertaken by the Indian Navy, viz. Passage Exercise (PASSEX); Coordinated Patrol (CORPAT); occasional exercises; institutionalised bilateral and multilateral exercises and high-level maritime strategic interactions (Ensuring Secure Seas: Indian Maritime Security Strategy, 2015: 86–91) follows below:

- PASSEX: the passage exercises are conducted when naval ships pass near each other's coast. The Indian Navy holds PASSEXs with Singapore and Cambodia to ensure freedom of navigation, countering piracy and providing coordinated responses to natural disasters.
- CORPAT: the patrolling exercises are conducted on either side of the International Maritime Boundary Line (IMBL) by naval ships and aircraft in a coordinated manner, aimed at enhancing mutual understanding, interoperability, surveillance and information-sharing. The Indian Navy conducts CORPATs with Indonesia (India-Indonesia Coordinated Patrolling/IND-INDOCORPAT; 33 editions as of March–April 2019), Myanmar (Indo-Myanmar CORPAT/

IMCOR; seven cycles till 2018) and Thailand (Indo-Thai CORPAT; 27 editions till November 2018). These include a gamut of activities related to the observance of regulations regarding protection and conservation of natural resources and marine environment, prevention and suppression of illegal fishing, drug trafficking, piracy, exchange of information on prevention of smuggling and illegal immigration and conduct of SAR operations at sea.

- Institutionalised bilateral exercises: the exercises are conducted on a regular basis in areas of maritime interest to stay apace with the evolving character of traditional and non-traditional maritime challenges. India has institutionalised bilateral exercises with Indonesia, Myanmar (India-Myanmar Naval Exercise/IMNEX), Singapore (Singapore-India Maritime Bilateral Exercise/SIMBEX), Vietnam, as well as EAS members like Australia (Australia-India Exercise/AUSINDEX) and Japan (Japan-India Maritime Exercise/JIMEX).

- Occasional exercises: these include maritime security exercises (including HADR) and overseas deployments. In a unique bid to celebrate the completion of two decades of India-ASEAN dialogue relations and a decade of summit-level partnership, INS *Sudarshini*, the sail training ship of the Indian Navy, embarked on a historical six-month voyage (September 2012–March 2013) of all the ASEAN countries (barring Laos). A collaborative venture of the Ministries of Defence and External Affairs, Government of India, this voyage conducted by India's "Ambassador at Large" not only retraced the civilisational and historical links between India and Southeast Asia, but also identified the contemporary maritime linkages of trade and technology as factors contributing to the holistic development and economic flourishing of India and ASEAN. Since then, the Indian Navy has sustained the tempo of operational deployments, ranging from two weeks to two months and more to the SCS, Southern Indian Ocean and Western Pacific, with port calls to Cambodia, Indonesia, Malaysia, the Philippines, Singapore, Thailand and Australia. In addition to demonstrating the enhanced outreach and fleet strength of the Indian Navy in its domains of maritime interest, by employing an array of vessels ranging from guided-missile stealth and multi-role frigates, warships, anti-submarine corvettes, missile destroyers, fleet tankers and support ships, these deployments facilitate strategic communication with counterparts, fostering familiarisation, professional communication and interoperability, particularly in the conduct of Table Top exercises.[6] Another significant matrix of non-traditional security collaboration between India and ASEAN where the Indian Navy has demonstrated its responsible role as the first responder is the HADR endeavours, undertaken in the wake of environmental disasters, particularly the devastating Indian Ocean Tsunami, cyclones and typhoons in Indonesia, Myanmar and the Philippines, as well as the conduct of SAR operations after the Malaysian Airlines aircraft, MH 370 went missing in 2014. Such assistance has been instrumental in reassuring the beneficiary communities and instilling their confidence in India's capabilities and readiness to address contingency issues, thereby bolstering its role as a "net security provider" and first responder in the Indo-Pacific region.

- High-level maritime strategic interactions: held periodically to improve strategic communication, share strategic maritime perspectives and review measures for maritime cooperation through the exchange of White Shipping information[7]; imparting training to Naval and Coast Guard personnel, in seamanship, navigation, ship handling, boat work, technical aspects, etc., and coordination of logistics and services support for repair and maintenance of naval ships, submarines and naval aircrafts, including ship-borne aviation assets. Furthermore, India's participation in the Cooperative Mechanism on the Strait of Malacca and Singapore and contribution to two of the six International Maritime Organisation (IMO) Projects (Project 1 and Project 4) with Malaysia for enhancement of navigational safety and environmental protection in the Strait has added heft to bilateral maritime interactions. As signatories of the Regional Cooperation Agreement on Combating Piracy and Armed Robbery of Ships in Asia (ReCAAP), India and ASEAN member-states have institutionalised a mechanism of seizure of ships or aircraft involved in piracy and armed robbery, besides cooperating in information sharing, capacity-building and cooperation for extradition and mutual legal assistance.

- Multilateral exercises: on the multilateral promenade, the navies of India and a majority of the littoral Southeast Asian and other Indo-Pacific nations have been engaged in naval exercises like MILAN and the trilateral MALABAR. MILAN, held biennially since 1995,[8] had started with India, Indonesia, Singapore, Thailand and Sri Lanka as members, and was subsequently extended to embrace Australia, Bangladesh, Brunei, Malaysia, the Maldives, Mauritius, Myanmar, New Zealand, the Philippines and Vietnam. The tenth edition of the MILAN, held in March 2018, has been hailed as the largest multilateral exercise to be conducted in the Andaman Seas. The wide range of both land and sea-phase exercises comprising of SAR, Visit-Board-Search and Seize, casualty evacuation, anti-air tracking, surface gun firing, practice approaches for replenishment at sea, close manoeuvring of fleet formations, helicopter operations and high-speed boat operations ("MILAN 2018", 2018) facilitated interoperability, in addition to demonstrating complementarities, coordination and goodwill among the participating navies. In addition to these exercises at the multilateral level, India is an integral part of strategic consultative fora in the region, among which the ADMM+8, IONS and IORA deserve mention. New Delhi's induction in the ADMM+8 mechanism in October 2010 is another strategic milestone, within the scaffold of which, Defence Ministers representing the ADMM+8 member-states[9] meet biennially and discuss, consult and explore areas of cooperation to address the conventional and non-conventional regional security threats. Additionally, it proposes to conduct joint exercises and training sessions between the defence establishments of the member countries. Besides, IONS, a voluntary initiative that seeks to increase maritime cooperation among the navies of the IOR littoral states, including Australia, India, Indonesia, Japan, Malaysia, Myanmar, Singapore and Thailand, in addition to 25 other regional counterparts, provides an open and inclusive forum for discussion of regionally relevant maritime issues. Since the 1st IONS "Conclave of Chiefs" was chaired by India in 2008, the forum has been meeting biennially, organising annual seminars and workshops, thus emerging as a podium for fostering maritime cooperation among the Indian Ocean littoral states. Having celebrated its tenth anniversary in November 2018, the IONS, led by India, has evolved as an extremely significant regional maritime security initiative for promoting a shared understanding of issues facing the region, formulating strategies and cooperative mechanisms to enhance regional security and strengthen capabilities to ensure speedy responses to requirements of HADR ("10th Anniversary of Indian Ocean Naval Symposium to be Hosted on 13–14 November 2018", 2018). Finally, the IORA, an organisation of 22 member-states, including regional states like Australia, India, Indonesia, Malaysia, Singapore and Thailand and nine Dialogue Partners belonging to the IOR, are committed to expand understanding and mutually beneficial cooperation for addressing the challenges facing the region. Through the conduct of flagship projects like the Indian Ocean Dialogue, the Association aims to work on its focus areas, with an emphasis on maritime safety and security, disaster risk management and exploring the blue economy, to fostering cooperation and to share knowledge, experiences and best practices ("Priorities and Focus Areas: Indian Ocean Rim Association", 2017) among the member-states.

1.3 Policy of internal balancing: complementing the external balancing strategy

The Indian Navy has traversed a long pathway since Independence. Regular alignment and planned up-gradation, in keeping with the ever transient nature of the regional environment and the complexity of traditional and non-traditional challenges, have catapulted the Navy to the redoubtable position it holds today. The enunciation of the Inaugural Maritime Strategy in 1988 has been followed up periodically with various editions of the Indian Maritime Doctrine (2004, 2007, 2009 and 2015), the Maritime Capability Perspective Plan (MCPP) and the Maritime Infrastructure Perspective Plan (MIPP) which focus on building infrastructure along with the blueprint for international collaboration and a roadmap for the development of Science and Technology and the Indian Naval Indigenisation Plan (INIP) (2015), thereby providing a concrete base for realising its vision of emerging as a blue water naval force, in addition to bolstering its strategy of internal balancing. The MCPP's impetus on capacity-building has laid down the template for the development and modernisation of the naval force through a 15-year window (2005–2022), aspiring to build a three-dimensional force, capable of addressing the slew of maritime challenges. The ambitious Plan is poised to raise the Navy into a "brand new" avatar by 2027 (Chand, 2012) and evolve into a "world-class navy" by 2050, galvanised with the proposed contingent of 200 ships, 500 aircraft and a handsome submarine fleet (Banerjee, 2018). As identified by the INIP, the Indian Navy has progressed substantially in the sphere of indigenisation within the framework of the Fifteen Year Indigenisation Plan prepared and promulgated in 2003, and revised and re-promulgated in 2008 for the period spanning 2008–2022, on its initial journey from a "Buyer's Navy" to a "Builder's Navy". It deserves mention in this context that prior to the introduction of the INIP, the equipment and machinery fitted on board ships in the three categories of "Float"[10], "Move"[11] and "Fight"[12] had been indigenised to the extent of 90 per cent, 60 per cent and 30 per cent respectively. Further, while sufficient and reasonable self-reliance has been achieved in the first and second categories, there is a large shortfall in the third category, which the present Plan endeavours to address, thereby facilitating its evolution into a "designer's navy".

Taking the indigenous route to development, flagged by the Make in India initiative introduced in 2014, the Plan presents itself not only as an enabler of national self-reliance in equipment and systems, but also as the facilitator of the Indian Navy's symbiosis with various sectors of the industry, cutting across the spectrum of Defence Public Sector Units, the large private industries or Medium, Small and Micro Enterprises to partake of the indigenous development of cutting-edge defence technologies. The aspiration to develop both indigenous capability and capacity across the spectrum of warship operations, surface ships design, submarine design, weapons system integration, armaments, etc., is aimed at addressing the lacunae in fostering credible research and development (R&D) in military sciences and technologies, the inadequate amalgamation between R&D and the manufacturing sector and the near absence of an integrated approach among users, designers and manufacturers (Indian Naval Indigenisation Plan, 2015–2030, 2015: Preamble, 2, 9). Furthermore, the latest version of the MIPP (2018) envisages the increase in the Navy's operational preparedness and surveillance capabilities, bolstering all aspects of induction of assets for various platforms, aircraft carriers and submarines by 2027, as a means to "ensur[e] training infrastructure is in sync with the induction of assets" (Hooda, 2018) Given this backdrop, the present section analyses the internal balancing strategy from the perspective of naval infrastructure development and up-gradation, with Make in India's thrust on the indigenisation and self-reliance in terms of equipment and infrastructure. The successful execution of the Make in India initiative finds manifestation in at least five projects, as the Indian Navy follows the upward trajectory of capacity expansion and self-reliance, within the wide ambit of implementing its policy of internal balancing. The projects are discussed below:

- Project 15A and 15B Destroyers: this project includes follow-on ships of the legendary Project 15 "Delhi" class Guided Missile Destroyers, which entered service in the late 1990s. A milestone in the Navy's self-reliance programme was reached, with the commissioning of INS *Kochi*, the second of the destroyers in 2015, close on the heels of INS *Kolkata* in 2014. Equipped with stealth concepts, INS *Kochi* has many firsts to her credit, including a very large component of indigenous combat-suite, the most sophisticated state-of-the-art weapons and sensors such as the vertically launched Long Range Surface to Air Missiles (LRSAM) and Multi-Function Surveillance, Track and Guidance Radar (MF-STAR), the advanced supersonic and long range BrahMos supersonic cruise missiles. Classified as a "Network of Networks", it is equipped with sophisticated digital networks, such as Asynchronous Transfer Mode based information highway, Integrated Ship Data Network, Combat Management System (CMS), used to integrate information from other platforms by an indigenous data-link system, in order to bolster Maritime Domain Awareness, the Automatic Power Management System and the Auxiliary Control System ("INS Kochi", 2015). Therefore, its commissioning reflects firm anchoring on self-reliance and indigenisation as the pivot of the Indian Navy's roadmap for expansion and growth ("INS Kochi Commissioned at Mumbai", 2015).

Of the four proposed ships to be built under the Project 15B, the maiden guided missile destroyer, INS *Visakhapatnam* was launched in 2015 and its delivery timeline will commence in 2021. Incorporated with new design concepts for improved survivability, sea keeping, stealth and manoeuvrability, its launch heralded the Navy's progressive step from a "Buyer's Navy" to a "Builder's Navy" ("INS Visakhapatnam, First Ship of Project 15 B Launched", 2015). Furthermore, the second and third guided missile destroyers attached to the project, INS *Murmagao* and INS *Imphal*, equipped with an array of state-of-the-art weapons and sensors, including MF-STAR and LRSAM for long-distance engagement of shore, sea-based and air targets and the capacity to carry and operate two multiple-role helicopters ("Launch of Yard 12706", 2019) were launched in September 2016 and April 2019 respectively.

- Project 17A: in 2017, the Indian Navy embarked upon the construction of a seven-fleet strong new class of advanced stealth frigates under this project. Equipped with the capacity to launch LRSAM, BrahMos missiles, anti-submarine weapons, comprising of a pair of rocket launchers[13] and a pair of triple-tube torpedo launchers, the first series of the three ships is expected to be delivered between 2023 and 2025 for sea trials (Mazumdar, 2018).
- Project 28: following the commissioning of the first indigenous Anti-Submarine Warfare (ASW) stealth corvette in 2014, three other ASW corvettes have been launched under this project, with the fourth ("Kavaratti" class) launched in 2015. These ships are equipped with a Total Atmospheric Control System, an Integrated Platform Management System, enhanced stealth features like the Low Radar Cross Section and reduced Infra Red Signature and are capable of carrying and operating one multiple role helicopter. In this context, the commissioning of the INS *Kadmatt* in 2016 and INS *Kiltan* in 2017, equipped to fight in nuclear, biological and chemical warfare conditions as well as featuring the integration of a host of weapons and sensors, mirrored the high level of indigenisation, marking "yet another milestone in our journey towards self-reliance and Make-in-India" and catapulting the Indian Navy into the elite club group of building stealth ships ("INS *Kadmatt* Commissioned at Visakhapatnam", 2016; Siddiqui, 2017). The weapons and sensor suite is predominantly indigenous and includes heavy weight torpedoes, ASW rockets, bow-mounted sonar and air surveillance radar "Revathi", among

others. Its uniqueness is contained in the successful consolidation of small and medium-scale industries towards constructing state-of-the-art ships under this project, steadily broadening the indigenisation efforts beyond ship-building (Bhattacharjee, 2017). This comes against the backdrop of INS *Arihant*, a nuclear armed submarine, which conducted its first deterrence patrol in November 2018, thereby operationalising the third and most long-lasting segment of India's nuclear triad.

- Project 75 (India/I): this project encompasses the construction of six stealth "Scorpene" submarines, based on indigenous design, in Indian shipyards (with international collaboration), with the objective of reversing India's status as one of the largest importers of submarines in the world. Presently, the Indian Navy has 13 conventional, one nuclear attack and four Howaldts-werke-Deutsche Werft (HDW) submarines as part of its underwater fleet. Following the induction of INS *Kalvari*, the first submarine of this project in December 2017, the second, INS *Khanderi* was inducted on September 28, 2019. The remaining four, namely INS *Karanj*, INS *Vela*, INS *Vagir* and INS *Vagsheer* are undergoing advanced, pre-induction trials. The Navy has also embarked upon a futuristic design plan following P 75 (I), which is expected to be launched by 2020, envisaging "all future submarines will be of our own design and will be made in India" (Pubby, 2018).

- Indigenous Aircraft Carriers (IACs): The onward trajectory of India fulfilling its cherished dream of operating a three-carrier naval force by 2030 is pro-gressing ambitiously as the first IAC, which would offer unmatched utility for a variety of tasks including anti-submarine warfare, is likely to be commis-sioned as INS *Vikrant* in 2020. This would provide a significant fillip to the Navy's blue water capability, enhancing the reach and impact of carrier-borne strike forces, both as a means of deterrence and during combat operations. On the other hand, the case of the second IAC, INS *Vishal* is awaiting official approval and the construction of the third, INS *Vikramaditya* is set to com-mence by 2021, thus ensuring that two carriers will be operationally available, even if the third undergoes a refit. Once inducted, a MiG-29 squadron would be positioned at the Eastern Naval Command in the Andaman and Nicobar Islands. The importance of these carriers for boosting the Navy's military sinews lies in their capacity to enhance the number of carrier battle groups (Gurung, 2018). A perfect complement of the submarine fleet, necessary for "sea denial", a carrier battle group is imperative for "sea control", beefing up the Navy's role in the Indo-Pacific. Moreover, lauding the quotient of self-reliance of the Steel Authority of India Ltd. in manufacturing the steel required to build submarines and warships, the Chief of Indian Naval Staff, Admiral Sunil Lanba expressed satisfaction regarding the possession of "self-sufficient and reliant teams of experts to make aircraft carriers to advanced submarines", weapons and sensors, thereby boosting the Navy's vision of inducting "more and more submarines, aircraft in coming days" ("Satisfied with Naval Fleet, More to be Inducted: Lanba", 2019). With significant indigenous content, these ships are a true hallmark of the self-reliance attained by India in warship design and shipbuilding and a shining example of the Make in India philosophy. In addition, eight Landing Craft Utility vessels, of which the first was commissioned in 2017, four Fast Attack Craft and 14 Immediate Support Vessels are in various stages of construction or launch, while the first prototype of Light Combat Aircraft (Navy), which will operate from the IAC, has successfully undergone tests. The acquisition of six indigenously built Next Generation Offshore Patrol Vessels fitted with a state-of-the-art sensor suite with increased endurance, for use in military operations for seaward defence, protection of offshore assets, maritime interdiction operations, surveillance missions, search and seizure operations and non-military operations like anti-piracy, counter-infiltration missions, HADR and SAR missions as a boost to its operational capacity, was approved by the Government of India in 2018. This is to be followed up with the acquisition of Next Generation Missile Boats, Frigates and Destroyers, currently under design. These platforms will bolster maritime security by undertaking a multitude of operational roles, both in blue-water and littorals (Shukla, 2018).

As the twin arm of enhancing the profile of India's defence acquisition drive and encouraging self-reliance in this sphere, the imperative of bolstering and developing infrastructure in the A&N Islands, rightly acknowledged to provide a "commanding presence in the Bay of Bengal as well as serve as India's window into East and Southeast Asia" ("INS 'Baaz' – Commissioned by Admiral Nirmal Verma as First Naval Air Station in Nicobar Group of Islands", 2012) cannot be overlooked. The commissioning of INS *Baaz* as the first naval air station (NAS) in 2012, followed up by INS *Utkrosh* and INS *Kohassa* provides India with the podium to keep a hawk-like eye on the strategic areas of interest of the Indian Navy, particularly the Malacca Strait and the Six Degree Channel. Although initially equipped to operate light to heavy aircraft capable of short field operations from the runway of about 3,500 ft (with projected plans to accommodate an extended airstrip of 6,000 ft) these bases are indispensable for information-gathering, based on airborne maritime surveillance using aircraft, Unmanned Aerial Vehicles (UAVs) and a robust radar network, pivotal to undertaking EEZ surveillance, anti-poaching, SAR and HADR missions, thus holistically contributing to the Navy's Maritime Domain Awareness. The strategic importance of the A&N Islands was revealed years back in 2001, with the construction of the 1st Tri-service Theatre Command[14] of the Indian Armed Forces, based at Port Blair (FENC) allowing it to keep a close watch on China's naval forays in the Indian Ocean, safeguarding the sea lanes converging on the Malacca Strait and also offering a good launch pad for India's anticipated role as a net security provider in the Indo-Pacific. This integrated Command was created to eventually build up a credible force and the capability to deploy these forces rapidly to safeguard India's strategic interests in the region. In 2001 NAS Shibpur was established as a forward operating air base for enhanced surveillance in North Andaman, and was intended to be developed as a fully fledged air base for round-the-clock operation with a 12,000 ft long runway. In order to bolster and further upgrade the FENC's infrastructure, India proposes to construct better-equipped runways at all NASs, in addition to improving surveillance capabilities, particularly at NAS Shibpur and Campbell Bay. In January 2019, the Indian Navy opened its third naval air facility at NAS Shibpur commissioned as INS *Kohassa*, while preparations to convert the NAS at Diglipur into a fully fledged base continue. The airstrips of the third base, with the operational capacity of short range maritime reconnaissance aircraft and helicopters, are proposed to be extended from the current 3,000 ft to 10,000 ft, so as to accommodate fighter jets and bigger planes of the ilk of the Indian Navy's Boeing P-8I long range maritime reconnaissance and anti-submarine aircraft. Moreover, these are to have extended jetties along the harbour for mooring aircraft carriers and large warships and a naval ammunition depot for replenishing the fleet during contingencies (Peri, 2019). Envisaged to serve as an extended arm and deterrent to the PLAN's expanding naval presence, the air bases will be instrumental in bringing a larger area under monitoring, surveillance, information dissemination and beefing up the A&N Command's sinews to operate independently from all the areas of this Union Territory. The base is self-contained with fuel storage, repair facilities and manpower under a commanding officer ("With 'INS Kohassa', India Set to Get Fourth Air Base in the Andamans", 2019).

In another first, the Indian Navy commissioned three of its indigenous Landing Craft Utility (LCU) ships at A&N in 2017–2018, to play a significant role in the transportation of military equipment such as main battle tanks, armoured vehicles with fully equipped troops, etc. Based in the A&N and with six LCUs inducted in the Navy as of July 2019 under this project, this initiative gives a significant boost to the Command's capability in undertaking multi-role activities such as beaching operations, HADR, SAR and supply and replenishment of distant islands ("Commissioning of Third Ship of Landing Craft Utility Mk-IV 'IN LCU L53' (GRSE Yard 2094) at Port Blair", 2018). Furthermore, in 2018, India inaugurated the laying of 1,450 miles dedicated submarine optical fibre cable, the "Chennai Andaman Nicobar Island" cable system, as a direct communication link between mainland (Chennai) and Port Blair and seven other islands, viz. Little Andaman, Car Nicobar, Havelock, Kamorta, Long, Rangat and Great Nicobar. Heralded as possessing "immense strategic significance to India in addition to assisting the Andaman and Nicobar Islands communications security, especially during natural disasters or failure of other systems", it would also enable the Navy to have access to real-time data on commercial ships and naval platforms, once India is authorised to patrol the Malacca Strait (Rohit, 2018). In 2017, the Indian Navy, in a bid to bolster its operational presence in the Indian Ocean littorals, transitioned a "new mission-based deployment", "maximising our time at sea with defined outcomes in our areas of interest" in addition to "assur[ing] our friends that the Indian Navy is available to assist in the event of any contingency". This involves enhancing the Navy's operational capacity by several notches through the deployment of combat-ready ships and aircraft along critical, vulnerable SLOC and choke points in the Indian Ocean, from the Persian Gulf and Gulf of Aden to the Malacca Strait and Sunda Strait. Envisaged as a ploy to challenge the almost ubiquitous nature of PLAN warships and submarines in the littorals, it proposes to "deploy mission-ready warships" and aircraft on a 24/7 basis round the year, with the warships being sustained and turned around on station. This would be a significant complement to the existing permanent positioning of 12–15 destroyers, frigates, corvettes and large patrol vessels in the IOR, supported by naval satellite "Rukmini" (GSAT-7) and daily sorties by Poseidon P-8I maritime patrol aircraft (Pandit, 2017). The developments discussed above, pertaining both to the strategies of external and internal balancing, are pointers to the Indian Navy's proportionate response through a strategy of counter power-projection and operational tempo in its areas of interest, resulting in bolstered maritime presence and outreach embellishing its credentials as an "outcome-oriented", vigilant security provider in the Indo-Pacific.

2 ASEAN'S response to India's balancing policy

ASEAN's response to India's policy of balancing discussed above is borne out by the willingness of the member-states to bolster defence cooperation with India, institutionalise Strategic Partnership and elevate it to the level of Comprehensive Strategic Partnership. This is in addition to ASEAN acknowledging officially in unison with India across a range of bilateral and multilateral fora the need to secure the regional littorals, as per international norms of freedom of navigation and overflight. Before embarking on a bilateral-level analysis of the policies undertaken by ASEAN member-states with respect to engaging with India diplomatically in the following sub-section, it should be remembered that, within the ambit of the LEP, India's steady graduation from a Full Dialogue Partner to attaining the membership of the ARF and subsequently becoming a "Plus One" (Summit-level) associate, followed by its inclusion within the EAS and ADMM+8 in 2005 and 2010 respectively and sharing Strategic Partnership with ASEAN since 2012 constituted an adroit edifice for the development and entrenchment of India-ASEAN ties. Thus, the legacy of the LEP, subsequently carried forward by the AEP, bolstered by its responsibility for ensuring regional peace and stability in the region and its demonstrated capabilities and aspirations, has been pivotal in evoking a positive response from ASEAN *vis-à-vis* India's position.

2.1 India's strategic engagement with ASEAN member-states: expanding the horizon

ASEAN has welcomed India's role as a responsible actor in the Indo-Pacific and acknowledged its ascendance as a net security provider in helping shape the regional strategic discourse that has been drifting towards uncertainty and militarisation. ASEAN expects India to play a more pro-active role in the regional security ambience, especially with reference to the SCS issue. This has been borne out not only within the organizational domain spelt out in various joint declarations, statements and agreements, but also at the bilateral level, as enumerated in this sub-section. To begin with, among the founding members of ASEAN, India has elevated relations to the level of Strategic Partnership with Malaysia, Singapore and Indonesia, while Thailand is seeking to establish the same. The Strategic Partnership established between India and Malaysia in 2010 forms the basis for their mutual cooperation for "peace, prosperity and security of the Asia-Pacific region and beyond", necessitated by their desire "to shape an open, transparent and inclusive regional order" (Joint Statement on the Framework for the India-Malaysia Strategic Partnership, 2010: Cls. 19, 23). Bilateral agreements on promoting joint collaboration in the defence sector, including the spheres of equipment and industry, research, training and capacity-building and establishing the mechanism for information-sharing on White Shipping and HADR, form important steps to this end (Joint Statement on Enhanced Malaysia-India Strategic Partnership, 2015: Cls. 18, 20). With the "long traditions of friendship based on mutual trust and respect and a shared history" forming the basis of bilateral ties between India and Singapore, the two countries have established a Strategic Partnership in 2015. Defence cooperation has been acknowledged to be its vital component, including collaboration in defence technology, co-development and co-production; bolstering cooperation in the sphere of maritime security to reaffirm a shared commitment to freedom of navigation, overflight, unimpeded commerce and safety of SLOC; operationalisation of the Technical Agreement on the Sharing of White-Shipping Information (Joint Statement on a Strategic Partnership between India and Singapore, 2015) and implementation of the agreement concerning Mutual Coordination, Logistics and Services Support for Naval Ships, Submarines and Naval Aircraft (including Ship borne Aviation Assets) visits (List of Memoranda of Understanding Signed between India and Singapore during the Visit of Prime Minister of India to Singapore, 2018). The signing of a New Comprehensive Strategic Partnership (2018) between India and Indonesia complemented the adoption of a "Shared Vision on Maritime Cooperation in the Indo-Pacific". Forming the basis for developing further maritime cooperation, the Vision Document envisages establishing "an open, inclusive and transparent cooperation, with the aim of delivering peace, security and prosperity to all associated with the region"; promoting "information-sharing related to maritime security in the Indo-Pacific region" and enhancing strategic technical cooperation on maritime security including an expanded maritime awareness, primarily to emerge as a force of immense stability in the region. These proposals are aimed at securing "sovereignty and territorial integrity, international law, in particular UNCLOS, freedom of navigation and over-flight and sustainable development" (Shared Vision of India-Indonesia Maritime Cooperation in the Indo-Pacific, 2018). Within the framework of the New Comprehensive Strategic Partnership, the identification of their defence industries for joint production of equipment, technology transfer, technical assistance and capacity-building as well as sourcing of defence equipment offers great potential to expand mutual cooperation in this sphere (India-Indonesia Joint Statement during the Visit of Prime Minister of India to Indonesia, 2018: Cl. 18). In a bid to provide a fillip to cooperation and comprehensive Maritime Domain Awareness, India and Thailand have been keen on securing SLOC; completion of the negotiation for the signing of the White Shipping Agreement; additionally Thailand has expressed interest in the Indian defence industry and its expertise for R&D. Furthermore, the new security cooperation mechanism under the JWG on Security Cooperation as well as the Joint Task Force on Maritime Security has been engaged in deepening maritime and defence cooperation covering ocean safety and disaster management (India-Thailand Joint Statement during the Visit of the Prime Minister of Thailand to India, 2016: Cls. 14–16). Recognising the imperative to strengthen defence and security cooperation, India and the Philippines have developed an impressive trajectory of mutual exchanges in military training and education, capacity-building, and regular goodwill naval visits, envisaging further collaboration in the spheres of Maritime Domain Awareness, intelligence sharing, capability-building, White Shipping and defence production. With respect to the volatile SCS issue, they have asserted "the importance of safeguarding the freedom of navigation and over-flight" and the settlement of all disputes by "peaceful means and of refraining from the threat or use of force, in accordance with universally recognised principles of international law" (Joint Statement of the 3rd India-Philippines Joint Commission on Bilateral Cooperation, 2015: Cls. 7, 11).

Among the later entrants of ASEAN, India and Vietnam elevated their Strategic Partnership (established in 2007) to a Comprehensive Strategic Partnership in 2016, which provides a "new direction, momentum and substance to our bilateral cooperation" and cements mutual efforts towards contributing to regional stability, security and prosperity. Acknowledging the need for complete compliance with international law, notably the UNCLOS, including the implementation of international legal obligations in good faith, the maintenance of freedom of navigation and overflight in the SCS, full respect for diplomatic and legal processes has been underscored by the two sides (India-Vietnam Joint Statement during the State Visit of President of Vietnam to India, 2018). Vietnam's burgeoning interest in engaging with India in the spectrum of defence has been reflected in the signing of the agreement on construction of offshore patrol boats and India's extension of a Defence Line of Credit to the tune of US$500 million in 2016 to facilitate extensive cooperation (Press Statement by the Prime Minister of India during his Visit to Vietnam, 2016). India and Myanmar have moved forward with the signing of an MoU on Maritime Security Cooperation; Sharing White Shipping Information and the Technical Agreement for providing Coastal Surveillance System (2017) in order to bolster capacity-building and bilateral maritime security collaboration (India-Myanmar Joint Statement Issued on the Occasion of the State Visit of Prime Minister of India to Myanmar, 2017: Cl. 9). The signing of the MoU on Defence Cooperation in July 2019 was another step towards strengthening maritime cooperation by joint surveillance and capacity-building, reviewing the conduct of joint exercises and training provided to the Myanmar Defence Services personnel by India (Senior General Ming Aung Hlaing, Commander-in-Chief of Myanmar Defence Services, Calls on Prime Minister Modi, 2019). It may be mentioned in this context that defence cooperation between India and Myanmar has scaled new heights with the latter's proposed acquisition of its maiden Kilo-class submarine from New Delhi by end-2019, along with a line of credit extended for Myanmar's military capacity enhancement (Pubby, 2019).

Prioritising SLOC security "to maintain peace and ensure safety and security of navigation in the Indo-Pacific Region" has been a common refrain of India and Cambodia, in addition to supporting the precepts of complete freedom of navigation and overflight and pacific resolution of maritime issues based on international law in the SCS (India-Cambodia Joint Statement during the State Visit of the Prime Minister of the Kingdom of Cambodia to India, 2018).

As India has embarked on the pathway of "reorienting our partnership in the twenty-first-century context to make it more pragmatic, action driven and result oriented" ("Keynote Address of the Minister of External Affairs of India at the Delhi Dialogue IX", 2017), identifying it as the necessary means of collectively addressing the various traditional and non-traditional security challenges ruffling regional peace and stability, the ASEAN member-states have explicitly alluded to the intensification of the dynamics of defence cooperation and linkages with India. This has been demonstrated and further facilitated within the Make in India ambit, which offers opportunities for FDI at 100 per cent, increasing the sectoral limit of existing sectors, simplifying other conditions of the FDI policy and removal of the clause requiring the single largest Indian ownership of equity to be 51 per cent and the lock-in period on equity transfer to be three years. The objective of the revamped FDI policy as an integral part of the Make in India scheme is to provide ease of doing business and flexibility of foreign investment in the defence industry, to reduce minimum capitalisation so as to foster cooperation in the spheres of defence equipment, technology and industry, and to encourage co-development, co-production, maintenance and up-gradation of defence platforms[15], R&D, training and military capacity-building. This is to be complemented by the continuation of regular high-level exchanges under the agreed dialogue mechanisms, joint naval exercises for enhancing mutual interoperability and closer consultation and coordination at the bilateral and multilateral levels, including EAS, ARF, ADMM+8, ASEAN-India Summits, etc. on maritime issues with a view to strengthening rule of law and ensuring freedom of navigation and safety of SLOC in the region.

2.2 ASEAN's imperative of maintaining the precarious balance between India and China

As ASEAN strives to constructively engage India in sustaining the architecture of regional peace and stability, it values the "unanimous and unwavering support for ASEAN centrality" accorded by India, and acknowledges it as a significant compatriot capable of maintaining the regional equilibrium (Lynn, 2013: 21). Notwithstanding these considerations, in order to emerge as a commensurate balancer to China, India continues a tight-rope walk, put forward by its asymmetric economic/trade and military capabilities *vis-à-vis* Beijing. This is of immense significance to ASEAN while computing and balancing its relational dynamics between India and China. China has come a long way since 1989, when its defence budget was roughly comparable to India (US$20 billion). By 2015, China's defence budget had leaped tenfold to US$215 billion, while that of India was US$51 billion. Furthermore, China's defence budget in 2016, which recorded

US$145 billion, was approximately equivalent to the sum of the budget allocation of Australia, India, Japan, the Philippines, Singapore and Vietnam (US$147 billion). This gap is projected to widen by 2030, as China is estimated to boast a Gross Domestic Product (GDP) of US$36.1 trillion, while the combined GDP of Australia, Japan, India, the Philippines and Vietnam will stand at US$27.7 trillion, implying its redoubtable capacity to bolster its military strength further (Rajagopalan, 2017: 12, 21). As the world's second largest spender on defence, China increased its military spending to US$250 billion in 2018, accounting for 14 per cent of global military expenditure. On the other hand, India's military expenditure accounted for US$66.5 billion in 2018, recording just 3.7 per cent of global military expenditure (Tian, Fleurant et al., 2019: 2). From the perspective of the latest defence budget (2019), China has increased it to US$177.61 billion from its previous year's figure of US$165 billion, posting a 7.5 per cent rise. The 2019 defence budget is over three times that of India, which accounts for US$44.6 billion ("At $177.6 billion, China's 2019 Defence Budget is over Three Times that of India", 2019), aptly indicating the skewed balance in favour of the former, given the escalating nature of security challenges in the region.

Second, with respect to trade with ASEAN, China outpaces India significantly. Poised to register US$1 trillion by 2020, as discussed in the preceding chapter, ASEAN-China trade in 2018 reached a record high of US$587 billion, pitching an increase of 14.1 per cent year on year and sustaining its position as ASEAN's largest trading partner for ten consecutive years ("China-ASEAN Trade Hits Record High in 2018", 2019). On the other hand, India-ASEAN trade hovers around US$81.3 billion (2017–2018) and US$86.8 billion (April 2018–February 2019), accounting for 10.12 per cent and 11.51 per cent of India's total trade value respectively (Export Import Data Bank, 2019). Although it is contended that the potential for India-ASEAN trade to develop further is huge but unexplored, realising it is incumbent on product integration and harmonisation, facilitating business to business connection, information exchange, mutual recognition of standards and the removal of non-tariff barriers (Gupta, 2018), the last factor in particular hindering the early conclusion of the Regional Comprehensive Economic Partnership (RCEP). Besides, India's trade relations are not uniform across the ASEAN spectrum, when analysed at the bilateral level: among the ten members, Singapore, Indonesia, Malaysia, Vietnam and Thailand feature among the top 25 trading countries accounting for US$24.2 billion, US$18.9 billion, US$15.7 billion, US$12.5 billion and US$10.8 billion respectively (April 2018–February 2019 data). These figures are in striking contrast to the meagre values posted by the remaining five member-states: the Philippines, Myanmar, Brunei, Cambodia and Laos, recording US$2.1 billion, US$1.5 billion, US$0.5 billion, US$0.2 billion and US$0.037 billion respectively (Export Import Data Bank, 2019).

In addition to the military and economic factors, it is equally important to underscore the position and predominance that China enjoys among the ASEAN-members, notwithstanding their contested and overlapping sovereignty claims in the disputed SCS, the reasons having been identified in the previous chapter. ASEAN and China are moving forward, subsequent to the conclusion of the framework agreement, or outline on the COC in August 2017; the concurrence on initiating negotiations for the text of a binding document on the SCS in November 2017, followed by the declaration of a shared commitment to promote peace and stability in the region at the ASEAN Retreat in February 2018 and the signing of the SDNT to provide the basis for further negotiations on specific provisions of the COC in 2019. Under the given circumstances, the organization, wary of being caught in a "cross-fire" (Saran, 2018) between New Delhi and Beijing, will be maintaining the precarious diplomatic balance. Simultaneously, as India consolidates and sustains both external and internal balancing strategies to bolster its engagement and capabilities, ASEAN is expected to be extremely forthcoming and appreciative of its role and responsible posture in the Indo-Pacific region.

Notes

1 Present Cambodia
2 Former South Vietnam
3 This strategy pressed for a moderate approach, conditioned by the consolidation of British-Indian territory within closed boundaries and accommodation with the rival European great powers
4 Other choke points include the Lombok and Sunda Straits which connect the SCS to the Indian Ocean; the Suez Canal and Red Sea; Six Degree Channel, Nine Degree Channel and the Horn of Africa
5 These included the Six Degree Channel; Eight/Nine Degree Channels; the Strait of Hormuz, Bab-el-Mandeb, Malacca, Singapore, Sunda and Lombok; the Mozambique Channel and the Cape of Good Hope and their littoral regions
6 A focused practice activity that places the participants in a simulated situation and tests their preparedness in mobilising resources in terms of HADR and SAR operations
7 Exchange of relevant advance information on the identity and movement of commercial non-military merchant vessels in order to facilitate Maritime Domain Awareness
8 The MILAN exercise was suspended in 2001 and 2005. In 2001, the Indian Navy hosted the International Fleet Review and, in 2005, the region was recovering from the grave effects of the December 2004 Indian Ocean Tsunami
9 ASEAN plus Australia, China, India, Japan, New Zealand, Russia, South Korea and the US
10 Includes all materials, equipment and systems associated with the hull structures and fittings of the ship
11 Includes Integrated Platform Management System/Automatic Power Management System of the ship
12 Includes all types of ship-borne weapons and sensor systems that directly improve the combat capability of the ship
13 Indigenous modification of the Soviet anti-submarine weapon rocket launcher, RBU 6000
14 Joint command of the Indian Army, Navy and Air Forces
15 Particularly beneficial for Malaysia and Vietnam as they share with India common lineage of military equipment of Russian origin

References

"10th Anniversary of Indian Ocean Naval Symposium to be Hosted on 13–14 November 2018". (2018). New Delhi: Ministry of Defence (Navy), www.indiannavy.nic.in/con

tent/10th-anniversary-indian-ocean-naval-symposium-be-hosted-13-14-november-2018 (accessed on 2019, May 12)

Admiral Sureesh Mehta. (2007). "Foreword", in *Freedom to Use the Seas: India's Maritime Military Strategy*. New Delhi: Ministry of Defence (Navy), http://aldeilis.net/mumbai/1686.pdf (accessed on 2019, April 1)

Admiral Sureesh Mehta, Interview with Rajat Pandit. (2006, November 1). "Blue Water Navy is the Aim", *Times of India*

"At $177.6 Billion, China's 2019 Defence Budget is over Three Times that of India". (2019, March 5), *Business Standard*

Banerjee, Ajay. (2018, December 4). "To Counter China, India to have 56 New Ships, Submarines", *The Tribune*

Bhattacharjee, Sumeet. (2017, October 16). "India in Elite Group with Stealth Ship", *The Hindu*

Chand, Naresh. (2012, December). "Indian Navy's Capability Perspective". *SP's Naval Forces*, 1, www.spsnavalforces.com/story/?id=184 (accessed on 2019, May 12)

"China-ASEAN Trade Hits Record High in 2018". (2019, March 13). *Xinhua*, www.xinhuanet.com/english/2019-03/13/c_137892383.htm (accessed on 2019, May 30)

"Commissioning of Third Ship of Landing Craft Utility Mk-IV 'IN LCU L53' (GRSE Yard 2094) at Port Blair". (2018, April 25). Press Information Bureau. New Delhi: Ministry of Defence, http://pib.nic.in/newsite/PrintRelease.aspx?relid=178918 (accessed on 2019, May 29)

Ensuring Secure Seas: Indian Maritime Security Strategy. (2015). New Delhi: Ministry of Defence (Navy), www.indiannavy.nic.in/sites/default/files/Indian_Maritime_Security_Strategy_Document_25Jan16.pdf (accessed on 2019, April 2)

Export Import Data Bank. (2019, April). New Delhi: Ministry of Commerce and Industry, https://commerce-app.gov.in/eidb (accessed on 2019, May 30)

Freedom to Use the Seas – India's Maritime Military Strategy. (2007). New Delhi: Ministry of Defence (Navy), http://aldeilis.net/mumbai/1686.pdf (accessed on 2019, April 1)

Gupta, Surojit. (2018, January 26). "Indo-ASEAN Trade Rises 10% to $72 Billion in FY 17, but is Long Way Off Potential", *Times of India*

Gurung, Shaurya Karanbir. (2018, December 3). "Navy Looking at Inducting 56 Warships and Submarines", *Economic Times*

Hooda, Deepshikha. (2018, July 11). "Navy Prepares Maritime Infrastructure Perspective Plan", *Economic Times*

India-Cambodia Joint Statement during the State Visit of the Prime Minister of the Kingdom of Cambodia to India. (2018, January 27). New Delhi: Ministry of External Affairs, https://mea.gov.in/incoming-visit-detail.htm?29394/IndiaCambodia+Joint+Statement+during+State+Visit+of+Prime+Minister+of+the+Kingdom+of+Cambodia+to+India+January+27+2018 (accessed on 2019, May 30)

India-Indonesia Joint Statement during the Visit of Prime Minister of India to Indonesia. (2018, May 30). New Delhi: Ministry of External Affairs, https://mea.gov.in/outoging-visit-detail.htm?29932/IndiaIndonesia+Joint+Statement+during+visit+of+Prime+Minister+to+Indonesia+May+30+2018 (accessed on 2019, May 30)

India-Myanmar Joint Statement Issued on the Occasion of the State Visit of Prime Minister of India to Myanmar. (2017, September 6). New Delhi: Ministry of External Affairs, https://mea.gov.in/outgoing-visit-detail.htm?28924/IndiaMyanmar+Joint+Statement+issued+on+the+occasion+of+the+State+Visit+of+Prime+Minister+of+India+to+Myanmar+September+57+2017 (accessed on 2019, May 30)

Indian Maritime Doctrine, 2004. (2004). New Delhi: Ministry of Defence (Navy)

Indian Maritime Doctrine, 2009. (2009). New Delhi: Ministry of Defence (Navy), www.indiannavy.nic.in/sites/default/files/Indian-Maritime-Doctrine-2009-Updated-12Feb16.pdf (accessed on 2019, May 12)

Indian Naval Indigenisation Plan, 2015–2030. (2015). New Delhi: Ministry of Defence (Navy), www.indiannavy.nic.in/sites/default/themes/indiannavy/images/pdf/naval_initiatives/INIP_2015-2030.pdf (accessed on 2019, May 19)

India-Thailand Joint Statement during the Visit of the Prime Minister of Thailand to India. (2016, June 17). New Delhi: Ministry of External Affairs, https://mea.gov.in/incoming-visit-detail.htm?26923/IndiaThailand+Joint+Statement+during+the+visit+of+Prime+Minister+of+Thailand+to+India (accessed on 2019, May 30)

India-Vietnam Joint Statement during the State Visit of President of Vietnam to India. (2018, March 3). New Delhi: Ministry of External Affairs, https://mea.gov.in/incoming-visit-detail.htm?29535/IndiaVietnam+Joint+Statement+during+State+visit+of+President+of+Vietnam+to+India+March+03+2018 (accessed on 2019, May 30)

"INS 'Baaz' – Commissioned by Admiral Nirmal Verma as First Naval Air Station in Nicobar Group of Islands". (2012, July 31). Press Information Bureau. New Delhi: Ministry of Defence, http://pib.nic.in/newsite/PrintRelease.aspx?relid=85620 (accessed on 2019, May 29)

"INS Kadmatt Commissioned at Visakhapatnam". (2016, January 7). New Delhi: Ministry of Defence (Navy), www.indiannavy.nic.in/content/ins-kadmatt-commissioned-visakhapatnam (accessed on 2019, May 19)

"INS Kochi Commissioned at Mumbai". (2015, September 30). New Delhi: Ministry of Defence (Navy), www.indiannavy.nic.in/content/ins-kochi-commissioned-mumbai (accessed on 2019, May 18)

"INS Kochi". (2015). New Delhi: Ministry of Defence (Navy), www.indiannavy.nic.in/content/ins-kochi (accessed on 2019, May 18)

"INS Visakhapatnam, First Ship of Project 15 B Launched". (2015, April 20). New Delhi: Ministry of Defence (Navy), www.indiannavy.nic.in/content/ins-visakhapatnam-first-ship-project-15b-launched (accessed on 2019, March 8)

Joint Statement of the 3rd India-Philippines Joint Commission on Bilateral Cooperation. (2015, October 14). New Delhi: Ministry of External Affairs, www.mea.gov.in/incoming-visit-detail.htm?25930/Joint+Statement++Third+IndiaPhilippines+Joint+Commission+on+Bilateral+Cooperation (accessed on 2019, May 30)

Joint Statement on a Strategic Partnership between India and Singapore. (2015, November 24). New Delhi: Ministry of External Affairs, https://mea.gov.in/outoging-visitdetail.htm?26060/Joint+Statement+on+a+Strategic+Partnership+between+India+and+Singapore+Renewed+Spirit+New+Energy++++++November+24+2015 (accessed on 2019, March 21)

Joint Statement on Enhanced Malaysia-India Strategic Partnership. (2015, November 23). New Delhi: Ministry of External Affairs, https://mea.gov.in/outgoing-visit-detail.htm?26057/Joint+Statement+on+enhanced+MalaysiaIndia+Strategic+Partnership+November+23+2015 (accessed on 2019, May 29)

Joint Statement on the Framework for the India-Malaysia Strategic Partnership. (2010, October 27). New Delhi: Ministry of External Affairs, https://mea.gov.in/bilateral-documents.htm?dtl/4764/Joint+Statement+on+the+Framework+for+the+IndiaMalaysia+Strategic+Partnership (accessed on 2019, May 29)

"Keynote Address of the Minister of External Affairs of India at the Delhi Dialogue IX". (2017, July 4). Media Centre. New Delhi: Ministry of External Affairs, www.mea.gov.in/Speeches-Statements.htm?dtl/28585/Keynote_Address_by_External_Affairs_Minister_at_ the_Delhi_Dialogue_IX_Charting_the_Course_for_India__ASEAN_Relations_for_the_Next_25_Years (accessed on 2019, May 30)

Kohli, S.N. (1978). *Sea Power and the Indian Ocean*, New Delhi: Tata McGraw Hill Publishing Co.

"Launch of Yard 12706". (2019, April 20). Press Information Bureau. New Delhi: Ministry of Defence, http://pib.nic.in/PressReleaseIframePage.aspx?PRID=1570912 (accessed on 2019, May 18)

List of Memoranda Signed between India and Singapore during the Visit of Prime Minister of India to Singapore. (2018, June 1). New Delhi: Ministry of External Affairs, https://mea.gov.in/outgoing-visit-detail.htm?29939/List+of+MoUs+signed+between+India+and+Singapore+during+visit+of+Prime+Minister+to+Singapore (accessed on 2019, May 30)

Lynn, Nyan. (2013). *Special Address of Deputy Secretary General for Political Security Community ASEAN Secretariat. Proceedings of the 1st Round Table on ASEAN-India Network of Think-Tanks*. New Delhi: Research and Information System for Developing Countries, http://aic.ris.org.in/sites/default/files/Publication%20File/AINTT-Proceedings-WEB.pdf (accessed on 2019, May 30)

Mazumdar, Mrintyunjoy. (2018, April 25). "India Reveals P-17A Frigate Configuration", *Jane's Defence Weekly*, www.janes.com/article/79583/india-reveals-p-17a-frigate-configuration (accessed on 2019, May 18)

"MILAN 2018". (2018). New Delhi: Ministry of Defence (Navy), www.indiannavy.nic.in/content/milan-2018MILAN 2018 (accessed on 2019, May 12)

Pandit, Rajat. (2017, October 25). "Eye on China, India Expands Naval Footprint in Indian Ocean", *Times of India*

Panikkar, K.M. (1943). *The Future of Southeast Asia*, New York: Macmillan & Co.

Panikkar, K.M. (1960). *A Survey of Indian History*, Bombay: Asia Publishing House

Peri, Dinakar. (2019, January 7). "Navy's New Air Base in North of Port Blair", *The Hindu*

Press Statement by the Prime Minister of India during his Visit to Vietnam. (2016, September 3). New Delhi: Ministry of External Affairs, https://mea.gov.in/outgoing-visit-detail.htm?27363/Press+Statement+by+Prime+Minister+during+his+visit+to+Vietnam+September+03+2016 (accessed on 2019, May 30)

Prime Minister of India, Manmohan Singh's Message. (2007). *Freedom to Use the Seas – India's Maritime Military Strategy*, New Delhi: Ministry of Defence (Navy), http://aldeilis.net/mumbai/1686.pdf (accessed on 2019, April 1)

"Priorities and Focus Areas: Indian Ocean Rim Association". (2017). Indian Ocean Rim Association, www.iora.int/en/priorities-focus-areas/overview (accessed on 2019, May 12)

Pubby, Manu. (2018, July 11). "Indian Navy's Submarines to be Made Locally; Rs 60000-Cr P 75 (I) will be Last Order from Abroad", *Economic Times*

Pubby, Manu. (2019, July 30). "Taking It to Next Level, India Readies Submarine for Myanmar", *Economic Times*

Raja Mohan, C. (2003). *Crossing The Rubicon: The Shaping of India's New Foreign Policy*, New Delhi: Penguin Books

Rajagopalan, Rajesh. (2017, September). "India's Strategic Choices: China and the Balance of Power in Asia", Carnegie Foundation (India), http://carnegieindia.org/2017/09/14/india-s-strategic-choices-china-and-balance-of-power-in-asia-pub-73108 (accessed on 2019, May 30)

"Remarks by External Affairs Minister of India, Sushma Swaraj at the 3rd Indian Ocean Conference". (2018, August 27). *Speeches and Statements*. New Delhi: Ministry of External Affairs, https://mea.gov.in/outgoing-visit-detail.htm?30327/Remarks+by+External+Affairs+Minis

ter+at+the+3rd+Indian+Ocean+Conference+Vietnam+August+27+2018 (accessed on 2019, April 24)

Rohit, T. K. (2018, December 24). "Andamans to Get Undersea Cable", *The Hindu*

Saran, Shyam. (2018, January 24). "India-ASEAN Ties: A Cup Half-Full?", *Hindustan Times*

"Satisfied with Naval Fleet, More to be Inducted: Lanba". (2019, April 21). *The Statesman*

Senior General Ming Aung Hlaing, Commander-in-Chief of Myanmar Defence Services, Calls on Prime Minister Modi. (2019, July 29). New Delhi: Ministry of External Affairs, www.mea.gov.in/press-releases.htm?dtl/31690/Senior_General_Min_Aung_Hlaing_CommanderinChief_of_Myanmar_Defence_Services_calls_on_PM_Modi (accessed on 2019, July 30)

Shared Vision of India-Indonesia Maritime Cooperation in the Indo-Pacific. (2018, May 30). New Delhi: Ministry of External Affairs, https://mea.gov.in/outoging-visit-detail.htm?29933/Shared+Vision+of+IndiaIndonesia+Maritime+Cooperation+in+the+Indo Pacific (accessed on 2019, May 30)

Shukla, Ajai. (2018, August 23). "Navy's Next-gen Patrol Vessels get Govt. Nod; Frigates, Destroyers to Follow", *Business Standard*

Siddiqui, Huma. (2017, October 19). "INS Kiltan Ready to Fight Nuclear, Biological Warfare, is Over 81 pct Indigenous". *Financial Express*, www.financialexpress.com/india-news/ins-kiltan-ready-to-fight-nuclear-biological-warfare-is-over-81-pct-indigenous/899155 (accessed on 2019, May 19)

Singh, Abhijit. (2015, January 26). "A 'PLA-N' for Chinese Maritime Bases in the Indian Ocean". http://csis.org/publication/pacnet-7-pla-n-chinese-maritime-bases-indian-ocean (accessed on 2019, May 12)

Tian, Nan, Aude Fleurant, Alexandra Kuimova, P.D. Wezeman and S.T. Wezeman. (2019, April). "Trends in World Military Expenditure, 2018". *SIPRI Fact Sheet*, Stockholm: International Peace Research Institute, www.sipri.org/sites/default/files/2019-04/fs_1904_milex_2018_0.pdf (accessed on 2019, May 23)

United Through Oceans – International Fleet Review. (2016). New Delhi: Ministry of Defence (Navy)

"Vision and Actions on Jointly Building Silk Road Economic Belt and 21st-Century Maritime Silk Road". (2019, May 12). *News Release.* Beijing: National Development and Reform Commission, http://en.ndrc.gov.cn/newsrelease/201503/t20150330_669367.html (accessed on 2019, May 12)

"With 'INS Kohassa', India Set to Get Fourth Air Base in the Andamans". (2019, January 24), *Hindustan Times*

5 The implications for India of great power shifts in priorities

The positions of Trump and Abe

The spectrum of India's AEP, following the experience of its predecessor, LEP, has expanded to integrate the countries of East Asia and the wider Indo-Pacific, including Japan and Australia within its ambit. As fellow members of the EAS, Japan, Australia and the most significant extra-regional power, the US, have been accommodative of the evolution of a concert of "like-minded" partners, tending to be "ambitious together" ("Raisina Dialogue Remarks by Admiral Harry B. Harris, Jr.", 2016) in providing a cooperative response to the present challenges posed by China's ambitious forays into the regional littorals. This willingness demonstrates the US strategy of selective engagement with like-minded countries, underscoring the objective of preserving its key alliances and safeguarding its vital strategic interests (Art, 2003: 9). Beyond the immediate ASEAN circuit, India's concerns *vis-à-vis* China's "expansionist" approach, "encroaching on the land and in the waters of other nations" ("Prime Minister of India, Narendra Modi's Keynote Address", 2014) has been successively and periodically voiced, in unison with other stakeholders, both at the bilateral and the multilateral fora, significant among them being the Indo-Japan-US Trilateral. At the Inaugural Trilateral Foreign Ministerial Meeting (2015), the three countries converged on the "importance of international law and peaceful settlement of disputes; freedom of navigation and over-flight; and unimpeded lawful commerce, including in the SCS", besides demonstrating their common move against the expanding trajectory of China's forays into the regional littorals ("Inaugural U.S.–India–Japan Trilateral Ministerial Dialogue in New York", 2015). The buttressing of Chinese territorial claims by building artificial islands, runways and radar facilities in the SCS and related activism pertaining to the militarisation of the South and East China Seas, China's recalcitrance *vis-à-vis* the PCA's ruling on the SCS (July 2016), the declaration of an Air-Defence Identification Zone (ADIZ) extending towards the Senkaku Islands, new fishing rules implemented on the Hainan coast and the PLAN's shadowing of passing vessels (Panneerselvam, 2016) have been a matter of concern. Additionally, China's fielding of a series of interrelated missile, sensor guidance and other technologies designed to challenge and deny freedom of movement to other littoral powers in the Indo-Pacific, or its Anti-access, Area Denial (A2/AD) programme, has been expanding its military outreach and vitiating the regional balance of power. It is believed that, the A2/AD capability will eventually be highly effective in extending a zone of exclusion out to or beyond the "Second Island Chain", referred to as a line that connects Japan, Guam and Papua New Guinea, thereby posing a major challenge to regional peace and stability (Biddle and Oelrich, 2016: 7).

Against this backdrop, Japan's "Discovery of India", implying the rediscovery of India as a partner armed with the ability and the responsibility to "nurture and enrich these seas [the Indian and Pacific Oceans] to become seas of clearest transparence" and sharing with it the values and interests of working "to enrich the seas of freedom and prosperity, which will be open and transparent to all" (Speech by the Prime Minister of Japan, H.E. Mr. Shinzo Abe , 2007), makes an Indo-Japan strategic partnership "indispensable" if peace and prosperity are to be ensured in the interconnected Asia, Pacific and Indian Ocean regions. India's rationale of greater strategic coordination with Japan fell in place seamlessly as the US, initially under the Barack Obama administration, unveiled the Pivot to Asia policy which identified India and Japan as solid pillars in its strategic pivot in the Indo-Pacific, while trying to undertake more concrete and decisive efforts to "constrain" China by a burgeoning counter-alliance, as the Trilateral Dialogue and the subsequent induction of Japan as a permanent participant in the MALA-BAR exercises indicate. As part of its anti-China "pivot", Washington's shoring up of strategic cooperation with India and Japan has continued unabated under the presidency of Donald Trump. The Trump administration's use of the "Indo-Pacific" label, not only reverberates the "importance of India's rise", but also acknowledges the vital role that India envisages playing in the region. Similar to the "pivot"/rebalancing strategy, it has been hailed as an embodiment of "a real pivot to Asia" (Remarks of the Acting Secretary of State, Michael Pompeo with Acting Secretary of Defense, Patrick Shanahan, Japanese Foreign Minister, Taro Kono, and Japanese Defense Minister, Takeshi Iwaya, 2019), facilitating and encouraging greater and sustainable coordination among the littoral powers. Furthermore, the US NSS (December 2017) and the NDS (January 2018) underscore the imperative of strengthening Indo-Pacific alliances through a policy of collective response with partners that uphold a shared respect for sovereign, fair, reciprocal trade practices and the rule of law. It is juxtaposed to China's dominance which "risks diminishing the sovereignty of many states in the Indo-Pacific". Therefore, its emphasis on reinforced commitment to free-dom of the seas and the peaceful resolution of territorial and maritime disputes in accordance with international law underscores Washington's stance of safe-guarding a Free and Open Indo-Pacific (FOIP) (National Security Strategy of the United States of America, 2017: 45–46).

It is in this context that the succeeding sections argue that the dovetailing of Japan's FOIP policy with India's AEP and the US thrust towards the Indo-Pacific is pulsating with the possibility of reviving what Dean Acheson called the "situa-tion of strength" (Jones and Moreland, 2017) developed by like-minded partners and premised on the common values of freedom, democracy and the rule of law. The first section will unfold the background providing strategic convergence between India, Japan and the US, as well as identify the common impulses guid-ing the same. The subsequent section will analyse the bilateral-level association of

India with Japan and the US respectively and conclude with brief comments on the evolving trajectory of this trilateral sojourn.

1 India–Japan–US trilateral convergence: backdrop and impulses

The inaugural impulses of the cementing of India–Japan–US strategic convergence may be discerned in the conduct of the maiden Foreign Ministerial (Trilateral) Meeting in September 2015, under the stewardship of the then US President, Barack Obama. Represented by the then Indian Minister of External Affairs, Sushma Swaraj, Japan's Minister for Foreign Affairs, Fumio Kishida and the US Secretary of State, John Kerry, the three leaders, in the course of this meeting, minced no words in articulating their increasing economic and strategic convergence on safeguarding the freedom of the SLOC as the lifeline of trade and commercial externalities. The Statement issued by the three Foreign Ministers at the conclusion of this meeting underscored "the importance of international law and peaceful settlement of disputes; freedom of navigation and over-flight; and unimpeded lawful commerce, including in the South China Sea" (George, 2015), and demonstrated their common move against China's aggressive forays into the regional littorals. This may also be viewed in the context of India's moves towards attaining a more significant role in the Indo-Pacific region, with its potential to emerge as an "anchor of stability and security", thus providing ample opportunities to buttress the dimensions of trilateral cooperation between India, Japan and the US. This was indicated by President Obama's acknowledgement that:

> We have elevated our trilateral cooperation with Japan. And we very much welcome India's increased ties with the region. It's clear that India can be an anchor of stability and security in the Asia Pacific and Indian Ocean region, and the United States looks forward to the work we can do together.
> ("U.S. President Barack Obama's Interview with Press Trust of India", 2016)

Furthermore, he resolved to expand the scope of military exercises and maritime cooperation in the trilateral sphere, such that the forces became interoperable, with India's AEP's demonstrated efforts at bolstering security partnerships forming the fulcrum. The above-mentioned Trilateral Dialogue was preceded by the inaugural Indo-Japan-Australia Trilateral Dialogue in June 2015 in course of which, the three neighbours on the "same page" with regard to China's "aggressive bid" in the region expressed their collective will to play a greater role in maritime security, besides mulling over the possibility of conducting a joint naval exercise. The Dialogue provoked speculation that the trilateral dimension could be extended to include its quadrilateral arm (the US) in future (Pubby, 2015), eventually realised by the rejuvenation of the QUAD – 2.0.

Japan's induction as a permanent member of the MALABAR naval exercise held in October 2015, as per the decision embarked upon in the 2015 Trilateral, was its immediate outcome. It may be recalled that MALABAR, initiated as an India-US bilateral naval exercise in 1992, had been witness to Japan's participation as a non-permanent participant in 2007 and its subsequent editions in 2009, 2011 and 2014, much to China's chagrin. The MALABAR is demonstrative of an impressive kaleidoscope of fleet strength, interoperability, coordination and development of a common understanding of procedures for Maritime Security Operations among the Indian, Japanese and US Navies, through professional interactions in harbour, a diverse range of activities at sea, including complex surface, sub-surface and air operations. In addition, it bears testimony to the US avowed policy of rebalancing the Indo-Pacific region, sending out signals to China on issues of freedom of navigation in international waters ("Exercise MALABAR 2016"). This collaboration is in addition to the Japan-India Maritime Exercise (JIMEX) held annually between India and Japan since January 2012. The last two editions of the MALABAR held in June 2018 (22nd edition) and September 2019 (23rd edition) showcased Japan's consecutive participation in the series since its regularised induction in 2015. In an apparent bid to ensure freedom of navigation in the East China Sea, as a deterrent to the Chinese presence therein, the latest edition of the trilateral exercise is conducted off the Japanese coast, in the midst of a major standoff between Vietnam and China in the SCS ("Mega Naval War Game among India, Japan & US Begins Today", 2019).

Three years after the trilateral dialogue was conducted at the level of Foreign Ministers, its graduation to trilateral summit caused no consternation among the international audience, as the triumvirate, in the course of their inaugural summit at the highest level, held in November 2018, embarked on the idea of building an "open and inclusive" regional architecture in the Indo-Pacific. While this inclusive architecture identified connectivity, sustainable development, maritime security, disaster relief and freedom of navigation as its basic parameters (Bagchi, 2018), the proposed outcome was aimed at reinforcing and sustaining the degree of cooperation and convergence of vision among India and its two strategic partners, skilfully and symbolically abbreviated "JAI" (Japan–America–India), towards "realising a free and open Indo-Pacific" (Remarks by President Trump, Prime Minister Abe of Japan and Prime Minister Modi of the Republic of India Before Trilateral Meeting, 2018). This seamlessly merges with India's Indo-Pacific policy, which is premised on openness, inclusiveness, without intending to single out any country as inimical, and the acknowledgement of ASEAN centrality and unity. It primarily seeks to promote, safeguard and evolve a common, rules-based regional order, which "equally appl[ies] to all individually as well as to the global commons", ensuring the prospects of "equal access as a right under international law to the use of common spaces on sea and in the air that would require freedom of navigation, unimpeded commerce and peaceful settlement of disputes in accordance with international law". The policy thus upholds New Delhi's commitment to multilateralism, regionalism and the rule of law, while fostering the "common pursuit of progress and prosperity" of all stakeholders ("Prime Minister of India, Narendra Modi's Keynote Address", 2018). Given China's expanding and increasingly assertive silhouette in the Indo-Pacific, this trilateral cooperation, hinged on the shared fundamental values of freedom, democracy and the rule of law has rightly been acknowledged to be "critically important for the stability and prosperity" of the region, particularly for bolstering maritime security and regional connectivity ("Japan-US-India Summit Meeting", 2018).

2 Analysing the bilateral beads in the trilateral chain: moving towards a concerted balance

Sharing a strong commitment to their values-based partnership in achieving a free, open and prosperous Indo-Pacific region where sovereignty and international law are respected, India, Japan and the US have cemented their partnership towards safeguarding and strengthening a rules-based order. At the trilateral echelon, President Donald Trump's strategy, which upholds the FOIP as an instrument for countering a "repressive vision of world order" with an alternative "free" vision of the world order, is in unison with the Japanese Prime Minister, Shinzo Abe and his Indian counterpart, Narendra Modi's policies of safeguarding a free, open and inclusive Indo-Pacific, premised on the principle of adherence to ASEAN's unity and centrality (Joint Statement of the 21st ASEAN-Japan Summit to Commemorate the 45th Anniversary of ASEAN-Japan Friendship and Cooperation, 2018: Cl. 3; Hussain, 2018). Having analysed the recent policies guiding such a seamless convergence in the preceding section, the sub-sections below will dwell on the bilateral-level association of India with Japan and the US respectively and conclude with brief comments on the evolving trajectory of this trilateral strategic endeavour.

2.1 Indo-Japan binomial under Prime Ministers Modi and Abe

Japan's efforts and policies pertaining to the forging and consolidation of a strategic alliance with India may be studied against the background of the unveiling of its NSS in 2013, which carved out the fundamental principles necessary to achieve national security, emphasising its role and "proactive" contribution to securing a FOIP. The inaugural NSS presented the bulwark for Japan's conduct of policies in areas related to national security, including sea, outer space, cyberspace, official development assistance and energy. The provisions in the preamble of the Strategy, while acknowledging Japan's contribution to "peace and stability in the Asia-Pacific region, by enhancing its alliance with the United States", in addition to "deepening cooperative relationships with other countries", advocated and substantiated the need to play a "more proactive role for peace and stability in the world", in a manner commensurate with the philosophy and spirit of "international cooperation", necessitated by an "increasingly severe security environment". Summarily then, Japan embarked on executing its responsibility as a "Proactive Contributor to Peace", based on the principle of international cooperation, by striving to secure regional and international peace and stability, culminating in the maintenance of international order and the rule of law. The primary objectives of the Strategy were identified unambiguously as being: to "strengthen the deterrence necessary for maintaining its peace and security and for ensuring its survival, thus deterring threats from directly reaching Japan"; to improve the regional security environment and prevent the "emergence of and reduce direct threats to Japan, through strengthening the Japan-U.S. Alliance"; and to enhance "the trust and cooperative relationships between Japan and its partners within and outside the Asia-Pacific region, and [to promote] practical security cooperation" (National

Security Strategy (Japan), 2013: 3–5). It identified "an increasing number of cases of unilateral actions in an attempt to change the status quo by coercion without paying respect to existing international law", clearly referring to China's ambitious overtures in the common maritime space including "the East China Sea and the South China Sea", thus vitiating its utilisation and free access. Furthermore, China's intrusion into Japan's territorial waters and airspace around the Senkaku Islands and infringement of the freedom of overflight above the high seas by declaring its ADIZ over the East China Sea were other serious concerns.

Japan's policy of addressing the challenges in the maritime sphere in particular, as unveiled in the NSS, inherently adopted a balancing approach, both internal and external. On the one hand, the Strategy outlined the development of a streamlined planning and programming process, encompassing the National Defense Program Guidelines (NDPG) and the Medium Term Defense Program (MTDP), to bolster its defence structure as a deterrent (internal balance). On the other hand, as a maritime nation with vital economic, energy and strategic interests in the SLOC stretching from the Persian Gulf, the Strait of Hormuz, the Red Sea and the Gulf of Aden to the surrounding waters of Japan, passing through the Indian Ocean, the Strait of Malacca and the SCS, it sought to play a pivotal role, in conjunction with regional littoral powers, by beefing up the "frequency and the quality of bilateral and multilateral cooperation on maritime security" (external balance). This was aimed at maintaining and developing "Open and Stable Seas" and upholding the maritime order, based on freedom and safety of navigation and overflight, and the peaceful settlement of disputes in accordance with relevant international law. Of particular significance for coastal states along the SLOC like India was the NSS's pronouncement of the imperative to assist in enhancing their maritime law enforcement capabilities and strengthening cooperation with partners "who share strategic interests with Japan" (National Security Strategy (Japan), 2013: 13, 16–17).

In this architecture of multilateral cooperation, Japan's traditional alliance with the US has not only served as the "core of its alliance network with countries in the region", but also has been readily cemented and expanded in a plethora of areas to ensure regional and international peace and stability, particularly in the context of the US Pivot to Asia" policy. With the Japan-US alliance forming the fulcrum, Japan sought to supplement this engagement with a wider network of cooperative relations with other partners, including India, premised on shared universal values, strategic interests and the Bilateral Global and Strategic Partnership, further emphasising cooperation in both ASEAN-centric multilateral fora like EAS, ARF, ADMM+, etc., and in triangular platforms, such as the Japan-India-US trilateral (National Security Strategy (Japan), 2013: 24–26). To this end, Prime Minister Abe named Japan's allies and friendly nations specifically, "including every leader of ASEAN member countries as well as the leaders of the United States, Australia, India, the United Kingdom, France and others", while acknowledging their explicit and enthusiastic support for its policy of "Proactive Contribution to Peace", in addition to attesting to his convergence with the US on strengthening trilateral cooperation with like-minded partners to promote regional peace and economic prosperity (Keynote Address by H. E. Mr. Shinzo Abe, Prime Minister of Japan, 2014).

Against this backdrop of emerging conviviality, Narendra Modi welcomed his counterpart, Abe's gesture of cooperation as a complement to the broader trilateral. The Prime Minister of India's enthusiasm to embrace Tokyo was reflected in his selection of Japan as his first port of call outside the immediate neighbourhood after assuming office in May 2014. This was not only concomitant with the strategic underpinnings of the AEP, but also demonstrated "the high priority that Japan receives in our foreign and economic policies" and "Japan's paramount importance in my vision for development and prosperity in India and in peace, stability and prosperity in Asia at large" (Prime Minister of India's Departure Statement Ahead of his Visit to Japan, 2014). Since 2014, which coincides with the first term of the NDA-II administration in India, the annual Prime Ministerial Summit[1] and the conduct of the Annual Strategic Dialogue at the Foreign Minister level,[2] the Annual Defence Ministerial Dialogue, the Defence Policy Dialogue, the National Security Advisors' Dialogue and the Staff-level Dialogue of each service, while reaffirming commitment to instituting a Foreign Ministerial and Defence Ministerial Dialogue (2+2 format), have provided an architecture for advancing strategic cooperation between the two countries. India and Japan have institutionalised a series of military and defence-related agreements in an endeavour to "transform the India-Japan Special Strategic and Global Partnership, a key relationship with the largest potential for growth, into a deep, broad-based and action-oriented partnership, which reflects a broad convergence of their long-term political, economic and strategic goals" (Joint Statement on India and Japan Vision 2025, 2015: Cl. 2). It may be recalled that the establishment of the "Special Strategic and Global Partnership" was preceded by the "Global Partnership between Japan and India" (August 2000) and the "Global and Strategic Partnership" (December 2006). It was then further elevated to "Special Strategic and Global Partnership" in the course of Narendra Modi's visit to Japan in September 2014.

Among the defence-related agreements, the Agreement concerning the Transfer of the Defence Equipment and Technology, providing a framework to enhance defence and security cooperation by making available to each other the defence equipment and technology necessary to implement joint R&D and/or production projects or projects; the Agreement concerning Security Measures for the Protection of Classified Military Information, which obligates both countries to protect classified military information exchanged, thereby facilitating more robust intelligence exchanges between their Forces (List of Documents Exchanged during the Visit of Prime Minister Shinzo Abe of Japan to India in New Delhi, 2015) and the Implementing Arrangements for Deeper Cooperation between the Navies to facilitate greater cooperation and information exchange in the sphere of Maritime Domain Awareness (List of Announcements/Agreements Signed between India and Japan during the Visit of Prime Minister to Japan, 2018) have been noteworthy. India and Japan should commence negotiations on an Acquisition and Cross Servicing Agreement (ACSA), similar to the Logistics Exchange and Memorandum of Agreement (LEMOA), in order to facilitate mutual use of and access to naval bases for fuel/servicing. In addition to this, the conduct of deliberations on a White Shipping Agreement will be pivotal to providing enhanced coordination and interoperability for their navies.

The unwavering commitment of the Prime Ministers of Japan and India to realising "a peaceful, open, equitable, stable and rule-based order in the Indo-Pacific region and beyond", while upholding "the principles of sovereignty and territorial integrity; peaceful settlement of disputes; democracy, human rights and the rule of law; open global trade regime; and freedom of navigation and over-flight", not only bolstered the foundation for cooperation for "peace, security and development of the Indo-Pacific region" (Joint Statement on India and Japan Vision 2025: Cl. 4) but also sent a clear message to China that its belligerent overtures in the regional waters would not go unchallenged. Referring to the SCS issue, they have sustained the view that:

> full and effective implementation of the 2002 Declaration on the Conduct of Parties in the South China Sea and early conclusion of the negotiations to establish a Code of Conduct by consensus will contribute to peace and stability of the region.
>
> (Joint Statement on India and Japan Vision 2025: Cl. 36)

Besides, the Joint Statement released at the end of the Indo-Japan Defence Ministerial Meeting held shortly afterwards vehemently criticised Beijing's rejection of the verdict of the PCA and urged the parties concerned to "show utmost respect for the UNCLOS" by "ensuring freedom and safety of navigation and over-flight as well as unimpeded lawful commerce in international waters". It also expressed "concern over recent developments" referring to China's actions such as the landing of planes on artificial islands and the tirade against the tribunal judges (Joint Statement after the Meeting between Raksha Mantri and Japanese Defence Minister, 2016: Cl. 4). On the whole, the two leaders' vision for the Indo-Pacific acknowledged ASEAN unity and centrality at its heart, professing a rules-based, inclusive and open order that respects the sovereignty and territorial integrity of nations, ensures freedom of navigation and over-flight as well as unimpeded lawful commerce, and seeks the peaceful resolution of disputes with full respect for legal and diplomatic processes in accordance with the universally recognised principles of international law. The burgeoning importance of bilateral ties was aptly envisioned in the Vision Statement released in the course of the India-Japan Annual Summit in October 2018, which not only upheld the transformation of relations "into a partnership with great substance and purpose", put forth as a "corner stone of India's Act East Policy", but also underscored the advance into the "new era in India-Japan relations" (India-Japan Vision Statement, 2018: Cl. 3) so as to further cooperate for peace, stability, inclusiveness and prosperity of the Indo-Pacific. Thus, Abe's FOIP concept, with the policy of Japan's Proactive Contribution to Peace forming its fulcrum, seeks to complement the US-Japan alliance by the forging of security and strategic ties with "like-minded" democracies such as India, which share the liberal values of freedom, democracy and the rule of law. On the whole, often regarded as the most proactive response to the Pivot to Asia policy, the FOIP envisages the development of a containment coalition with countries like India that are capable of deterring China's aggressive bids in the region.

2.1.1 India–Japan collaboration in defence: Make in India as the gateway

The Government of India's Make in India initiative, particularly its defence manufacturing component, has opened greater avenues of collaboration between India and Japan with respect to joint development and the production of defence equipment. The Make in India project provides Japan with investment opportunities in sectors like defence products manufacturing, supply chain sourcing and defence offsets, legal trade practices in the aerospace and military industries and arrangements in which the seller of a defence product or service agrees to buy products or services from its client as an inducement. New Delhi's decision to allow defence FDI up to 100 per cent with a rider that the project should involve "modern technology" has enthused the Japanese defence industry with respect to its investment prospects, facilitated by Tokyo's relaxation of the rules on export of defence equipment and technology introduced in April 2014, which hitherto concentrated exclusively on the domestic market in order to demonstrate its commitment to peace. Japan's ShinMaywa Industries, the manufacturer of US-2i SAR amphibious aircraft, offered to set up a plant in New Delhi (under the 30 per cent offset clause) to meet international demands. India and Japan have moved closer to concluding the first-ever bilateral defence deal, following a pricing agreement for the 12 SAR aircraft. With Japan offering ShinMaywa US-2i amphibious aircraft at a price concession of more than 10 per cent per aircraft, the deal is in the penultimate stage of finalisation. However, the deal is far from done yet, as the Japanese Ministry of Defence is intent on India establishing its procurement policy at the earliest, succeeding which Japan would flexibly respond to any request from India for cooperation.

Since 2014, several initiatives have been undertaken both by New Delhi and Tokyo to promote greater participation and investment in the defence sector, facilitated by the revisions in the Defence Procurement Procedure (DPP) within the Make in India framework, particularly aided by the introduction of the Strategic Partnership Model, an increase in FDI through an automatic route to 49 per cent; restricting licensing requirements for critical items; de-notifying several items previously produced only by Ordnance Factory Boards, etc. On the other hand, bilateral convergence pertaining to cooperation in the defence sector has been facilitated by a significant transformation in legislation instituted by the Abe administration since his assumption of office in 2012. To begin with, demonstrating a marked departure from Japan's Post-Second World War pacifism, in September 2015, the Japanese Parliament (Diet) enacted two security laws, removing some of the key legal restrictions that the war-renouncing Constitution hitherto imposed on the Japanese Self-Defence Forces (SDF) during overseas missions, including the long-standing ban on collective self-defence enshrined in Article 9. It also established a new permanent law that allows Japan to deploy the SDF overseas to provide logistic support for UN-authorised military operations involving a foreign or multinational force. Under the new laws, Japan will theoretically be allowed to use collective self-defence to come to the aid of an ally under three conditions: if Japan's "survival" is at stake; there is no alternative; and the use of force is kept to the "minimum necessary" (Yoshida and Aoki, 2015). Therefore, though the new security legislation is not country-specific, in the event of a regional conflict, India being Japan's "Strategic Partner" will certainly benefit from its provisions. Besides, Japan's decision to exercise the right of Collective Self Defence when "people's right to life, liberty and the pursuit of happiness is fundamentally undermined" is a bold and commendable move as it will help arrest the increasing anxiety in the region. Since both India and Japan depend on the SLOC for their trade and resource supplies through the Malacca Strait and the Indian Ocean, any impediment in the freedom of navigation by state or non-state actors may undermine their economic interests as maritime security is directly linked to economic security (Mishra and Khan, 2015).

Second, Japan's new security legislation, in consonance with the *National Defense Programme Guidelines for Financial Year 2014 and Beyond*, offers a huge number of opportunities to realise the optimum level of strategic cooperation with India. While paving the way for complementing each other in the maritime security domain in particular, the Guidelines recognise India's ascendance among the regional players, noting that "Japan will strengthen its relationship with India in a broad range of fields, including maritime security, through joint training and exercises as well as joint implementation of international peace cooperation activities" (National Defense Programme Guidelines for FY 2014 and Beyond, 2013: 11). As the latest NDPG for FY 2019 and Beyond recognises China's forceful, large-scale and rapid reclamation of maritime features and their conversion into military facilities in the SCS, as well as its "lack of transparency surrounding its defense policy and military power" pose a "serious security concern for the region including Japan", it therefore aims to balance the emerging situation by further strengthening cooperation with India and the US (National Defense Programme Guidelines for FY 2019 and Beyond, 2018: 5, 16). Moreover, among its two allies under discussion, the strategy aspires to fortify alliance with the US by enhancing the domain of cooperation in a wide range of spheres, including implementing measures to facilitate the stationing of US forces on its soil, as an instrument of improving operational readiness and deterrent capabilities, the consolidation of operational cooperation and policy coordination, particularly in comprehensive air and missile defence; personnel training and exercises; intelligence, surveillance and reconnaissance (ISR) operations; providing logistic support for US force activities and protection of its ships and aircraft, thereby bolstering the Extended Deterrence Dialogue. Moreover, for the purpose of enhancing strategic partnership with India, Japan aims to promote joint training and exercises as well as collaboration in defence equipment and technology in a broad range of areas including maritime security (National Defense Programme Guidelines for FY 2019 and Beyond, 2018: 13–14).

Third, closely related to these developments, the Japanese Cabinet approved a defence budget allocating ¥5.05 trillion (US$42.1 billion) in December 2015 for FY 2016–2017 in light of the SDF's preparation to assume an expanded role and greater collaboration with other powers under the new security legislation. This may be considered in conjunction with Japan's urge to steadily improve its defence capabilities during FY 2016, as the third fiscal year of Japan's effort to develop a dynamic Joint Defence Force (Medium Term Defense Program for FY 2014–2018, 2013: 1–2). Since 2014, defence-related expenditure has been on the increase for six years in a row and when compared to FY 2017, it was increased by ¥39.2 billion in FY 2018. Additionally, the supplementary budget for FY 2018 contained an appropriation of ¥234.5 billion (approximately US$2.13 billion) as necessary expenses for securing stable operation of the SDF, including responding to ballistic missile attacks (Defense of Japan, 2018: 229). As the present data indicate, based on the adoption of the NDPG for FY 2019 and Beyond and a new procurement plan, MTDP for FY 2019–FY 2023 (in December 2018) the Diet approved a "record high" defence budget of ¥5.26 trillion (US$47.2 billion) for FY 2019, which has increased by almost 12 per cent over seven years, to develop and invest in new capabilities and equipment ("Japan's Diet Passes Record 101 Trillion Yen Budget with Spending Hikes for Defense and Social Security", 2019). It marks the seventh consecutive increase in the defence budget under the Abe administration, and a year-on-year increase of 1.3 per cent (Takahashi, 2018) as Tokyo aspires to invest in new capabilities and equipment, prominent among which is the introduction of two of the US military's Aegis Ashore land-based missile interceptor systems, with "offensive" aircraft carrier capabilities, accommodating F-35A and 35B stealth jets including short take-off and vertical landing versions to help bolster defences along its islands at the edge of the East China Sea, cyber space and enhanced ISR capabilities. This is part of the Ministry of Defense's plan to spend ¥27 trillion (US$239.5 billion) on its military over five years starting April 2019 (Kelly, 2018). Additionally, the MTDP for FY 2019–FY 2023 endorsed setting aside US$240 billion to pave the way for beefing up weapons and defence equipment.

In summary, Japan's escalated allocation to the defence budget augurs well for its strategic congruence with India, further facilitated by the policies introduced within the scaffold of Make in India and the amended DPP (2016). It introduced the Indigenously Designed, Developed and Manufactured (IDMM) as a category for acquisition, which, along with the "Buy and Make Indian" categories will assist global Original Equipment Manufacturers (OEM) and Indian companies to forge a partnership for co-development and co-production (Defence Procurement Procedure 2016: Backgrounder, 2016: 2–4; Basu, 2016). Incidentally, the outlines of the DPP were in sync with Japan's launching of the guidelines of the Ministry of Defense's Acquisition, Technology and Logistics Agency in October 2015, which proposed the effective management of defence equipment acquisition and promoting defence equipment cooperation with its allies, thereby boosting its involvement in international development programmes. The result of placing the growth of Japan's defence industry at the core of the national defence strategy has not only been a valuable incentive to strengthen the country's industrial base, but also a key element in a new strategic approach to counter Beijing's regional influence by strategically coordinating with countries (Grevatt, 2015; "Defense

Ministry Launches New Equipment Management Agency", 2015) and allies in the region. Furthermore, India's latest Defence Production Policy (2018) attempts to build on these initiatives and provide a focused, structured and significant thrust to the development of indigenous defence design and production capabilities. It ambitiously aims to achieve a turnover of US$26 billion in defence goods and services by 2025 (Draft Defence Production Policy, 2018, 2018: 4).

2.2 India–US defence collaboration

The Indo-Pacific region has become a crucial base for Indo-US maritime strate-gising, as envisioned in the US-India Joint Strategic Vision for the Asia-Pacific and Indian Ocean Region (2015), the NSS (2017) and the NDS (2018) and reflected in the signing of a series of defence-related agreements like the Indo-US LEMOA and the Communications Compatibility and Security Agreement (COMCASA). Akin to Japan's NDPG for 2019 and Beyond, the (US) NSS clearly acknowledges China's spree of building and militarising outposts in the SCS as a threat to "the free flow of trade", the "sovereignty of other nations" and "regional stability", in addition to rueing Beijing's ambition to sustain a military modernisation campaign to constrain US access in the region, thereby providing China with a freer hand therein. It thus underscores the "real world integration of our complementary strategic visions" as the region countenances an increasingly complex security ambience. As Washington identifies its commitment to respond to the "calling" by the regional states as a guarantor of the balance of power in the Indo-Pacific, it welcomes "India's emergence as a leading global power and stronger strategic and defense partner", as well as a compatriot in the QUAD architecture (National Security Strategy of the United States of America, 2017: 45–46). The NDS cate-gorises China both as a "revisionist" power that employs coercive policies to undermine the rules-based international order and a strategic competitor using "predatory economics to intimidate its neighbors while militarizing features in the South China Sea", thus posing a central challenge to US prosperity and security in the Indo-Pacific region. Under such circumstances, Washington aspires to main-tain a favourable balance of power by strengthening regional alliances and part-nerships and coordinating bilateral and multilateral security relationships to preserve the free and open international system, and to facilitate the creation and sustenance of a networked security architecture "capable of deterring aggression, maintaining stability, and ensuring free access to common domains" (Summary of the 2018 National Defense Strategy of the United States of America: 4–9). Therefore, spurred on by the common threat to regional peace and stability emanating from China, the triumvirate alliance of India, Japan and the US are intent on bolstering strategic relations, both at the bilateral and trilateral levels and the rest of this section enumerates the pillars and trajectory of the Indo-US component of defence collaboration.

Recognising India's stature as a US Major Defense Partner (MDP) under the National Defense Authorisation Act in 2017, bilateral defence relations have been upgraded to the highest level of institutionalised security engagement, manifest in the 2+2 Dialogue and the signing of the LEMOA[3], one of the four "foundational agreements" that the US enters into with its defence partners. The LEMOA enables the defence forces to use mutual assets and bases for repair and replenishment of supplies on a reimbursable basis, thus facilitating "practical engagement and exchange" and the logistics of joint operations ("India and the United States Sign the Logistics Exchange Memorandum of Agreement/LEMOA", 2016). Of the four foundational agreements, the General Security of Military Information Agreement (GSMIA) and COMCASA, the India-specific version of the Communications and Information Security Memorandum of Agreement (CISMOA) were signed in 2002 and 2018 respectively, while the Basic Exchange and Cooperation Agreement (BECA) for Geospatial Intelligence is pending signature. Committed to expanding the scope of India's MDP status, by embarking upon "mutually agreed upon steps to strengthen defense ties further and promote better defense and security coordination and cooperation" (Joint Statement on the Inaugural India-US 2+2 Ministerial Dialogue, 2018) the two countries are intent on collaborating in advanced defence equipment and technology "at a level commensurate with that of the closest allies and partners of the United States", facilitated by the developing strides of the Make in India scheme. India's designation as Washington's MDP has provided a framework for facilitating innovative and advanced opportunities in defence technology and trade cooperation, for which, the US has agreed to elevate defence trade and technology-sharing with India to a level commensurate with its closest allies and partners (George, 2016). These initiatives have been supplemented with the US offer to consider selling Sea Guardian Unmanned Aerial Systems to India, building on the implementation of their "White Shipping" data sharing arrangement to facilitate Maritime Domain Awareness and India's invitation to the US to join the IONS as an observer (Joint Statement – United States and India: Prosperity through Partnership, 2017).

In particular, the launch of the 2+2 Dialogue in September 2018, proposed to become an annual feature thereafter, reflected the US and India's shared commitment to catalyse an institutionalised architecture to provide "a positive, forward-looking vision for the India-US strategic partnership and to promote synergy in their diplomatic and security efforts", premised on the democratic values of freedom, justice and adherence to the rule of law. An important outcome of this inaugural dialogue was their convergence on working together on "regional and global issues, including in bilateral, trilateral, and quadrilateral formats", in addition to establishing secure communication between India's Ministry of External Affairs (MEA) and the US Secretary of State, on the one hand, and between India's Minister of Defence and the US Secretary of Defense, on the other, in a bid to sustain "regular high-level communication on emerging developments". The most significant outcome of the Dialogue, heralded as a "milestone" in boosting India's defence preparedness and capabilities, and indicating "growing trust between the two countries", has been the signing of the COMCASA. It will provide facilitated access to advanced defence systems, thereby enabling India to optimally utilise and fully exploit its existing[4] and proposed/purchased[5] (Thakur and Padgett, 2018) platforms of US origin. Additionally, it signifies US willingness to continue negotiations on an Industrial Security Annex to support closer defence industry collaboration and offer real-time data-sharing with the Indian military over secure channels, thus providing greater awareness and intelligence inputs, through accessing the Combined Enterprise Regional Information Exchange System (CENTRIXS) mounted on-board naval ships (Peri, 2018). With its signing, the US will be in a position to transfer highly secure, coded communication equipment with the military platforms it sells to India, reversing the latter's dependence on commercially available, less secure systems on high-end platforms like C-130Js and the P8I maritime surveillance aircraft, among others ("Seven Reasons why COMCASA is so Important for India", 2018). Its signing will also fulfil the mandatory requirement for India to procure the armed version of the Sea Guardian drones from the US, since they are critically dependent on a highly secure data and communication system link (Singh, 2018). Regarded as the great enabler in ship-to-ship operational dialogue in both text and Web-based formats, the CENTRIXS operates through a collection of coalition-wide area networks or "enclaves", with CENTRIXS-J operational for the US and Japan (Bailey, 2007). Therefore as a beneficiary of the CENTRIXS, India will be able to avail itself of the advantages offered by the system on a par with Japan. This provides a platform for the three countries to bolster Maritime Domain Awareness and interoperability in this region.

These developments have been accompanied by the decision to establish an Indo-US tri-services exercise in order to enhance personnel exchange and interoperability. In an endeavour to support and facilitate bilateral coordination in the maritime domain, India and the US are determined to commence exchanges between the US Naval Forces Central Command and the Indian Navy. In addition, the inaugural 2+2 Dialogue beckons a plethora of possibilities for India and US to collaborate, in cognisance of the former's inclusion among the top tier of countries entitled to license-free exports, re-exports and transfers under License Exception Strategic Trade Authorization (STA-1). It also reinforces the commitment to explore other means of expanding bilateral trade in defence items and defence manufacturing supply chain linkages, taking advantage of the amended provisions of the Government of India's Make in India scheme (Joint Statement on the Inaugural India-U.S. 2+2 Ministerial Dialogue, 2018). Of special mention in this regard is the bilateral affirmation to prioritise co-production, co-development and innovation projects through the Defense Technology and Trade Initiative (DTTI), initiated in 2012. New Delhi and Washington identified "pathfinder efforts" in 2015 "in principle to pursue co-production and co-development". While the first component included four pathfinder projects, namely next-generation Cheel (Raven) mini-unmanned aerial vehicle (UAV)s; roll-on/roll-off kits for C-130 aircraft; mobile, electric hybrid power sources; and next-generation protective ensembles, the formation of working groups to explore possible cooperation in aircraft carrier and jet engine technology-sharing and design was recommended in the second component (Joint Statement during the Visit of the President of USA to India, 2015). Thus, the DTTI, in consonance with the first-ever country-specific India Rapid Reaction Cell (IRRC), which was established in the Pentagon in 2015, in order to expedite the overall "operational tempo" and process of co-development and co-production of hi-technology military equipment in India ("Pentagon Sets Up India Rapid Reaction Cell", 2015), will find its perfect complement in the Make in India programme, and further upgrade the complexion of bilateral defence cooperation, embellished by the signing of the COMCASA.

Furthermore, recognising the "increasing connectivity between the Indian and Pacific Oceans", the rechristening of the US Pacific Command (USPACOM), vested with the responsibility of military activities and stability in the greater Pacific region, based on "partnership, presence, and military readiness", as the US Indo-Pacific Command (USINDOPACOM) is a significant symbol of the escalating importance of New Delhi in Washington's strategic computations. To further its objective of ensuring a FOIP in association with "a constellation of like-minded Allies and Partners", sharing concerns of mutual security, interests and values, the USINDOPACOM envisages the implementation of a combat credible deterrence strategy against adversarial policies ("US Indo-Pacific Command Holds Change of Command Ceremony", 2018). Besides, India and the Indo-Pacific Navies have been conducting one of the world's largest US-led, biennial multilateral maritime exercises, named RIMPAC (Rim of the Pacific). Hosted and administered by the USPACOM (now USINDOPACOM), the inaugural RIMPAC was held in 1971. In its 23rd edition (June 2012) China, India and the Philippines made their RIMPAC debut as observers. While not contributing any ships, observer nations are involved in RIMPAC at the strategic level, thus using the platform to interact with navies from other nations, including Australia, Indonesia, Japan, Malaysia, New Zealand, Singapore, South Korea and Thailand, across the Indo-Pacific region. In 2014, Indian naval participation was enhanced by deployment of INS *Sahyadri* in its 24th edition, providing it with an opportunity to interact with the regional navies and enhance interoperability and development of common understanding critical to ensuring SLOC safety. The latest (26th) edition, held in 2018 was witness to the display of capabilities ranging from disaster relief and maritime security operations to sea control and complex war-fighting exercises, thereby bolstering mutual confidence and ensconcing "India's contribution in ensuring peace and stability in the Indo-Pacific region" (Majumder, 2018).

It follows from the discussion above that the converging concerns of India, Japan and US regarding the security, openness/freedom and accessibility of the Indo-Pacific are pivotal to their attempts at deterring the increasing silhouette of China in the region. As the trio converge on balancing China by employing mechanisms that exert both internal and external balance, they simultaneously maintain the sanctity of ASEAN centrality in all matters pertaining to the Indo-Pacific, thus demonstrating their endeavour to uplift the liberal norms of international order, particularly the regional maritime order, while respecting the anchorage provided by ASEAN to the region. Finally, the three countries, whether in bilateral or trilateral collaboration, have clearly sent out the message that they are not pursuing either hegemonic or expansionist designs. On the contrary, on the one hand, they are committed to advancing a free, open and inclusive Indo-Pacific region, premised on the liberal tenets of respect for sovereignty, territorial integrity, rule of law, good governance, free and fair trade and freedom of navigation and overflight, as a means of securing the trade and energy-related interests of the regional states. On the other hand, while understanding the geostrategic importance of the littorals, they have recognised the imperative of cooperation in infrastructure and connectivity projects to establish the transparent and responsible development of the region. Significantly enough, the Indo-Japanese geo-economic endeavour to explore the development of industrial corridors and networks for the growth of Asia and Africa is projected to benefit various stakeholders in the Indo-Pacific region and is germane to the potential to emerge as a counterweight to the BRI. Indo-Japanese collaboration related to the development of India's Northeast fosters further synergy between AEP and Japan's FOIP strategy. The evolving architecture in the Indo-Pacific region is poised to revive the semblance of a "situation of strength" by like-minded partners, thus exerting a deterrent effect on China's unabated geostrategic expansionist bid in the SCS as well as its geo-economic BRI blueprint, through which it attempts to propagate domination and apply conditions of debt and dependency on stakeholders.

Notes

1 The 13th edition was held in October 2018
2 The 10th edition was held in January 2019
3 LEMOA was signed in 2016 and has been operational since 2018
4 P-8 Poseidon anti-submarine warfare aircraft, SH-3 anti-submarine warfare helicopters, C-17 transport aircraft, C-130 Hercules aircraft and the M2.50 caliber machine gun
5 Chinook helicopters, M 777A2 howitzers, Stinger missiles and Apache helicopters

References

Art, Robert J. (2003). *A Grand Strategy for America*, Ithaca, NY: Cornell University Press
Bagchi, Indrani. (2018, December 1). "In First Ever Trilateral Summit, India-Japan-US Focus on 'Inclusive' Indo-Pacific", *Times of India*
Bailey, Jessica M. (2007, July 16). "CENTRIXS Provides Vital Communication". Washington, DC: Department of Navy, www.navy.mil/submit/display.asp?story_id=30603 (accessed on 2019, April 19)
Basu, Nayanima. (2016, March 29). "Defence Procurement Policy Pushes 'Make in India'". *Hindu Business Line* (accessed on 2019, May 28)
Biddle, Stephen and Ivan Oelrich. (2016). "Future Warfare in the Western Pacific: Chinese Anti-access/Area Denial, U.S. Air, Sea Battle, and Command of the Commons in East Asia", *International Security*, 41(1)
Defence Procurement Procedure 2016: Backgrounder. (2016). New Delhi: Ministry of Defence, www.mod.nic.in/writereaddata/Background.pdf (accessed on 2019, May 28)
"Defense Ministry Launches New Equipment Management Agency". (2015, October 1). *Japan Times*, www.japantimes.co.jp/news/2015/10/01/national/politics-diplomacy/defense-ministry-launches-new-equipment-management-agency/#.V7ZgRZh97IU (accessed on 2019, May 28)

Defense of Japan. (2018). Tokyo: Ministry of Defense, www.mod.go.jp/e/publ/w_paper/pdf/2018/DOJ2018_Full_1130.pdf (accessed on 2019, April 15)

Draft Defence Production Policy, 2018. (2018). New Delhi: Ministry of Defence, https://ddpmod.gov.in/sites/default/files/Draft%20Defence%20Production%20Policy%202018%20-%20for%20website.pdf (accessed on 2019, May 30)

"Exercise MALABAR 2016". (2016). Press Release. New Delhi: Ministry of Defence (Navy), http://indiannavy.nic.in/content/exercise-malabar-2016 (accessed on 2019, May 26)

George, Varghese K. (2015, October 1). "India, U.S., Japan Say Interests in Indo-Pacific Converge", *The Hindu*

George, Varghese K. (2016, August 30). "India, US Sign Military Logistics Pact", *The Hindu*

Grevatt, John. (2015, October 2). "Japan Launches New Procurement Agency". *Jane's Defence Weekly*, www.janes.com/article/54984/japan-launches-new-procurement-agency (accessed on 2019, May 28)

Hussain, Zakir. (2018, August 3). "US Remains Committed to ASEAN Centrality, Mike Pompeo Tells Foreign Ministers", *The Straits Times*, www.straitstimes.com/politics/us-remains-committed-to-asean-centrality-mike-pompeo-tells-foreign-ministers (accessed on 2019, May 26)

"Inaugural U.S.–India–Japan Trilateral Ministerial Dialogue in New York". (2015, September 30). Press Release. New Delhi: Ministry of External Affairs, https://mea.gov.in/press-releases.htm?dtl/25868/inaugural+usindiajapan+trilateral+ministerial+dialogue+in+new+york (accessed on 2019, May 12)

"India and the United States Sign the Logistics Exchange Memorandum of Agreement/LEMOA". (2016, August 30). Press Information Bureau. New Delhi: Ministry of Defence, http://pib.nic.in/newsite/mbErel.aspx?relid=149322 (accessed on 2019, April 19)

India-Japan Vision Statement. (2018, October 29). New Delhi: Ministry of External Affairs, www.mea.gov.in/outoging-visit-detail.htm?30543/IndiaJapan+Vision+Statement (accessed on 2019, April 15)

"Japan's Diet Passes Record 101 Trillion Yen Budget with Spending Hikes for Defense and Social Security". (2019, March 27). *Japan Times*, www.japantimes.co.jp/news/2019/03/27/business/economy-business/diet-passes-record-%C2%A5101-trillion-fiscal-2019-budget-spending-hikes-defense-social-security/#.XLVVkokzZkg (accessed on 2019, May 12)

"Japan-US-India Summit Meeting". (2018, November 30). Tokyo: Ministry of Foreign Affairs of Japan, www.mofa.go.jp/s_sa/sw/in/page3e_000969.html (accessed on 2019, April 12)

Joint Statement – United States and India: Prosperity through Partnership. (2017, June 27). New Delhi: Ministry of External Affairs, www.mea.gov.in/bilateral-documents.htm?dtl/28560/Joint_Statement__United_States_and_India_Prosperity_Through_Partnership (accessed on 2019, April 17)

Joint Statement after the Meeting between Raksha Mantri and Japanese Defence Minister. (2016, July 14). Press Information Bureau. New Delhi: Ministry of Defence, http://pib.nic.in/newsite/PrintRelease.aspx?relid=147097 (accessed on 2019, April 15)

Joint Statement during the Visit of the President of USA to India. (2015, January 25). New Delhi: Ministry of External Affairs, www.mea.gov.in/bilateral-documents.htm?dtl/24726/Joint_Statement_during_ (accessed on 2019, April 15)

Joint Statement of the 21st ASEAN-Japan Summit to Commemorate the 45th Anniversary of ASEAN-Japan Friendship and Cooperation. (2018, November 13). Jakarta: ASEAN

Secretariat, https://asean.org/storage/2018/11/ASEAN-Japan-Joint-Statement.pdf (accessed on 2019, May 26)

Joint Statement on India and Japan Vision 2025: Special Strategic and Global Partnership Working Together for Peace and Prosperity of the Indo-Pacific Region and the World. (2015, December 12). New Delhi: Ministry of External Affairs, www.mea.gov.in/incoming-visit-detail.htm?26176/Joint+Statement+on+India+and+Japan+Vision+2025+Special+Strategic+and+Global+Partnership+Working+Together+for+Peace+and+Prosperity+of+the+IndoPacific+Region+and+the+WorldDecember+12+2015 (accessed on 2019, May 12)

Joint Statement on the Inaugural India-US 2+2 Ministerial Dialogue. (2018, September 6). Press Information Bureau. New Delhi: Ministry of Defence, http://pib.nic.in/newsite/PrintRelease.aspx?relid=186956 (accessed on 2019, April 15)

Jones, Bruce and Will Moreland. (2017, March 24). "To Negotiate from Strength, Team Trump has to Build 'Situations of Strength'", www.brookings.edu/blog/order-from-chaos/2017/03/24/to-negotiate-from-strength-team-trump-has-to-build-situations-of-strength/ (accessed on 2019, May 24)

Kelly, Tim. (2018, December 11). "Japan to Ramp Up Defense Spending to Pay for New Fighters, Radars". *Reuters,* www.reuters.com/article/us-japan-defence-budget/japan-to-ramp-up-defense-spending-to-pay-for-new-fighters-radar-idUSKBN1OA0VP (accessed on 2019, April 15)

Keynote Address by H.E. Mr. Shinzo Abe, Prime Minister of Japan at the 13th IISS Asian Security Summit "Shangri-La Dialogue". (2014, May 30). Tokyo: Ministry of Foreign Affairs of Japan, www.mofa.go.jp/fp/nsp/page18e_000087.html (accessed on 2019, April 14)

List of Announcements/Agreements Signed between India and Japan during the Visit of Prime Minister to Japan. (2018, October 29). New Delhi: Ministry of External Affairs, www.mea.gov.in/bilateral-documents.htm?dtl/30542/List_of_AnnouncementsAgreements_signed_between_India_and_Japan_during_visit_of_Prime_Minister_to_Japan (accessed on 2019, April 14)

List of Documents Exchanged during the Visit of Prime Minister Shinzo Abe of Japan to India in New Delhi. (2015, December 12). New Delhi: Ministry of External Affairs, www.mea.gov.in/incoming-visit-detail.htm?26177/List+of+documents+exchanged+during+the+visit+of+Prime+Minister+Shinzo+Abe+of+Japan+to+India+in+New+Delhi+December+12+2015 (accessed on 2019, May 12)

Majumder, Soumyajit. (2018, June 27). "India's INS Sahyadri Reaches Pearl Harbour for Strategic Exercise", www.ndtv.com/india-news/rimpac-18-indias-ins-sahyadri-reaches-pearl-harbour-for-strategic-exercise-1873753 (accessed on 2019, May 31)

Medium Term Defense Program for FY 2014–FY 2018. (2013, December 17). Tokyo: Ministry of Defense, www.mod.go.jp/j/approach/agenda/guideline/2014/pdf/Defense_Program.pdf (accessed on 2019, April 15)

"Mega Naval War Game among India, Japan & US Begins Today". (2019, September 26), *The Statesman*

Mishra, Rahul and Shamsad A. Khan. (2015, December 11). "How Shinzo Abe's Visit will Strengthen India's Ties with Japan", www.dnaindia.com/analysis/standpoint-how-shinzo-abe-s-visit-will-strengthen-india-s-ties-with-japan-2154332 (accessed on 2019, April 6)

National Defense Programme Guidelines for FY 2014 and Beyond. (2013). Tokyo: Ministry of Defense, www.mod.go.jp/j/approach/agenda/guideline/2014/pdf/20131217_e2.pdf (accessed on 2019, April 6)

National Defense Programme Guidelines for FY 2019 and Beyond. (2018, December 18). Tokyo: Ministry of Defense, www.mod.go.jp/j/approach/agenda/guideline/2019/pdf/20181218_e.pdf (accessed on 2019, April 15)

National Security Strategy of the United States of America. (2017, December). Washington, DC: The White House, www.whitehouse.gov/wp-content/uploads/2017/12/NSS-Final-12-18-2017-0905-2.pdf (accessed on 2019, May 24)

National Security Strategy (Japan). (2013, December 17). Tokyo: Ministry of Foreign Affairs of Japan, www.cas.go.jp/jp/siryou/131217anzenhoshou/nss-e.pdf (accessed on 2019, April 7)

Panneerselvam, Prakash. (2016, August). "Advancing India's Relationship with Japan and South Korea: Quest for Middle Power Cooperation". *Issue Brief,* 262, www.ipcs.org/issue-brief/india-the-world/advancing-india39s-relationship-with-japan-and-south-korea-quest-for-262.html (accessed on 2019, May 12)

"Pentagon Sets Up India Rapid Reaction Cell". (2015, September 15), *Hindu Business Line*

Peri, Dinakar. (2018, September 7). "COMCASA will Help India Track China's Indian Ocean Moves Better", *The Hindu*

"Prime Minister of India, Narendra Modi's Keynote Address at the 17th Asia Security Summit in Singapore". (2018, June 1), www.narendramodi.in/pm-%20modi-%20to%20-deliver%20-keynote-%20address%20-at%20-shangri-la-%20dialouge-%20in%20-singapore-540324 (accessed on 2018, September 16)

"Prime Minister of India, Narendra Modi's Keynote Address at the Luncheon Hosted by Nippon Kiedanren, Japanese Chamber of Commerce and Industry and the Japan-India Business Cooperation Committee". (2014, September 1), www.narendramodi.in/pms-keynote-address-at-the-luncheon-hosted-by-nippon-kiedanren-the-japanese-chamber-of-commerce-and-industry-and-the-japan-india-business-cooperation-committee (accessed on 2019, May 12)

Prime Minister of India's Departure Statement Ahead of His Visit to Japan. (2014, August 29). Press Information Bureau. New Delhi: Prime Minister's Office, http://pib.nic.in/newsite/PrintRelease.aspx?relid=109178 (accessed on 2019, April 14)

Pubby, Manu. (2015, June 8). "India Kicks Off Trilateral Talks with Japan and Australia; Joint Training, Naval Exercises on Agenda", *Economic Times*

"Raisina Dialogue Remarks by Admiral Harry B. Harris, Jr.". (2016, March 2). Speeches/Testimony. Hawaii: US Pacific Command, www.pacom.mil/Media/Speeches-Testimony/Article/683842/raisina-dialogue-remarks-lets-be-ambitious-together/ (accessed on 2019, May 12)

Remarks by President Trump, Prime Minister Abe of Japan and Prime Minister Modi of the Republic of India Before Trilateral Meeting. (2018, November 30). Washington, DC: The White House, www.whitehouse.gov/briefings-statements/remarks-president-trump-prime-minister-abe-japan-prime-minister-modi-republic-india-trilateral-meeting/ (accessed on 2019, April 12)

Remarks of the Acting Secretary of State, Michael Pompeo, with Acting Secretary of Defense, Patrick Shanahan, Japanese Foreign Minister, Taro Kono, and Japanese Defense Minister, Takeshi Iwaya, at a Joint Press Availability for the US-Japan 2+2 Ministerial. (2019, April 19). Washington, DC: US Department of State, www.state.gov/secretary/remarks/2019/04/291254.htm (accessed on 2019, April 21)

"Seven Reasons why COMCASA is so Important for India". (2018, September 7), *Economic Times*

Singh, Sushant. (2018, June 27). "COMCASA: Why US, India Can't Connect". *Indian Express*

Speech by the Prime Minister of Japan, H.E. Mr. Shinzo Abe at the Parliament of the Republic of India. (2007, August 22). Tokyo: Ministry of Foreign Affairs of Japan, www.mofa.go.jp/region/asia-paci/pmv0708/speech-2.html (accessed on 2019, May 12)

Summary of the 2018 National Defense Strategy of the United States of America, Sharpening the American Military's Competitive Edge. (2018). Washington: Department of Defense, https://dod.defense.gov/Portals/1/Documents/pubs/2018-National-Defense-Strategy-Summary.pdf (accessed on 2019, May 30)

Takahashi, Kosuke. (2018, December 21). "Japan Self-Defense Forces Receive Significant Boost in 2019 Budget", *Jane's Defence Weekly*, www.janes.com/article/85398/japan-self-defense-forces-receive-significant-boost-in-2019-budget (accessed on 2019, April 15)

Thakur, Arvind and Michael Padgett. (2018, May 31). "Time is Now to Advance US–India Defence Cooperation", *National Defense*, www.nationaldefensemagazine.org/articles/2018/5/31/time-is-now-to-advance-us-india-defense-cooperation (accessed on 2019, April 15)

"US Indo-Pacific Command Holds Change of Command Ceremony". (2018, May 30), US Indo-Pacific Command, www.pacom.mil/Media/News/News-Article-View/Article/1535776/us-indo-pacific-command-holds-change-of-command-ceremony/ (accessed on 2019, May 31)

"U.S. President Barack Obama's Interview with Press Trust of India". (2016, January 25), *The Statesman*

Yoshida, Reiji and Mizuho Aoki. (2015, September 19). "Diet Enacts Security Laws, Marking Japan's Departure from Pacifism". *Japan Times*, www.japantimes.co.jp/news/2015/09/19/national/politics-diplomacy/diet-enacts-security-laws-marking-japans-departure-from-pacifism-2/#.VqY9CPl97IV (accessed on 2019, April 6)

6 Conclusion

The SCS dispute is intricately complex and has been identified as a function of various factors like the overlapping claims to sovereignty among four of the ASEAN member-states,[1] China and Taiwan. The nature of the dispute has complicated the applicability and interpretation of international law pertaining to the jurisdiction and access to natural resources in the littorals. The issue has been further compounded by China's binge of territorial reclamation and island-construction, enhanced by military surveillance, communications and logistics infrastructure-building in the SCS. A retrospective perspective of the trajectory of the dispute unveils its intractable nature, exacerbated by the interconnectedness of two principal factors: the legal/jurisdictional and organisational/institutional. The chequered nature of claims to sovereignty among the claimant nations and the quest for access to its rich natural resources constitutes the first factor. Institutional determinants like ASEAN's inability to present a concerted stance in conflict resolution, wherein the priorities, interests and equations of individual member-states have overridden the interests of the organisation; the languid pace of the institutional mechanism, as manifested in the progression of ASEAN-China negotiations since the adoption of the Spratly Declaration in July 1992 and the limitations of the principal agreements, form the second factor. Tracing the chronology of the development in ASEAN-China negotiations, it is pertinent to note that the DOC, acknowledged to be a reference point and the guiding document for framing the COC, particularly with the enshrinement of Article 10, which reaffirmed the commitment of the concerned parties to a COC, was signed in 2002, a decade after the adoption of the Spratly Declaration. Although the signing of the "Guidelines for the Implementation of the DOC" in 2011 had generated hope that the COC would be adopted at the tenth anniversary of the signing of the DOC, the progress has belied expectations. As the present circumstances indicate, ASEAN and China have agreed on adopting a Framework of the COC that "will facilitate the work for the conclusion of an effective COC on a mutually agreed timeline" and the SDNT to provide the basis for further negotiations on specific provisions of the COC ("China, ASEAN Arrive at Single Draft Negotiating Text of COC in SCS", 2018). ASEAN has acknowledged enthusiasm for the future trajectory of the SDNT, while stressing the imperative to maintain an ambience conducive to expedited negotiations on the COC and confidence-building among the parties concerned (Chairman's Statement of the 34th ASEAN Summit, 2019: Cl. 53). It is significant to note that the "cherishable" objective of concluding the first reading of the SDNT was achieved (on July 31, 2019) ahead of its scheduled deadline (end 2019) ("The First Reading of the Single Draft Negotiating Text of the Code of Conduct in the South China Sea Completed Ahead of the Schedule", 2019). Although the two sides hope to conclude the agreement by 2021 limitations pertaining to the most sensitive issues like the agreement's geographic scope, potential dispute settlement mechanisms and details of resource exploration and development (Thayer, 2018), in addition to the definitiveness of its legal sanctity, are the principal stumbling blocks to its successful culmination.

1 ASEAN's precarious balancing dynamics in the South China Sea: India's policy response summarised

The complex nature of the dispute has not only contributed to retarding the pace of progress towards a negotiated settlement, but also cut a deep wedge into the organisational unity of ASEAN, in turn providing a leeway for China's forays and ambitions in the SCS. The disarray among the ASEAN members on this issue has been particularly in evidence since 2012, posing a major challenge to ASEAN centrality and role in safeguarding the vitality of its norms and identity. Its ability to reconcile the divergent strains of adherence to the normative motivations contained in the ASEAN Way, on the one hand, and the primacy of individual national interests of the member-states, on the other, have been seriously constrained. For its part, China has been adeptly employing its economic, soft power and geo-economic potential to draw its ASEAN neighbours into a more close-knit core of partnership, envisaged in the concept of "community of common destiny". This posture finds reflection in its attempts to neutralise the "China threat" thesis with the tenets of "Peaceful Rise" and "Peaceful Development" and the introduction of the BRI. Therefore, China has been able to influence the policies of individual ASEAN member-states to varying degrees and succeeded in establishing its niche as an almost indispensable and invincible neighbour in the ASEAN psyche. ASEAN has generally been accommodative of China, evading a direct confrontational posture. Simultaneously, it has welcomed the role of prominent maritime nations like India, Japan, Australia and the US, which nurture significant geostrategic stakes in the maintenance of peace and order in the Indo-Pacific region as potential balancers, in an attempt to deter China's aggressive posture. To this end, ASEAN has focused on the policy of "omni-enmeshment" through the institutionalisation of bilateral and multilateral engagements and erecting a cooperative security framework of dialogue and defence/strategic interactions with major stakeholding nations (Goh, 2007–2008: 129). Acknowledged as the most viable means of safeguarding a "stable, predictable regional order in which countries big and small can prosper together", ASEAN's "omni-enmeshment" has been undertaken to achieve indirect balancing of China by the organisation.

1.1 India's policy in the South China Sea: rationale and responses

Although India is neither a SCS littoral state, nor claimant to any territory therein, a host of factors and geostrategic concerns determine and stimulate its policy on and responses to the issue. This book identified the following factors in rationalising India's concerns and engagement:

First, India's commitment to safeguarding and maximising the stability of the Indo-Pacific region in general and the freedom of navigation and overflight of the SCS in particular, which has been identified as the Indian Navy's "primary area of interest", has served as a principal consideration. This rationale has been embodied in its vision of realising and upholding "a peaceful, open, equitable, stable and rule-based order in the Indo-Pacific region and beyond" (Joint Statement on India and Japan Vision 2025, 2015, Cl. 4).

Second, the geostrategic salience of the SCS, a significant "global commons" site, connecting with the Indian Ocean through the Malacca Strait to the southwest and commanding access to the East China Sea to the northeast, is enhanced by its role as a vital naval lifeline for India, facilitating the passage of vessels and accounting for the transportation of more than 55 per cent of its sea-borne trade (Answer of the Minister of State in the Ministry of External Affairs, Gen. V. K. Singh (Retd.) to Unstarred Question No. 808 in Rajya Sabha, 2017). In addition to commercial interests, India's engagement with Vietnam for oil exploration in the SCS is another substantive issue, with the potential to facilitate the nation's energy security in the face of burgeoning demands.

Third, in cognisance of its stakes in sustaining the overall security and balance of power in the region, India intends to play a more direct role in the dynamics of the SCS littorals and the wider Indo-Pacific, with the objective of emerging as the net security provider and an "anchor of stability and security". This is in conformity with the Indian Navy's conduct of military, diplomatic, constabulary and benign functions as a responsible naval force. The responsible execution of this four-pronged role will bolster its sustenance as a "stabilising force" in the region, in addition to facilitating its geostrategic objectives and imperatives. In other words, India seeks to balance "against prevailing threats, meeting risks and rising challenges through continuous monitoring, and a containment strategy for non-traditional challenges" in the region (Ensuring Secure Seas: Indian Maritime Security Strategy, 2015: 8–9).

Fourth, as India embarks on playing a more direct and responsible role in the dynamics of the Indo-Pacific region, the successful execution of the LEP and AEP, premised on the adherence to the principle of ASEAN centrality, complemented its strategy of containing Chinese footprints in its "extended" neighbourhood by putting its weight behind countries caught in the dispute over overlapping claims to sovereignty in the SCS with Beijing.

Fifth, as China engineers and sustains heavy investments across strategic locations in the South Asian neighbourhood, over a string of states like Bangladesh, the Maldives, Nepal, Pakistan and Sri Lanka, either at the bilateral level or within the scaffold of the ambitious BRI project, India deems it a strategic imperative to explore the advantages of its geographical position and emerging naval profile as well as the legacy of goodwill and cooperation with ASEAN to balance its eastern neighbour.

Finally, the manifestation of India's concerns in the context of the unfolding events in the SCS gains currency when compared to China's not too dissimilar "aggressive and expansionist" strategy pertaining to the undemarcated Line of Actual Control on the Sino-India border. Beijing practises the classic "salami slicing tactic" of being non-committal on territorial demarcation and employing it as a means of further expansion and claim. Such a consideration is borne out by their historical legacy, refreshed by the Doklam standoff in 2017. Taking cognisance of the history of Sino-India relations as well as the contemporary circumstances, a realist approach, tempered by strains of tangible, critical geopolitical imperatives, complemented by the constructivist logic of intangibles, in the form of images and perceptions in state-level interactions and policy-making, underline the rationale behind India's responses *vis-à-vis* the dispute and its overall binary with China.

India's posture pertaining to the SCS dispute has been coherent through the successive administrative tenures of the UPA and NDA-II governments, under review. While following a nuanced and balanced approach in the strategic dynamics of the region, India's official policy has acknowledged the importance of maintaining and promoting peace, stability, maritime safety and security, freedom of navigation and overflight and unimpeded lawful maritime commerce, in addition to resorting faith in ASEAN centrality to promote peaceful resolutions of disputes, in keeping with the universally recognised principles of international law. This was manifested when India welcomed the

> collective commitment by the concerned countries to abide by and implement the 2002 Declaration on the Conduct of Parties in the SCS and to work towards the adoption of a Code of Conduct in the SCS on the basis of consensus.
>
> (Answer of the Minister of State in the Ministry of External Affairs, Gen. V. K. Singh (Retd.) to Starred Question No. 568 in Lok Sabha, 2016)

With the LEP and AEP forming the fulcrum of India's engagement with Southeast Asia in particular and the greater Indo-Pacific in general, the ascendance of its strategic profile and maritime cooperation with the littoral ASEAN states, non-ASEAN maritime powers like Japan and Australia and even extra-regional navies has been demonstrative of its potential to emerge as an "anchor of stability and security" in its "legitimate area of interest" stretching from the Persian Gulf to the Strait of Malacca.

India's policy response to the issue is based on the realist balance of power logic, as it aims to deter China's ambitions in the SCS, acting as a perfect complement to ASEAN's stance of the indirect balancing of China, by the fostering of an alliance, premised on the principle of cooperative security. India's approach to the issue is contingent upon the principles of internal and external balancing, trailing its origin to Kenneth Waltz's espousal of states balancing by internal and external efforts, which synergises with the logic of cooperative security. In this context, India's strategy of internal balancing has been demonstrated in the bolstering of defence capabilities, raising stronger forces, indigenising weapons procurement capacities and developing infrastructure, towards which the Make in India initiative has provided a major boost. It has also found expression in various editions of the *Indian Maritime Doctrine* (2004, 2007, 2009 and 2015), Maritime Capability Perspective Plan (MCPP), Maritime Infrastructure Perspective Plan (MIPP) and the Indian Naval Indigenisation Plan (INIP). Its posture of internal balancing has been adequately supplemented by the external balancing strategy of forging bilateral and multilateral security mechanisms with ASEAN and other regional navies; strengthening engagement in relevant institutional mechanisms like ARF, EAS, ADMM+8, conducting regular maritime and Coast Guard exercises to facilitate interoperability, at the bilateral, trilateral and multilateral levels as demonstrated by MILAN and MALABAR, and multilateral institutional linkages fostered through the IONS, the IORA and the rejuvenation of the QUAD among Australia, India, Japan and the US. The developments in the policies of external and internal balancing have been borne out by the Indian Navy's proportionate responses to challenges in the region by charting a strategy of counter power-projection, enhancing operational tempo, outreach and strategic communication with its partners and regional allies.

1.2 ASEAN's acknowledgement of India's response: move towards greater convergence

ASEAN's positive response to India's profile and responsible role is borne out by the increased level of strategic cooperation, institutionalised in the Strategic and Comprehensive Strategic Partnership agreements. Accredited as an outcome of India's steady graduation from a Full Dialogue Partner to attaining the membership of ARF and subsequently becoming a "Plus One" (Summit-level) associate, followed by its inclusion within the EAS and ADMM+8 in 2005 and 2010 respectively, the LEP and AEP have constituted the bulwark for the development and entrenchment of India-ASEAN ties. Besides, it has also erected the foundation for India's enhanced participation and assumption of responsibility in Indo-Pacific affairs. As ASEAN strives to constructively engage India in sustaining the balance of power in the regional architecture, it values the "unanimous and unwavering support for ASEAN centrality" accorded by India, and acknowledges it as a significant compatriot capable of maintaining the regional equilibrium (Lynn, 2013: 21).

ASEAN has and is expected to continue to appreciate and acknowledge India's twin strategies of external and internal balancing, as it attempts to bolster the level of engagement and capabilities in the region. India's AEP has received a further boost with the dovetailing of Japan's FOIP policy and the US policy regarding the Indo-Pacific, as enumerated in the NSS and NDS, with the objective of creating an overarching concert of "like-minded" partners, who emphasise reinforced commitment to freedom of the seas and the peaceful resolution of territorial and maritime disputes in accordance with international law. This triangular convergence of India, Japan and the US has been institutionalised in the Trilateral Dialogue and the induction of Japan as a permanent participant in the MALABAR naval exercise. The outcome of this convergence at the strategic level has been reflected in the graduation of the Dialogue to the highest grade from that of Foreign Ministers, and New Delhi is further committed to multilateralism, regionalism and the rule of law, while fostering the "common pursuit of progress and prosperity" in this endeavour ("Prime Minister of India, Narendra Modi's Keynote Address", 2018).

As a means of encouraging trilateral cooperation, the Government of India's Make in India initiative, particularly its defence manufacturing component, has opened greater avenues of collaboration between India, Japan and the US, with respect to joint development and production of defence equipment. It has also unveiled investment opportunities in sectors like defence products manufacturing, supply chain sourcing and defence offsets and fortified legal trade practices. Within the Make in India framework, factors like major revisions in the DPP, introduction of the Strategic Partnership (SP) Model, an increase in opportunities for foreign direct investment through an automatic route, restricting licensing requirements for critical items and de-notifying several items previously produced only by Ordnance Factory Boards, among others are aimed at promoting greater participation and investment in the defence sector. This signature programme of the Government of India under the tutelage of Prime Minister, Narendra Modi has facilitated the investment climate in India. The defence sector has benefited considerably from its introduction and the defence-industrial base has received a facelift as well. Besides, in specific areas, where the domestic industry has not developed adequate capacity to meet schedule requirements, it emphasises the necessity of maintaining its combat-readiness and narrow critical capability gaps.

The accent on collaboration in defence technology, co-development and co-production, offering investment opportunities in defence products manufacturing, supply chain sourcing opportunities and defence offsets has been a unique feature of Make in India. This has been boosted by reforms in legislation and the relaxation of measures introduced in the FDI policy in defence, begun in June 2016, and followed up in January 2018. In keeping with New Delhi's vision of promoting the twin facets of the domestic defence industry and international collaboration, the avenues of defence cooperation and investment have been widened further with the adoption of the Defence Production Policy (DProP) (2018), which is germane to the objective of catapulting India into the world's top five manufacturers of defence platforms. The policy envisages exporting US$26 billion in defence goods and services by 2025, including exports to the tune of US$5 billion by the same time. In order to boost FDI into defence production, DProP 2018 proposed 74 per cent FDI under the automatic route for "niche technology areas" (Shukla, 2018) a considerable leap from the current 49 per cent. The policy clearly spells out the provision of promoting export through Government-to-Government agreements and line of credit/funding. The thrust to open up the defence sector for private partnership facilitates foreign OEMs to enter into Strategic Partnerships with Indian firms, so as to leverage opportunities in the domestic and global markets. Since 2015, India's state-owned arms manufacturer, Defence Research and Development Organisation (DRDO) has developed over 24 platforms, like the Arjun tank, the Tejas fighter, the airborne early warning and control system, the advanced towed artillery gun system, weapon locating radar, the high-speed heavyweight ship-launched torpedo and anti-torpedo decoy system. Besides, the DProP's stipulation of 13 areas where India must achieve self-reliance by 2025, viz. manufacturing fighter aircraft, medium lift and utility helicopters, warships, land combat vehicles, autonomous weapon systems, missile systems, gun systems, small arms, ammunition and explosives, surveillance systems, electronic warfare systems, communication systems and night fighting enablers, emerges as a stimulant. Additionally, the avenues to share real-time intelligence, by extending assistance to other countries, particularly Indonesia, Malaysia, Singapore and Vietnam, in establishing and developing the Command, Control, Communications, Computers, Intelligence, Surveillance, Reconnaissance (C4ISR) systems (Anand, 2018) are worth exploring for which the Make in India programme offers an excellent promenade. These initiatives clearly fall in line with the announcement made by the Indian Defence Public Sector Undertakings of its intentions regarding defence exports. For instance, Bharat Dynamics Limited proposes to explore the market to export a variety of anti-tank guided missiles and surface to air missiles (Akash missile systems). The Akash missile system can target aircraft, helicopters and drones up to 25 kilometres away, which is vital to balance China's buttressing of aerial defences over reclaimed land in the disputed SCS littorals. Bharat Dynamics has identified 15 weapon systems for export including Astra beyond-visual range air to air missiles, Prahar surface to surface missiles, light combat aircraft, BrahMos supersonic cruise missiles, SONARs, Arjun Mk-2 battle tanks, airborne early warning systems, battlefield radars and a variety of unmanned systems.

The defence component of Make in India has encouraged the Japanese defence industry with respect to its investment prospects, further facilitated by India's relaxation of rules on the export of defence equipment and technology that was introduced in April 2014.[2] Besides, Japan's new security legislation, in consonance with the NDPG for FY 2014 and Beyond, offers immense opportunities to realise the optimum level of strategic cooperation with India. In this context, the significance of the bilateral defence deal, following an agreement on price for purchasing 12 ShinMaywa US-2i amphibious SAR aircraft for the Indian Navy, cannot be exaggerated, given the geostrategic necessity prompted by China's burgeoning forays in the Indo-Pacific littorals. Once finalised, this acquisition will meet a wide array of requirements pertaining to: the coastal/inter island ferrying of personnel and cargo; supply of critical spares to units at sea; rapid response missions for HADR; visual/radar surveillance at long range; and long range SAR missions and casualty evacuation at sea. Furthermore, major developments brought about by the signing of a series of defence-related agreements such as the Indo-US LEMOA and COMCASA and the DTTI and the DTTI's emphasis on co-production, co-development and innovation projects have complemented the Make in India programme and encouraged defence cooperation between India and the US.

The trilateral strategic convergence between India, Japan and the US has been unveiled in spirit and practice through the AEP, FOIP, NSS and NDS, and reflects their determination to deter the increasing silhouette of China in the region, and upholds the security, openness, freedom and accessibility of the Indo-Pacific maritime domain. The policy of balancing China, which is inherent in this trilateral mechanism, has been extended to include a fourth arm, by reviving the QUAD and introducing Australia into the trajectory, following the first official parleys of the QUAD members in November 2017. The imperative of securing its maritime neighbourhood in consonance with its allies has been acknowledged as Australia's pragmatic foreign policy objective. Even before the official revival of the QUAD in its present manifestation (QUAD 2.0), Australia's "Defence White Paper" (2016) envisaged unequivocally that instability or conflict in Southeast Asia and the Pacific would endanger national security and "our vital and growing economic relationships in that region". The document also underscored:

> Stability is important in South East Asia to countering other threats including transnational crime and terrorism. Australia's reliance on maritime trade with and through South East Asia, including energy supplies, means the security of our maritime approaches and trade routes within South East Asia must be protected, as must freedom of navigation, which provides for the free flow of maritime trade in international waters.
>
> (Australia's Defence Strategy, 2016: 69)

Canberra has identified India as among the "front rank of Australia's international partnerships", in addition to outlining the congruence of mutual economic and security intent with like-minded partners, Japan and the US, particularly in maintaining the stability and openness of the regional littorals. While ASEAN forms the principal pillar of defence and strategic cooperation, its rejuvenated interest in QUAD 2.0 with a commitment to ensuring increased prosperity and security in the region and to working together to guarantee that it remains "free and open" ("Australia-India-Japan-United States Consultations on the Indo-Pacific", 2017) unveils the assumption of a more responsible regional role for Canberra. As a cornerstone of the convergence of complementary visions harboured by its members, the QUAD, by affirming ASEAN centrality and upholding the rules-based regional order, increasing connectivity consistent with international law and standards and coordinating on counter-terrorism and maritime security (Indo-Pacific Strategy Report, 2019: 48), provides a concerted balance to China in the Indo-Pacific littorals. Therefore, although India has hitherto seldom experienced the centripetal pull towards synchronisation with prominent regional powers, it would be wise and pragmatic to seize the "quadri-polar" moment, temporally appropriate as "every single country in the ASEAN region wants India to be more engaged in the region in every possible way" (Indian Ambassador to the Philippines, Jaideep Mazumdar, quoted in Mohan, 2017).

Parallel to the strategic commitment to advancing a free, open and inclusive Indo-Pacific architecture, the regional stakeholders have acknowledged the necessity of mutual cooperation through economic, infrastructure, connectivity and capacity-building initiatives, for the purpose of fostering transparent and sustainable development of the region. In this domain, mention may be made of India's "holistic vision for engagement with the region" ("Remarks by External Affairs Minister of India, Sushma Swaraj at the 3rd Indian Ocean Conference", 2018), christened SAGAR, and its collaboration with Japan with regard to the development of India's Northeast, which is acknowledged as the geostrategic gateway to Southeast and East Asia, thereby emphasising the complementarity of security, economic growth and development. The third prong of India's policy in the security-economic complex is its focus on reviving the cultural syncretism that the region shared in the days of yore through Project Mausam: Maritime Routes and Cultural Landscapes across the Indian Ocean. These three components, defence/security; connectivity and infrastructure; culture/soft power are discussed below.

Unveiled in 2015, the doctrinal vision of SAGAR has been entwined with the prospects of maritime security and a sustainable blue economy to enhance the opportunities for trade, commercial, cultural and communication linkages with the maritime nations of the Indo-Pacific. Within the scaffold of SAGAR, India is not only committed to strengthening economic and security cooperation with its maritime neighbours, but also to assisting in developing their maritime security capabilities, primarily by facilitating information exchange, coastal surveillance and the building of infrastructure capabilities (Padmaja, 2018). In addition, the security arm of SAGAR was bolstered by the inauguration of the Indian Navy's Information Fusion Centre for the Indian Ocean Region (IFC – IOR) in 2018, as a collaborative hub for coordinating and disseminating analysed maritime security and safety information with neighbouring littoral countries and international agencies (Siddiqui, 2018). The security aspect of SAGAR, which supplements its economic domain, endorses the need to promote a more integrated and cooperative future in the region that enhances the prospects for sustainable development of the blue economy, facilitating greater collaboration in trade, tourism and investment, infrastructure development, marine science and technology, sustainable fisheries and protection of the marine environment ("Prime Minister of India's Remarks at the Commissioning of Offshore Patrol Vessel Barracuda in Mauritius, 2015"). Its rationale emerges from the burgeoning dependence on the seas for national and regional development, particularly since maritime economic activities continue to expand and the conduct of seaborne trade, shipping and fishing calls for securing and maintaining freedom of navigation of the SLOC and ISL. Therefore, Prime Minister of India, Narendra Modi's determination to not only secure the Indian Ocean maritime domain against traditional and non-traditional challenges, but also to provide the means to ensure sustainable and balanced development, by establishing and maintaining a climate of trust and transparency; respect for international maritime rules and norms; sensitivity to mutual interests; and a peaceful resolution of maritime issues must be read in the context of China's increasing footprint, for which the maritime component of BRI, namely the MSR, acts as a pivot.

At the level of implementation, SAGAR incorporates a three-pronged project to: first, promote hinterland linkages and strengthen regional connectivity; second, link South Asia to Southeast Asia by proactively pursuing AEP; and, third, play an active and constructive role in strengthening regional maritime security. Among these initiatives, the SAGARMALA focuses on developing hinterland linkages and encouraging regional connectivity through the construction of new ports, modernising old ones and developing inland waterways and hinterland, aimed at institutionalising a broad-based and strong maritime logistics infrastructure ("Remarks by External Affairs Minister of India, Sushma Swaraj at the 3rd Indian Ocean Conference", 2018). With the robust objective of revolutionising maritime logistics and port-led development in India, SAGARMALA has identified more than 600 projects worth US$120 billion, proposed to be operational by 2020. In this ambitious scheme, the ports and coastal economic zones are envisioned to emerge as a "microcosm of the blue economy", emphasising the growth of sea-dependent industries and contributing to global trade through sea connectivity ("Shri Nitin Gadkari Addresses the Sustainable Blue Economy Conference in Nairobi, Says Blue Economy a Critical Aspect of India's Economic Development Agenda", 2018).

Significantly enough, the Indo-Japan geo-economic endeavour to explore the development of industrial corridors and connectivity networks, to propel the growth of Northeast India is projected to benefit various stakeholders in the Indo-Pacific region and is germane to its potential to emerge as a counterweight to the BRI. To this end, the launch of the Japan-India Coordination Forum for Development of the North-eastern Region in August 2017 as the dedicated bilateral forum and Tokyo's decision to invest Rs. 13,000 crore in a slew of ongoing and new projects; the Northeast Road Network Connectivity Improvement Project (Assam and Meghalaya) and the Northeast Network Connectivity Improvement Project (Meghalaya) are particularly encouraging developments (Singh, 2019). These projects are integral parts of a wider Indo-Japan corridor for the Indo-Pacific region extending to eastern Africa, within the framework of the Asia-Africa Growth Corridor. On the whole, engagement and cooperation in India's Northeast is a prerequisite to contributing not only to the development of this particular region, but also its neighbourhood and beyond, with the potential to transform the corridor into the "epicentre of the Act East Policy" ("Keynote Address of the Chief Minister of Assam, Sarbananda Sonowal at the Workshop on India-Japan Partnership for Economic Development in Northeast Region", 2017).

Finally, in a "soft" power-based response to the MSR, India launched "Project Mausam: Maritime Routes and Cultural Landscapes across the Indian Ocean" during the 38th World Heritage Session in Doha in June 2014. A transnational initiative for the revival of its ancient maritime routes and cultural linkages with 39 countries in the IOR that were linked through sea trade routes in the past, the project collates archaeological and historical research in order to document the diversity of cultural, commercial and religious interactions, extending from East Africa, the Arabian Peninsula, the Indian subcontinent and Sri Lanka to the Southeast Asian archipelago. While at the macro level it aims to reconnect communication among these countries through an enhanced understanding of cultural values and ethos, at the micro level the focus is on understanding national cultures. The project also aims to gather together regional researchers and academics on a common platform to shed more light on the subcontinent's maritime history, by reviewing archaeological sites, architectural and industrial heritage and cultural landscapes along the Indian Ocean coast. Furthermore, the project aims to promote research on themes related to the study of maritime routes through international scientific seminars and meetings and by adopting a multidisciplinary approach to encouraging the production of specialised work and publications to widen the understanding of the concept of a common heritage and multiple identities (Project 'Mausam'– Mausam/Mawsim: Maritime Routes and Cultural Landscapes, 2014). The duration of the project has been extended up to 2020, with the pre-approved fund of Rs. 60,039,297 (approx. US$1 million) ("Project 'Mausam' Extended up to 2020 with the Pre-approved Fund of Rs 60,039,297: Dr. Mahesh Sharma", 2018). Through its emphasis on re-inventing ancient maritime interactions between countries and communities connected by the shared cultural heritage of the Indian Ocean "world", the project offers an alternative to the soft power component of MSR.

In addition to this initiative, the restoration and boosting of the age-old ties of culture and connectivity between India and ASEAN have been resuscitated through efforts like the construction of the Stilwell Road; the 3,200 km-long India-Myanmar-Thailand (IMT) Trilateral Highway, running from Moreh to Maesot via Tamu, Mandalay and Myawaddy; the Kaladan Multimodal Transit and Transport facility (KMMTT) project; revival of the Nalanda-Srivijaya University through the collaboration of the Governments of India and Singapore; opening of border towns in Moreh and Tamu; and the re-construction of archaeological structures and heritage sites in various countries, either funded or monitored by the Archaeological Survey of India (ASI). As a significant component of providing modern content to a historical relationship, the ASI's engagement in archaeological restoration in a host of ASEAN countries is commendable. Following its post-earthquake restoration of the Prambanan temples in Indonesia (2006) and the successful completion of the Angkor Wat Project in Cambodia, the ASI was assigned an important project for restoration of the famous twelfth-century Ta Prohm complex, a monastic complex built by Jayavarman VII, the most famous of the Khmer rulers. These were followed by the ASI's project assistance in the restoration of the sixth-century temple complex of Vat Phou in the province of Champassak (Laos) in 2010 by painstakingly piecing the heritage of the past and converting the heaps of stones into living monuments as relics of the highest form of architecture and aesthetics. In Vietnam, India pledged aid to help conserve the World Heritage Site, My Son Sanctuary, in addition to supervising restoration of Bagan's twelfth-century Ananda Temple (in Myanmar) in 2010. The Government of India has allocated US$3 million towards its restoration ("PM Visits Ananda Temple, Bagan", 2017). The enthusiasm with which the ASI restored some of the architectural elements of the original temple and its environs, making the complex both accessible and safe for tourists elicited praise from APSARA (Authority for the Protection and Management of the Angkor Region), the body of the

Cambodian Government in overall charge of this famous World Heritage Site. Additionally, in October 2011, the ASI decided to restore Cham temples in Vietnam, in order to heal the scars inflicted by US bombings during the Vietnam War. Interestingly enough, the tragic fate of the last kings of India and Myanmar has "intertwined" the history of the two nations. This was expressed in no uncertain terms by the former Indian President, A.P.J. Abdul Kalam during his visit to the mausoleum of the last Mughal emperor, Bahadur Shah Zafar in Yangon in March 2006. Thereafter, the Indian Vice President, Hamid Ansari, during his visit to the same site in February 2009 recalled how the last king of Myanmar, Thebaw, had encountered a similar end in Ratnagiri, Maharashtra, after he was taken there by the British. While reiterating this "tragic example of the intertwining of the history of India and Myanmar" ("Ansari Prays at Bahadur Shah Zafar's Yangon Tomb", 2009), Ansari identified these shrines as part of our shared historical-cultural legacy. Thus, it is obvious that cultural collaboration between India and the countries of this region forms a major dynamic in the development of holistic linkages within the scaffold of LEP/AEP. As India and ASEAN have embarked on the threshold of a qualitatively more substantive and reinvigorated betrothal through the Plan of Action for the Period 2016 to 2021, New Delhi aims to not only strengthen the third pillar of engagement, i.e. the socio-cultural pillar, but also to ardently bring it to the forefront of the relationship.

In summary then, the potential strength that India demonstrates and further aspires to in the near future in the spheres of economy, security/defence and culture, in conjunction with its strategy of practising internal and external balancing, clearly emboldens ASEAN's impression and appreciation of its capability to act as an adequate, emergent balancer to China.

2 Limitations of India's policy responses: thoughts on the future trajectory

Notwithstanding these considerations and positive activities, India still walks a tight-rope on the path of its emergence as a commensurate balancer, put forward by its asymmetric economic and military capabilities *vis-à-vis* Beijing. In addition to the military and economic factors, the present book, in its introductory chapters, has underscored the position and predominance that China enjoys among the ASEAN member-states, in spite of the contested and overlapping sovereignty claims that half of the member-states share with China in the disputed SCS. Besides, the progressive trajectory of the ASEAN-China negotiations regarding the SCS, with the conclusion of the framework agreement, or outline, on the COC in August 2017, followed by the declaration of a shared commitment to promote peace and stability in the region at the ASEAN Retreat in February 2018 and the signing of the SDNT to provide the basis for further negotiations on specific provisions of the COC in 2019 emphasise the pragmatism of maintaining an ambience conducive to expedited negotiations on the COC and confidence-building among the parties concerned (Chairman's Statement of the 34th ASEAN Summit, 2019: Cl. 53). Against this backdrop, ASEAN, wary of disturbing the evolving alchemy with China, will be intent on maintaining the precarious balance in its relations with India and China. Furthermore, India's policy responses are encumbered by certain limitations, which are analysed in the following subsection.

2.1 Identifying the challenges to India's responses

The challenges to India's policy response on the issue under review follows from a host of factors as discussed below, which potentially limit the adequate and effective pursuit of its internal and external balancing endeavours:

- *First*, India's defence collaboration with Vietnam and Japan: India and Vietnam have been locked in protracted negotiations over the former's sale of the supersonic BrahMos missile[3] to Vietnam to equip its coastal defence unit in Phu Yen, north of Cam Ranh, after vacillating on its request since 2011. Similarly, India and Japan have been engaged in protracted negotiations over the purchase of US-2i aircraft by the Indian Navy for the past three years. Under such circumstances, ironing out the differences over the acquisition procedure and technicalities at the earliest stage with respect to Vietnam and Japan augurs well for future defence collaboration within the Make in India ambit.
- *Second*, technicalities of the Make in India programme: in view of the technicalities pertaining to the Make in India initiative, the procurement policy that emphasises local manufacturing needs fine-tuning, failing which it will be difficult to achieve the desired result in the absence of an adequate manufacturing ecosystem and dithering among some manufacturers to part with sensitive, cutting-edge technology. The same holds true for the impediments in procurement policy, particularly under the SP model. Although the SP model attempts to designate a few private sector firms as system integrators for collaborating with foreign OEMs to erect a robust defence-industrial foundation, limitations have been identified with respect to execution, and a dearth of institutional capacity and capability to steer it to its logical conclusion. Furthermore, the success of the offset programme would impinge on identifying and removing restrictions, in addition to extending offsets to the civil sector for implementation (Bharadwaj, 2018). Finally, the apprehension emanating from pricing issues and non-adherence to specific production deadlines (Banerjee, 2018) could also tarnish the prospects of Make in India in the defence sphere.
- *Third*, constraints in the Defence Budget affecting Make in India: The competent implementation of the Make in India project in the defence sphere necessitates a proportionate increase in the budgetary allocation for modernisation outlays. Given the commitment of the Government of India regarding the defence modernisation and indigenisation components within the Make the India programme, the budgetary allocation has been a disappointment to the defence forces of the country. It has generally exhibited a trend of declining modernisation outlays for new projects with approximately 80 per

cent of outlays earmarked for "committed liabilities", which include instalments for arms deals inked previously and a skewed ratio of revenue and capital expenditure (Pandit, 2018). As per the defence budgetary allocation for the fiscal year 2019–2020 estimated at around 1.6 per cent of the GDP, the capital allocation of the Ministry of Defence under Budget Estimate 2019–2020 is 31.97 per cent of the Central Government's total capital expenditure ("Defence Budget 2019: Rs 3.18 Lakh Crore Allocated to Defence Budget", 2019) which is considered incommensurate with its projected aspiration for modernisation.

- *Fourth*, missed and extended deadlines and other challenges regarding connectivity projects: It is acknowledged that adequate connectivity infrastructure in India's Northeast will improve its potential as the hub of economic activity as well as its opening up to Southeast Asia and the wider Indo-Pacific. Realising this imperative, the AEP has not only taken forward the momentum of connectivity projects, but also encouraged the inauguration of new ones, in a bid to improve its connectivity potential and tap the region's eastern gateway for international trade and commerce. The legacy of cultural and trade ties and connectivity has been resuscitated through efforts like the upgrading of the Kalewa-Kalemyo Road in Myanmar across Manipur and a road connecting Sittwe to Lawngtlai in Mizoram, India; New Delhi's active exploration of the opening of the Stilwell Road to Myanmar, in conjunction with a telecommunication network connecting Moreh through a 6 km optic fibre link to Tamu; the 3,200 km-long IMT Trilateral Highway, running from Moreh to Mae Sot via Tamu, Mandalay and Myawaddy;[4] the proposed extension of the IMT Highway to Vietnam, Laos and Cambodia in the second phase; the KMTTT[5] designed to connect Mizoram with Sittwe through construction of a Kaladan inland waterway; and improvement of the Sittwe deep sea port, after being operationalised, which will open the direct sea trade from Kolkata to Northeast India and further to Southeast Asia through Sittwe port, etc. These are some of the game-changing projects at various stages of progress which, once operational, would be able to further reorient the strategic and developmental dynamics of the region. However, the execution of a majority of the identified projects has been mired in hurdles and consecutively missed deadlines. For instance, the IMT Highway project, which has been a work in progress since 2002, is facing inordinate delays, and having already missed a couple of deadlines, is now proposed to be operational by end-2019. The main hindrances stem from the slow progress in rebuilding 69 dilapidated bridges on the Indian side and other procedural issues like Myanmar's demand to renegotiate the trilateral Motor Vehicles Agreement (Chakraborti and Chakraborty, 2018: 272) and its applicability on the Highway. Incidentally, India and Myanmar have opened two land crossings through Moreh in Manipur and Zokhawthar in Mizoram to travellers with valid visas and passports, in order to facilitate free movement of people and goods between India and Southeast Asia. Besides, the progress of the KMMTT has been circumscribed by three missed deadlines owing to poor weather conditions, remoteness and inaccessibility as well as the prevailing security considerations and sensitivity of the region (Bhattacharyya, 2018). The sustained emphasis on and the follow-up of the ambitious projects would indeed go a long way to linking India with its eastern neighbours, thus serving as significant channels for augmenting connectivity between them, by optimally utilising and thereby developing the North-eastern corridor. Thus, there is a crucial need for completing road, rail and air connectivity projects either undertaken or under negotiation within the stipulated time.

In the light of the discussion above, as ASEAN finds itself situated at the nucleus of the Indo-Pacific region, it appreciates and encourages India's "positive" role and emergence as "a very important component for peace, prosperity and stability" in the region (Transcript of Media Briefing by Preeti Saran (Secretary, East) on ASEAN-India Commemorative Summit, 2018). The importance attached to India by ASEAN has been exemplified by the Prime Minister of Singapore, Lee Hsien Loong's assertion that it would "make a major contribution to regional affairs, helping to keep the regional architecture open, balanced and inclusive" ("Prime Minister, Lee Hsien Loong's Opening Remarks for the ASEAN-India Commemorative Summit Plenary Session, 2018"). Furthermore, the attendance of the heads of all the ASEAN member-states as chief guests at the 69th Republic Day celebrations in New Delhi in January 2018 was unprecedented, symbolising the acknowledgement of India's emerging status as a decisive and responsible power in the region. While, on the one hand, it provided the opportunity to showcase the country's military might, technological innovations and achievements in all three wings of the defence forces to the other guests, it demonstrated the historical, civilisational, educational, religious and cultural linkages with ASEAN through tableaux performances, on the other ("Curtain Raiser – Republic Day 2018", 2018). It is interesting to note in this context that the chief guest at India's 1st Republic Day (January 26, 1950) celebration was the then Indonesian President, Sukarno.

In the present circumstances, the importance that India attaches to the Indo-Pacific region has been further exemplified by the Ministry of External Affair's establishment of an Indo-Pacific division in April 2019 with the objective of integrating the IORA, ASEAN region and QUAD within the core of its regional diplomacy (Bagchi, 2019). This significant development has added further credence to India's outlook on the wider Indo-Pacific, converging seamlessly with ASEAN's emphasis on encouraging external partners "to support and undertake cooperation with ASEAN on the key areas" (Chairman's Statement of the 34th ASEAN Summit, 2019: Cl. 56) as outlined in the *ASEAN Outlook on the Indo-Pacific*, which constitutes the building blocks for establishing the ASEAN-centred regional architecture, facilitating its contribution to sustaining peace, freedom, stability and prosperity in the region. ASEAN recognises the Indo-Pacific, geostrategically represented as the Asia-Pacific and Indian Ocean regions, as closely integrated and interconnected regions, though geographically non-contiguous territorial spaces. Reading through the AOIP carefully, one discerns the emphasis that ASEAN places on sustaining an "inclusive regional architecture", acknowledging the organisation's centrality and its continued momentum as an "honest broker" with respect to issues of competing regional strategic interests (ASEAN Outlook on the Indo-Pacific, 2019: Cl. 3–4). India ardently supports the AOIP, and warmly welcomed it as having synchronised with India's Indo-Pacific vision, "especially from the standpoint of principles, as well as its approach and ASEAN's listing of areas of cooperation". This has been further echoed in Narendra Modi's pronouncement of a "free, open, inclusive and rules-based Indo-Pacific, of which India is an important part" (Raveesh Kumar, Official Spokesperson of Ministry of External Affairs' Response, 2019). The acknowledgement and staunch support of ASEAN centrality and the importance of ASEAN-led regional architecture in governing the dynamics of the region has not only found expression unilaterally in India's official pronouncement, but also within the multilateral framework of the QUAD ("QUAD Backs ASEAN-led System for Indo-Pacific", 2019). In summary, the AOIP emerges as the pivot of "upholding the principles of peacekeeping, fostering a culture of dialogue and strengthening cooperation" (President of Indonesia Joko Widodo, quoted in Septiari, 2019) representing ASEAN's holistic perspective on peace and confidence-building as well as promoting a culture of dialogue, cooperation and prosperity, in consonance with the partners concerned, with ASEAN and ASEAN-led mechanisms, like EAS, ARF, ASEAN+1, ADMM+ etc., adorning the driver's seat.

It is clear from the discussion above that India's Look East journey has accumulated major achievements and enhanced cooperation in a plethora of areas that have been supported by the AEP as well. Significantly enough, in the domestic sphere, India has enjoyed political consensus on the LEP's implementation, and the desirability of closer engagement with Southeast Asia and the further East has gone unquestioned by the different governments in power. Thus, New Delhi has demonstrated sincere pragmatism in moulding and developing its relations with these countries, by adopting a proactive, mature and sustainable foreign policy posture in its totality, which was sadly lacking during the Cold War epoch. Nonetheless, having examined the major achievements that have adorned the Look East/ Act East sojourn, it may be contended that this policy has not been immune to challenges and there are avenues for future improvement. In fact, the challenges and opportunities of taking this policy forward are like the proverbial two sides of the same coin, with deft diplomatic handling the encumbrances can be transformed into potential vistas of cooperation.

Viewed from the other end of the spectrum, ASEAN intends to revert to its position of strength and coordination, asserting organisational centrality and expressing willingness to assume responsibility for issues pertaining to preserving regional order and stability and fostering development. While, on the one hand, ASEAN understands that if left unattended, other regional powers will be found exerting their influence, given the geostrategic stakes attached to the SCS, it also comprehends the essence of exploring the development-related opportunities embarked upon by India and Japan, which could provide alternatives to BRI, weighed down by its myriad limitations and conditions, on the other. Given the status of negotiations with China on the SCS, though ASEAN has acknowledged its optimism with respect to the future trajectory of the SDNT, the early 2020s will be critical in determining the strategic architecture of the region, given the deadline for concluding the readings of the SDNT, which will be a decisive factor in expediting negotiations on the COC and confidence-building. The successful culmination of the first reading of the SDNT before its proposed schedule has not only fostered confidence-building, but also "streamlined the framework and essential elements of the COC". It has been hailed as a "positive development" in the unfolding trajectory of ASEAN-China negotiations on SCS. ASEAN has "welcomed the completion of the first reading of the Single Draft COC Nego-tiating Text ahead of schedule" (Chairman's Statement of the 26th ASEAN Regional Forum, 2019) and also underscored the concerns emanating from "land reclamations, activities and serious incidents in the area, which have eroded trust and confidence, increased tensions and may undermine peace, security and stabi-lity in the region". To this end, ASEAN has reiterated the "non-militarisation and self-restraint in the conduct of all activities by claimants and all other states" and the "the need to enhance mutual trust and confidence, exercise self-restraint in the conduct of activities and avoid actions that may further complicate the situation, and pursue peaceful resolution of disputes in accordance with international law, including the 1982 UNCLOS." (Joint Communiqué of the ASEAN Foreign Ministers' Meeting, 2019: Cl. 76)

As ASEAN undertakes its role as a united agenda-setter and fulcrum for the Indo-Pacific, it finds as its arms and conduits responsible balancers in India, Japan and the US, which unilaterally and in unison have the capability to sustain regional order and balance, while upholding ASEAN's vision and focus. The confidence that India has successfully generated has been attested to by Vietnam seeking New Delhi's support, exhorting it to "exert diplomatic pressure on Beijing", as part of its efforts to mobilise international opinion against China in the wake of the lat-ter's "interference" with ongoing oil and gas activities in SCS. Since India has a direct stake in the matter, which concerns exploration activities undertaken by OVL, Vietnam's urgency in garnering New Delhi's vocal support against China's "infringement upon its (Vietnam's) sovereign rights and jurisdiction over the SCS" (Peri, 2019) indicates greater acceptance of India as a power capable of offsetting China's ambitions in the region, to a considerable extent. The challenge faced by Vietnam is reminiscent of that shared by Malaysia near an oil and gas block in the Luconia Shoals in May 2019, when Chinese Coast Guard vessels tried to prevent drilling operations in areas within the Malaysian continental shelf. It is further apprehended that the Philippines may be subjected to a similar situation, in the case of its decision to explore the Recto Bank, which lies within its EEZ. Such a posture exposes the irreconcilable dyad of China's oft-repeated commitment to peace and stability and assurances of adherence to international law pertaining to the SCS issue and its actions on the ground, aptly summed up by the Philippine Defence Secretary, Delfin Lorenzana as a "consolation" and "optics" (Mangosing, 2019) a rather elusive and illusory rhetoric. Therefore, as China continues its policy of "bullying" and intimidating ASEAN member-states which have commercial stakes and disputes over territorial claims in the SCS littorals, international opinion against this unilateral infringement on a state's sovereign rights and jurisdiction, bolstered by voices of regional powers like India, will have a deterrent effect on Beijing. In light of this, the Government of India's announcement in September 2019 that it is allocating US$130 billion for fleet modernisation of its armed forces between 2019 and 2026 gains prominence, particularly with its emphasis on bolstering the capacity of its navy with the proposed addition of 200 ships, 500 aircraft and 24 submarines, improving upon its present contingent of 132 ships, 220 aircraft and 15 submarines ("India Firms up $130 Billion Plan to Enhance Military Capability", 2019). This reference is not, however, intended to suggest that India's enhanced engagement in the region and proportional increase in military capacity as a means of internal balancing strategy will trigger Sino-India military competition in the SCS. On the contrary, it is argued that, deterrence in itself is a significant guarantee of maintaining the status quo and respect for the tenets of a peaceful and stable maritime order. India and China are distinct political systems and hail from distinct political cultures. India harbours no pretension to hegemony or territorial expansion, though it has the capacity to "respond" appropriately to circumstances that threaten or jeopardise the security of global commons, particularly situations in which its own stakes or those of its allies are high. Furthermore, its response to sensitive circumstances need not necessarily be military, they may be diplomatic in nature, as the successful handling of the Doklam issue testifies. Finally, in this age of complex global interdependence, the "fates" of nations are believed to be intertwined. In such a scenario, a rational response to exigent circumstances by a responsible actor like India, which has generated adequate goodwill in the region through its track record of association with ASEAN and its member-states, both at the organisational and bilateral levels, would serve the aggregate interests of the stakeholders, rather than its own constricted and realist interests.

Notes

1 Brunei, Malaysia, the Philippines and Vietnam
2 Prior to this relaxation, Japan concentrated exclusively on the domestic market in order to demonstrate its commitment to peace
3 More than 50 per cent of the missile was made in India
4 Proposed to be fully operational by December 2019. India is undertaking two sections of the Trilateral Highway namely, (i) construction of the Kalewa-Yagyi road section in Myanmar, and (ii) construction of 69 bridges on the Tamu–Kyigone–Kalewa road section in Myanmar
5 Conceived in 2003 and agreed upon for implementation in 2008; proposed to be operational by 2020

References

Anand, Vinod. (2018, March 1). "Strengthening the Comprehensive Strategic Partnership between India and Vietnam", Vivekananda International Foundation, www.vifindia.org/article/2018/march/01/strengthening-the-comprehensive-strategic-partnership-between-india-and-vietnam (accessed on 2019, February 4)

"Ansari Prays at Bahadur Shah Zafar's Yangon Tomb". (2009, February 8), *The Hindu*

Answer of the Minister of State in the Ministry of External Affairs, Gen. V. K. Singh (Retd.) to Starred Question No. 568 in Lok Sabha. (2016, April 27). New Delhi: Ministry of External Affairs/Lok Sabha, www.mea.gov.in/lok-sabha.htm?dtl/26684/QUESTION_ NO568_SOUTH_CHINA_SEA (accessed on 2019, January 20)

Answer of the Minister of State in the Ministry of External Affairs, Gen. V. K. Singh (Retd.) to Unstarred Question No. 808 in Rajya Sabha. (2017, February 9). New Delhi: Ministry of External Affairs/Rajya Sabha, www.mea.gov.in/rajya-sabha.htm?dtl/28041/QUES TION_NO808_TRADE_THROUGH_SOUTH_CHINA_SEA (accessed on 2019, January 20)

ASEAN Outlook on the Indo-Pacific. (2019, June 23). Jakarta: ASEAN Secretariat, https://asean.org/asean-outlook-indo-pacific (accessed on 2019, July 19)

Australia's Defence Strategy. (2016). Canberra: Department of Defense, www.defence.gov. au/whitepaper/Docs/2016-Defence-White-Paper.pdf (accessed on 2019, May 12)

"Australia-India-Japan-United States Consultations on the Indo-Pacific". (2017, 12 November). Media Release. Canberra: Department of Foreign Affairs and Trade, http://dfat.gov. au/news/media/Pages/aus-india-japan-us-consultations-on-the-indo-pacific.aspx (accessed on 2019, May 12)

Bagchi, Indrani. (2019, April 15). "In a Show of Intent, External Affairs Ministry Sets Up Indo-Pacific Wing", *Times of India*

Banerjee, Ajay. (2018, February 4). "Battle for Make-in-India Defence", *The Tribune*

Bharadwaj, Dalip. (2018, May 7). "Make in India in Defence Sector: A Distant Dream", www.orfonline.org/expert-speak/make-in-india-defence-sector-distant-dream (accessed on 2019, February 6)

Bhattacharyya, Rajeev. (2018, December 31). "Slow Progress Mars Mizoram-Myanmar Kaladan Project as India Misses Deadline for Road Third Time in a Row". *First Post*, www.firstpost. com/india/slow-progress-mars-mizoram-myanmar-kaladan-project-as-india-misses-deadline-for-road-third-time-in-a-row-5817371.html (accessed on 2019, June 23)

Chairman's Statement of the 26th ASEAN Regional Forum. (2019, August 2). Jakarta: ASEAN Secretariat, https://asean.org/storage/2019/08/26th-ARF-Chairmans-State ment_FINAL.pdf (accessed on 2019, August 15)

Chairman's Statement of the 34th ASEAN Summit. (2019, June 23). Jakarta: ASEAN Secretariat, https://asean.org/storage/2019/06/Final_Chairs-Statement-of-the-34th-ASEAN-Summit_as-of-23-June-2019-12....pdf (accessed on 2019, June 24)

Chakraborti, Tridib and Mohor Chakraborty. (2018). *Expanding Horizon of India's Southeast Asia Policy: "Look", "Move" and "Act" East,* New Delhi: KW Publishers

"China, ASEAN Arrive at Single Draft Negotiating Text of COC in SCS". (2018, August 2). *China Daily,* www.chinadaily.com.cn/a/201808/02/WS5b62c87da3100d951b8c8460. html (accessed on 2019, June 2)

"Curtain Raiser – Republic Day 2018". (2018, January 25). Press Information Bureau. New Delhi: Ministry of Defence, http://pib.nic.in/newsite/PrintRelease.aspx?relid= 175907 (accessed on 2019, April 25)

"Defence Budget 2019: Rs 3.18 Lakh Crore Allocated to Defence Budget". (2019, July 7), *Economic Times*

Ensuring Secure Seas: Indian Maritime Security Strategy. (2015, October). New Delhi: Ministry of Defence (Navy), http://indiannavy.nic.in/sites/default/files/Indian_Maritime_ Security_Strategy_Document_25Jan16.pdf (accessed on 2019, May 12)

Goh, Evelyn. (2007–2008). "Great Powers and Hierarchical Order in Southeast Asia: Analysing Regional Security Strategies". *International Security,* 32(3)

Indian Ambassador to the Philippines, Jaideep Mazumdar, quoted in Mohan, Archis. (2017, November 13). "India Holds First 'QUAD' Meet with US, Japan, Australia", *Business Standard*

"India Firms up $130 Billion Plan to Enhance Military Capability". (2019, September 10), *The Hindu*

Indo-Pacific Strategy Report – Preparedness, Partnerships and Promoting a Networked Region. (2019, June 1). Washington, DC: Department of Defense, https://media.defense.gov/2019/May/31/2002139210/-1/-1/1/DOD_INDO_PACIFIC_STRAT EGY_REPORT_JUNE_2019.PDF (accessed on 2019, June 17)

Joint Communiqué of the ASEAN Foreign Ministers' Meeting. (2019, July 31). Jakarta: Ministry of External Affairs, https://asean.org/storage/2019/07/CIRCULATE-Joint-Communique-of-the-52nd-AMM-FINAL.pdf (accessed on 2019, August 15)

Joint Statement on India and Japan Vision 2025: Special Strategic and Global Partnership Working Together for Peace and Prosperity of the Indo-Pacific Region and the World. (2015, December 12). New Delhi: Ministry of External Affairs, www.mea.gov.in/incoming-visit-detail.htm?26176/Joint+Statement+on+India+and+Japan+Vision+2025+Special+Strategic+and+Global+Partnership+Working+Together+for+Peace+and+Prosperity+of+the+IndoPacific+Region+and+the+WorldDecember+12+2015 (accessed on 2019, May 12)

"Keynote Address of the Chief Minister of Assam, Sarbananda Sonowal at the Workshop on India-Japan Partnership for Economic Development in Northeast Region". (2017, March 29), https://indiafoundation.in/india-japan-partnership-for-economic-development-in-ner/ (accessed on 2019, June 23)

Lynn, Nyan. (2013). *Special Address of Deputy Secretary General for Political Security Community ASEAN Secretariat. Proceedings of the 1st Round Table on ASEAN-India Network of Think-Tanks.* New Delhi: Research and Information System for Developing Countries, http://aic.ris.org.in/sites/default/files/Publication%20File/AINTT-Proceedings-WEB.pdf (accessed on 2019, May 30)

Mangosing, Frances. (2019, July 31). "Lorenzana Admits China's 'Bullying', Says Beijing's Peace 'Rhetoric' Just 'Optics'", *The Inquirer*, https://globalnation.inquirer.net/178403/lorenzana-admits-chinas-bullying-says-beijings-peace-rhetoric-just-optics (accessed on 2019, August 1)

Padmaja, G. (2018, April 26). "Revisiting 'SAGAR' – India's Template for Cooperation in the Indian Ocean Region", National Maritime Foundation, http://maritimeindia.org/View%20Profile/636602941847320911.pdf (accessed on 2019, June 23)

Pandit, Rajat. (2018, February 1). "Budget 2018: Government Hikes Defence Budget by 7.81%, but it's just 1.58% of GDP and Lowest since 1962", *Times of India*

Peri, Dinakar. (2019, July 30). "Vietnam Briefs India on Standoff with China in the South China Sea", *The Hindu*

"PM Visits Ananda Temple, Bagan". (2017, September 6). Press Information Bureau. New Delhi: Prime Minister's Office, https://pib.gov.in/newsite/PrintRelease.aspx?relid=170572 (accessed on 2019, August 15)

President of Indonesia, Joko Widodo, quoted in Septiari, Dian. (2019, June 23). "ASEAN Leaders Adopt Indonesia-led Indo-Pacific Outlook". *The Jakarta Post*, www.thejakartapost.com/seasia/2019/06/23/asean-leaders-adopt-indonesia-led-indo-pacific-outlook.html (accessed on 2019, July 19)

"Prime Minister of India, Narendra Modi's Keynote Address at the 17th Asia Security Summit at Singapore". (2018, June 1), www.narendramodi.in/pm-%20modi-%20to%

20-deliver%20-keynote-%20address%20-at%20-shangri-la-%20dialouge-%20in%20-singa
pore-540324 (accessed on 2018, September 16)

*Prime Minister of India's Remarks at the Commissioning of Offshore Patrol Vessel Barracuda in
Mauritius.* (2015, March 12). New Delhi: Ministry of External Affairs, www.mea.gov.in/
outoging-visit-detail.htm?24912/Prime+Ministers+Remarks+at+the+Commissioning+of+
Offshore+Patrol+Vessel+OPV+Barracuda+in+Mauritius+March+12+2015 (accessed on
2019, June 23)

*Prime Minister, Lee Hsien Loong's Opening Remarks for the ASEAN-India Commemorative
Summit Plenary Session.* (2018, January 25). Singapore: Prime Minister's Office, www.pm
o.gov.sg/Newsroom/pm-lee-hsien-loong-asean-india-commemorative-summit-plenary-ses
sion (accessed on 2019, June 23)

"Project 'Mausam' Extended up to 2020 with the Pre-approved Fund of Rs 60,039,297:
Dr. Mahesh Sharma". (2018, December 17). Press Information Bureau. New Delhi:
Ministry of Culture, http://pib.nic.in/newsite/PrintRelease.aspx?relid=186490 (acces-
sed on 2019, April 29)

Project 'Mausam' – Mausam/Mawsim: Maritime Routes and Cultural Landscapes. (2014).
Indira Gandhi National Centre for the Arts – Research Programme 2014–2019. New
Delhi: Ministry of Culture, http://ignca.nic.in/mausam_objectives.htm (accessed on
2019, March 7)

"QUAD Backs ASEAN-led System for Indo-Pacific". (2019, June 1), *Hindustan Times*

*Raveesh Kumar, Official Spokesperson of Ministry of External Affairs' Response to a Query on
India's View on the Recently Announced ASEAN Outlook on the Indo-Pacific.* (2019,
June 26). New Delhi: Ministry of External Affairs, https://mea.gov.in/response-to-
queries.htm?dtl/31470/Official_Spokespersons_response_to_a_query_on_Indias_view_
on_the_recently_announced_ASEAN_Outlook_on_the_IndoPacific (accessed on 2019,
July 19)

"Remarks by External Affairs Minister of India, Sushma Swaraj at the 3rd Indian Ocean Conference". (2018, August 27). *Speeches and Statements.* New Delhi: Ministry of External Affairs,
https://mea.gov.in/outoging-visit-detail.htm?30327/Remarks+by+External+Affairs+Minis
ter+at+the+3rd+Indian+Ocean+Conference+Vietnam+August+27+2018 (accessed on 2019,
April 24)

"Shri Nitin Gadkari Addresses the Sustainable Blue Economy Conference in Nairobi, Says
Blue Economy a Critical Aspect of India's Economic Development Agenda". (2018,
November 28). Press Information Bureau. New Delhi: Ministry of Shipping, http://pib.
nic.in/newsite/PrintRelease.aspx?relid=185994 (accessed on 2019, June 23)

Shukla, Ajai. (2018, 23 March). "Vision 2025: Draft Defence Policy Eyes Place for India in
Producers' Club", *Business Standard*

Siddiqui, Huma. (2018, December 23). "India's SAGAR Inaugurated, to Help Fight
Maritime Piracy and Terrorism", *Financial Express*, www.financialexpress.com/defence/
indias-sagar-inaugurated-to-help-fight-maritime-piracy-and-terrorism/1422761 (accessed
on 2019, June 23)

Singh, Bikash. (2019, June 12). "Japan to Invest Around Rs 13000 Cr in Various Projects
in India's Northeast States", *Economic Times*

Thayer, Carlyle A. (2018, August 3). "A Closer Look at the ASEAN-China Single Draft SCS
Code of Conduct", https://thediplomat.com/2018/08/a-closer-look-at-the-asean-china-
single-draft-south-china-sea-code-of-conduct (accessed on 2019, June 2)

*The First Reading of the Single Draft Negotiating Text of the Code of Conduct in the South
China Sea Completed Ahead of the Schedule.* (2019, August 1). Beijing: Ministry of

Foreign Affairs, www.fmprc.gov.cn/mfa_eng/zxxx_662805/t1685674.shtml (accessed on 2019, August 15)

Transcript of Media Briefing by Preeti Saran (Secretary, East) on ASEAN-India Commemorative Summit. (2018, January 26). New Delhi: Ministry of External Affairs, www.mea.gov.in/media-briefings.htm?dtl/29399/Transcript_of_Media_Briefing_on_ASEANIndia_Commemorative_Summit_January_26_2018 (accessed on 2019, June 23)

Index

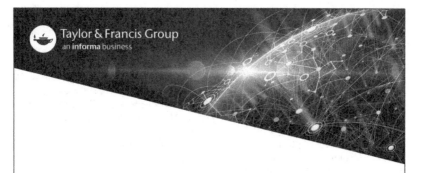